D1131122

TRADE UNION OFFICERS

OFFICERS

*A Study of Full-Time Officers, Branch Secretaries and
Shop Stewards in British Trade Unions*

BY

H. A. CLEGG
Fellow of Nuffield College, Oxford

A. J. KILLICK
Sometime Research Assistant, Nuffield College, Oxford

AND

REX ADAMS
*Staff Tutor, Department of Extra-Mural Studies
University of Sheffield*

ST. JOSEPH'S UNIVERSITY   STX
HD6664.C3872
Trade union officers;

3 9353 00052 7117

HD
6664
.C 3872

HARVARD UNIVERSITY PRESS
CAMBRIDGE, MASSACHUSETTS
1961

172243

© Basil Blackwell & Mott, Ltd., 1961

PRINTED IN GREAT BRITAIN

PREFACE

THE collection of the material on which this study is based was started towards the end of 1956 as one of several projects financed out of a grant from the Leverhulme Trust to Nuffield College for research in industrial relations. Rex Adams worked on it along with other projects during his two years as a Research Assistant in the College from 1956 to 1958. His place was taken by A. J. Killick, who worked full-time on the project during the following year. Both of them have continued to give me their help in the period of writing-up and preparation for publication.

Besides the gratitude we owe to the Warden and Fellows of Nuffield College, and to the Leverhulme Trustees, I should like to record our thanks to the many trade union officers, from general secretaries to shop stewards, who have given so liberally of their time to assist us, and been so patient with our ignorance and our follies. In addition, officers of all the unions whose records we used have read draft copies and suggested many improvements. Amongst them I should like to single out Mr. H. W. Howard, of the Transport Salaried Staffs Association, whose close attention and command of detail saved us from a multitude of errors. I must also thank two of my colleagues, Alan Fox and Bill McCarthy; Arthur Marsh, Staff Tutor in the Oxford University Delegacy of Extra-Mural Studies; and Piet Thoenes, of the University of Leyden. All of them read drafts of the study and made valuable comments and suggestions. Mrs. Yates typed successive drafts with great patience and skill.

We are deeply indebted to the thirty-six ex-students of Ruskin College who went to great trouble to circulate our questionnaires for trade union officers during their Easter vacation in 1959; and to the Principal of Ruskin College for his co-operation in the matter. Without their help the study could not have been completed.

Finally, I have to acknowledge permission to make use, in our questionnaires, of the Hall-Jones scale from *Social Mobility in Great Britain*, edited by Professor D. V. Glass and published by Routledge & Kegan Paul Ltd.

H. A. CLEGG

Nuffield College

v

CONTENTS

PART I: INTRODUCTORY

TABLES

Chapter 4

Chapter 5

Chapter 6

Chapter 7

Chapter 8

Chapter 9

PART I

INTRODUCTORY

CHAPTER I

THE NATURE OF THE INQUIRY

DOUBTS about the quality of British trade union officers have been voiced often in recent years, by politicians (of both parties), business-men, civil servants, trade union members and trade union officers themselves. Sometimes the complaint is that trade union officers are not of the quality of the great men of the past, fifty, thirty, or perhaps only ten years ago. Offices once held by men whose mission was to change the world (so it is said) have now become just another profession. Since it is thought to be badly paid, it is only to be expected that it does not attract capable recruits. Post-war nationalization and the practice of appointing trade union officers to positions on the boards and in the labour departments of the nationalized industries is thought to have denuded the unions of their best men. There are fears for the future. When the 1944 Education Act has taken full effect, it is said, every child with high intelligence will find a place in a university, and wage-earning occupations will be left to the duller minds. Trade unions will then be administered by men of small intelligence unless the unions revolutionize their methods of recruitment and build up a staff of graduate officers.

Introducing the General Council's proposals for expanding its training college to the 1957 Trades Union Congress, Wilfrid Beard said:[1]

I should like to recall a meeting that I had only a few weeks ago with the headmaster of probably one of the greatest schools in Britain, a school that has provided some of the finest men and brains in many walks of life. I was attending a conference, and he was there and we had some discussion, and he said to me: 'Do you know, Mr. Beard, I am wondering where you are going to get your trade union leaders of the future. When you were younger many of you were forced to go into industry and you devoted your time to educating yourself to serve the Movement which has become so great. But what is going to happen in the future? That kind of boy is not going to go into industry, he is going to come to me. He is going to go through my school, he is going to go through the University, and he is going into the highest walks of life in many fields. What are you going to do about the future of your trade union officers?'

[1] 1957 T.U.C. Report, p. 389.

B

3

Mr. Beard's subsequent remarks showed that he shared the head-master's fears. From discussions with leaders of most of the major unions we have learned that many of them feel this to be one of the most serious of the problems which face them. But are they justified? Do the facts support them?

In two issues of February 1959 the *Economist*[1] published 'The Anatomy of British Trade Unions—A Special Survey in Two Parts'. Its first section, entitled 'The Men Who Matter', describes trade unions as 'to some extent a trained (not always a particularly skilfully trained) corps of bargainers, whose say has been increased, but whose spirit has been eroded, by the power and security that full employment brings'. 'Dues and the salaries of most trade union officials', it says, 'are now kept so low by the votes of the members themselves (much lower in real terms than before the war) as seriously to prejudice both the quality of service that the unions offer and their staying power in disputes.'

Of full-time officials the *Economist* boldly states 'there are only 3,000 of these', but quotes no source, and later says that whether they are appointed or elected, 'it is usual for the people already in control eventually to get their own way about who their colleagues shall be'. An even bolder estimate follows: 'The problems that occasionally arise about the election of some of the 3,000 full-time trade union officials in Britain are as nothing, however, besides the problems that can be set by the power wielded by some of the 200,000 trade union organizers [from the context this means shop stewards] on the factory floor.'

'Almost all unions', says the *Economist*, 'maintain a thriving education department. . . .' Amongst other remarks about the job of the trade union officer, it says: 'It is surprising how often one meets a union official who spends most of his time arguing with his members—or more often with local shop stewards—in favour of management schemes for introducing piecework, streamlining production and the like.'

'. . . Too few men', we are told, 'have recently been seeking union office.' Trade union 'rule books see to it that officials have as few privileges as possible'. As a means to full-time office 'in general, life service is a must. Thus the next generation of union leaders will have to come through the secondary modern schools and apprenticeship courses, at a time when neither is geared to the needs of the really able child.'

---

[1] February 21st and 28th.

One or two of these statements can be corrected without deep inquiry—for example, the number of trade union education departments. Others, such as the contents of trade union rule books, can be checked without too much trouble. But most of the *Economist's* statements could be substantiated only by lengthy and detailed research. It gives figures of 3,000 full-time officers and of 200,000 shop stewards without quoting a source because there is no source worth quoting. No one knows how trade union officers spend their time, so that the *Economist's* guess that many of them spend most of it talking to their members about specified subjects is as good as another. The *Economist* may be correct in its forecast that future full-time trade union officers will be drawn from the secondary modern schools, but the fact that few unions appoint university graduates to full-time posts is not sufficient to establish the proposition.

Consequently the main objective of this study has been to discover the facts and to set them down, so that future discussions of the subject may be more informed. Where our information has allowed us to draw conclusions about quality, we have drawn them; but we have also included much more that seems to us to be important; and we have pursued a number of problems which arose in the course of our work. We began, for example, by collecting statistics about full-time trade union officers from trade union head offices. It is impossible, however, to collect meaningful figures without some definition of the categories concerned, and it soon became clear to us that there was no accepted definition of a full-time trade union officer. The term is not synonymous with 'trade union employee', still less with 'fully employed on trade union work'. A trade union typist is clearly not a trade union officer, but the line between officers and 'staff' or 'clerks' is variously drawn by different unions. The full-time branch secretary may or may not be a full-time trade union officer according to rule. Sometimes he is not even a full-time employee of his union, and the full-time convenor of shop stewards is rarely, if ever, a union employee.

These are not marginal quibbles. According to the definition given, the officer force of at least one trade union can be doubled or trebled. Few trade unions know exactly how many of their members are working full-time on their behalf, and some can give only a very approximate estimate. All this means that we were required to do a good deal of digging before we could interpret and compare the experience of different unions.

We soon came to the view that the best way of presenting most of our findings was by comparing officers in one union, or group of unions, with others. There are many important differences between unions, and this method allows us to reveal these differences, to ask why they exist and which practice is the best. In order, therefore, to make the comparisons intelligible we now turn to a brief account of the main characteristics of the major unions, and an account of the classification which we have used for different types of union.

CHAPTER 2

UNIONS AND UNION TYPES

THE 'BIG SIX'

IN recent years the six largest British trade unions have become known as the 'Big Six'. They are: the Transport and General Workers' Union (1,266,023 members);[1] the Amalgamated Engineering Union (888,363); the National Union of General and Municipal Workers (774,940); the National Union of Mineworkers (674,088); the National Union of Railwaymen (355,440); and the Union of Shop, Distributive and Allied Workers (353,131). The total membership of these unions has for some years added up to a little more than half of the total trade union membership affiliated to the Trades Union Congress (8,176,252) and rather less than half the total membership of all British trade unions (9,616,000).[2]

Many of the comparisons we shall make will be between two or more of the big six. Whatever can properly be said about any one of them is thereby true of a significant section of the trade union movement. We therefore give a brief outline of the major characteristics of each one of them.

THE TRANSPORT AND GENERAL WORKERS' UNION

The Transport and General Workers' Union is the direct descendant of Ben Tillett's dockers' union which leaped to fame in the Dock Strike of 1889. It took on its present name and constitution in an amalgamation of 1921. At that time it was still predominantly a union of dockers and road transport workers, but subsequent developments (particularly amalgamation with the Workers' Union in 1928) have spread its interests far and wide.

[1] We have brought all our series of figures up to December 31st, 1958, or to the latest possible date in 1958. Except where the text makes clear that it is otherwise, it is this final figure which is quoted. See Appendix 2.

[2] This figure is published annually in the *Ministry of Labour Gazette*. Besides T.U.C. affiliates it includes the National and Local Government Officers' Association (246,578) and the National Union of Teachers (229,594, including 14,966 associate members at Teachers' Training Colleges). Amongst the smaller organizations are some that cannot be trade unions at law, and might not be generally accepted as trade unions, but these do not make a very large contribution to the total.

Although other unions organize some dockers and some road transport workers, the Transport and General Workers is *the* union in these industries. It is of no significance on the railways or amongst most classes of seamen. Elsewhere it organizes labourers in building, in shipbuilding and in certain other industries, and production workers in a wide range of manufacturing, foodstuff and service industries (above all in the huge, sprawling engineering industry). This by no means exhausts the list (the union, for example, includes some farmworkers, and has its own clerical and administrative section) but it is sufficient to give some notion of the wide scope of the union and of the different aspect which the union wears in different industries. It also reveals the dualism of the union between strike-prone sections, such as the dockers, and some of the more pacific groups of general workers. Engineering workers (especially in the motor-car industry) come somewhere between the two. This dualism has been to some extent reflected in the leadership. In his early years as general secretary, Ernest Bevin had a reputation as a militant strike-leader as well as a brilliant negotiator. After 1926 the negotiator took over, and the tradition established by the later Bevin was turned almost into a gospel by his successor, Arthur Deakin. The present general secretary, Frank Cousins, has moved once more towards militancy.

The union's constitution is also dualistic. Whether his branch is a 'general branch', or confined to workers from one industry, each member belongs both to a region and to a trade group. The affairs of the region are administered by a Regional Secretary, and those of the trade group (which deals with industrial matters) by its national and regional trade group secretaries. Both regions and trade groups have their own conferences and committees, and both elect representatives on to the union's General Executive Council.

All full-time officers of the union are appointed, except the general secretary (and one or two officers whose posts are governed by amalgamation settlements). Moreover, on the three occasions on which this office has fallen vacant, the previously appointed assistant general secretary has been chosen, so that it seems likely to become virtually an appointed office. The chairman of the General Executive Council is not a full-time officer.

At one time the Communists were a considerable minority in the conferences, committees and staff of the union, but in 1949 the rules were amended to debar members of Communist and Fascist parties from office.

THE AMALGAMATED ENGINEERING UNION

The Amalgamated Engineering Union was founded as the Amalgamated Society of Engineers in 1851, and adopted its present title on a further amalgamation in 1920.

Despite its part in two of the most famous disputes of the nineteenth century (the Engineers' Lock-Outs of 1852 and 1897) its reputation in that period was generally as an aristocratic, conservative and wealthy association of time-served craftsmen, as much concerned with friendly benefits as with improving wages and conditions.

Two factors have wrought great changes. Before the end of the nineteenth century the union had made its first moves towards including less-skilled workers. Further relaxation in the rules began to take effect during the economic expansion of the later 'thirties until to-day apprenticed craftsmen form a minority of the total membership. Secondly, the rise of the shop stewards' movement in the First World War affected the engineers more than any other union, and ever since then a section of shop stewards have provided a militant and politically 'left-wing' element within the union.

These factors produced a swing to the left in the union's leadership. After the last war there followed a gradual groping back towards the right which has taken on firmness and resolution under the Presidency of W. J. Carron. But on too many occasions conflicts between the right and the left have gone unresolved and this has led to confused and vacillating policies.

As a result of changes in its composition the union now consists of skilled craftsmen, labourers working with engineering craftsmen, and production workers in engineering factories (including women). The first group is to be found as maintenance workers in almost every industry in the country. Where they choose to do so, these craftsmen can often persuade their assistants to join their union. In most sections of the engineering industry proper skilled workers are now confined to the tool-room, to maintenance and to other specialized departments, and the general run of productive workers can be classified as semi-skilled. In one factory they may be organized by the Amalgamated Engineering Union, in another by the Transport and General Workers, and in another by the National Union of General and Municipal Workers. In many undertakings, including some of the biggest (such as Fords at Dagenham), all three are in competition.

The branches are supposed to be based on place of residence, and no branch is confined to a single undertaking except by chance or by some local arrangement. Branches are grouped into relatively small districts whose secretaries and committees (on which shop stewards as well as branches are represented) play an important part in the union's affairs.

The full-time officers of the union are elected. Since 1958 they have been subject to re-election at five-yearly intervals. Before that, re-election was required each third year. The Executive Council of seven members serves full-time, and the union has a full-time President (who is the eighth member of the Executive Council), as well as a general secretary. Besides ranking as the senior officer the President is responsible for industrial matters.

The frequent elections required by the union rules serve as a constant focus for factions within the union. The union has never been 'Communist-controlled', although more than once since the war the National Committee (the annual conference and main policy-making body) of the union, and its Executive Council, have almost come under Communist sway. Even after a determined counter-attack by their opponents the Communists retain considerable power through their influence in several of the main industrial centres and district committees.

The National Union of General and Municipal Workers

The General and Municipal Workers trace their descent from Will Thorne's Gasworkers' Union of 1889, and took on their present form in an amalgamation of 1924. Their major characteristics may be drawn out by comparison with the Transport and General Workers, whom they resemble in so many respects.

The industrial coverage of the union is almost identical with the Transport and General Workers. In some instances they work as equal partners, but in many industries the one is clearly in the lead and the other has only a minority interest. The General and Municipal Workers have only a few isolated pockets of membership in transport, but take the lead in municipal employment, gas, electricity and water supply.

Consequently the General and Municipal Workers lack any large militant section. They have had difficulties with their shop stewards, but these have been contained. Since the amalgamation, the union has always stood to the right of the movement. Communists have been effectively debarred from full-time office since 1926, and have never constituted an effective power within the union.

Although the different industrial interests of the union are allocated between a group of national officers, the union has never adopted the trade group structure of the Transport and General Workers. All branches, whether general or specialized, take part in the affairs of the national union only through the medium of their district.[1] The ten district secretaries serve with fourteen 'lay' members of the union on the General Council of the union, and five of them constitute half the membership of the National Executive Committee. It is normally one of these district secretaries who serves as chairman of the union, but the general secretary is unquestionably the chief executive of the union, and there is no assistant general secretary to provide an automatic succession.

The union preserves a nominal electoral procedure for full-time officers. In the first place, officers are appointed. After two years' satisfactory service their names are submitted to a ballot in their district, in which they may be opposed by any other member of the district. Contests are the rule, but no appointed officer has yet been defeated. Once elected, officers may be promoted by the appropriate committee to the posts of national officer or district secretary, although for special reasons a ballot has occasionally been held for a district secretaryship. The last contest for the general secretaryship was a real and close-fought contest.

THE NATIONAL UNION OF MINEWORKERS

At first sight, the National Union of Mineworkers should be the most simply and easily described amongst the major unions, since it has very little membership outside the employment of the National Coal Board, and covers the vast majority of the Coal Board's employees. In fact, however, this simplicity is deceptive, for the change from the old Miners' Federation of Great Britain (1888) to the new National Union of Mineworkers (1945) left the union still federal in form, and each of its constituent areas has retained its own sometimes complex and invariably individual structure.

The core of the union is provided by the underground face-workers, but the union includes almost all manual workers, both underground and on the surface. It has arrangements with the two general unions, the engineers' and certain other unions, concerning

[1] The National Union of General and Municipal Workers' District is equivalent in size to the Transport and General Workers' Regions.

craftsmen and some other minor groups. It also includes the majority of the Coal Board's clerical and supervisory employees; although here again it has arrangements with other unions.

The great majority of its members are in branches (or 'lodges') covering a single colliery. The branches are grouped in Areas. Most of these Areas are the old constituent associations of the Federation, except that several small associations in the Midlands have been grouped into a Midlands Area. Besides the geographical Areas there are several occupational 'Areas': the Cokemen, the Colliery Officials and Staffs, two groups of mechanics and enginemen, and two 'power groups' constituted by the mining membership of the two general workers' unions.

The national union has two full-time officers, the President and the General Secretary, a part-time Vice-President (who is invariably a full-time Area Officer, although the post is also open to lay members); and a considerable staff. Each Area has its own staffing arrangements and these differ considerably from each other. All full-time officers are elected, however (but not subject to re-election), and each post requires national approval.

The members of the National Executive Committee are elected by the Areas. Both full-time officers and lay members are entitled to stand, but, in fact, very few laymen are successful in elections. In 1958 only five of the twenty-seven members elected by the Areas (excluding the representatives of the two 'power' groups, who are national officers of the general unions) were lay members. Each of the major Areas includes its chief officer (Secretary or President as the case may be) amongst its representatives, and this, of course, increases the strength of federal tendencies within the union. Each of these officers is reluctant to interfere with his peers lest he suffer in his turn.

For some years past, the Communists have controlled the major offices in the Scottish and South Wales Areas, and have had some influence elsewhere. The present general secretary is a Communist, as was his predecessor. For all that, the Communists have not succeeded in exerting a predominant influence on the policy of the union at any time since the war.

THE NATIONAL UNION OF RAILWAYMEN

The National Union of Railwaymen claims to be the union for all railwaymen. It is, in fact, the only considerable union for all the conciliation grades (wage-earners) apart from footplate staff, most of whom are in the Associated Society of Locomotive Engineers and Firemen. It includes some of the railway salaried staffs, most of whom are in the Transport Salaried Staffs Association, and it organizes about two-thirds of the 120,000 railway shopmen. Many of the skilled workers in the workshops, however, are in other unions.

It is the most centralized of the major unions. For most purposes its branches are in direct contact with Head Office, and its districts have only limited significance in the union's constitution. Each has its own organizer, but he has no staff, and most administrative matters are handled by headquarters.

The full-time officers of the union are elected for life. The members of the Executive Committee hold office for three years, one-third being elected annually. The work of the Committee and its sub-committees has always been more onerous than that of similar committees in other unions, and in recent years it has reached such proportions that its members rarely, if ever, have time to give to their nominal posts in the railway service, although they are not officially full-time employees of the union. Since two consecutive periods of office are debarred by rule, the members of the committee must return to their railway posts at the end of their periods of office. The President is elected annually, and is eligible for re-election up to a total of three consecutive years of office.

The union has the reputation of being on the left of the Trades Union Congress and the Labour Party, but has never been controlled by the Communists. For many years the Independent Labour Party had a greater following amongst its members than in most unions.

THE UNION OF SHOP, DISTRIBUTIVE AND ALLIED WORKERS

The Union of Shop, Distributive and Allied Workers descends from the Amalgamated Union of Co-operative Employees through amalgamations with other groups of warehousemen, shop assistants and the like in 1921 and 1946. The core of its membership is still in co-operative employment, which includes a number of manufacturing and food-processing industries as well as retail shops. In addition the union has a considerable membership in the private retail trade and in private firms in a number of industries and services, including some manufacturing industries.

Its structure bears resemblances to those of the two other general unions. National officers deal with the affairs of its various industries, and administration is primarily in the hands of divisional officers. The divisions play a smaller part in the union's affairs than do the powerful districts of the General and Municipal Workers. On the other hand, although the union holds an Annual Trade Conference for each major section of its membership, in addition to its Annual Delegate Meeting, these sections are not so powerful as the trade groups of the Transport and General Workers. The officers (other than the general secretary) are appointed without any pretence at elections.

The union has a reputation for independence of opinion and a bias to the left rather than to the right, but its small minority of Communists have never amounted to more than an occasional embarrassment to it.

TRADE UNION TYPES

Besides collecting the fullest possible information about the 'Big Six' we have collected information about a considerable number of medium-sized unions. Comparisons between a large number of units cannot be conveniently presented or comprehended, so that it is necessary to find some method of grouping all unions (including the 'Big Six') by common characteristics in order to present our results. The customary classifications are: craft unions (unions which recruit from one skilled occupation or a related group of occupations), industrial unions (which organized one industry completely) and general unions (whose membership is so diverse as to defy classification). Students have long agreed that these classifications do not suffice to distinguish the main types of British trade unions, but have not agreed on a new set of categories. Accordingly we have found it necessary to develop our own system of five types. We do not claim any universal significance for it, and put it forward only as a useful means of analysing certain information about British trade unions. The five types are: General, Single-Industry, Skilled, Ex-Craft, White Collar.

GENERAL UNIONS

General unions have a coverage so wide that they cannot possibly be pressed into any other category. We place three British unions in this group. The Transport and General Workers' Union and the National Union of General and Municipal Workers are obvious candidates. Along with them we include the Union of Shop, Distributive and Allied Workers.

Most of that union's members are co-operative employees, but co-operative employment straddles a number of occupations and industries. Shop assistants form the largest single section of the union's members, but the others are spread over a very diverse range of occupations. For some time we debated whether or not it should be included in what we call the 'Single-Industry' group, but decided in the end that it should be treated as a General union, and this decision was confirmed as our inquiries developed.

We have included no unions outside the big six under this heading.

SINGLE-INDUSTRY UNIONS

The classification 'industrial union' is of little value in grouping British unions, for it suggests a union which includes all the workers (or at least all the manual workers) in a given industry, and no one else. There are no such unions in Britain. The National Union of Boot and Shoe Operatives comes very close to the mark, and the National Union of Mineworkers could be slipped by without too much dishonesty, but industrial unionism is merely an aspiration with the National Union of Railwaymen. They share their field with two other considerable railway unions. They are not even consistent in their aspiration, for they have no intention of sacrificing their busworkers.

On the other hand there is need for a term to cover unions which are confined to a single industry, or have their predominant interest in a single industry; which are not limited to skilled workers or to White Collar workers; and which do not share the craft traditions and characteristics of the group we describe as 'Ex-Craft' unions.

Amongst other important unions in this group are the National Union of Railwaymen, the Iron and Steel Trades Confederation (also known as the British Iron, Steel and Kindred Trades Association), the National Union of Seamen, the National Union of Dyers, Bleachers and Textile Workers (although this covers cotton finishing as well as the woollen industry), the Amalgamated Weavers' Association, the Amalgamated Association of Card, Blowing and Ring Room Operatives, and the Union of Post Office Workers. We have also included the National Union of Public Employees. Its membership is spread over municipal employment, the Health

Service and one or two other public utilities, but we regarded these as sufficiently closely associated as to be treated as one industry.

Skilled Unions

None of the big six, not even the Amalgamated Engineering Union, can be classified as a craft union, and, for many years past, the share of this type of union amongst British workers has been on the decline. There are still some important unions, however, which are wholly or mainly confined to skilled or supposedly skilled workers. The United Society of Boilermakers, Ship-Builders and Structural Workers is an example. We have also included the Amalgamated Society of Woodworkers, who now include some 'allied process' workers, but not many.[1] The United Patternmakers' Association is usually quoted as the purest of the craft unions.

In addition to these and similar unions which are still based on the apprenticeship system we have also included in this group another type of union in which skill is acquired by promotion from grade to grade on the job. The Associated Society of Locomotive Engineers and Firemen, for instance, takes in the firemen who have not yet qualified as drivers, and the engine cleaners who have not yet qualified as firemen, in addition to full drivers. The Amalgamated Association of Operative Cotton Spinners and Twiners similarly includes all assistant minders and piecers along with the minders themselves. In neither union can the junior grades be termed apprentices, because promotion depends on vacancies (which may be twenty or more years delayed) and not on the satisfactory completion of a fixed period of training. All the junior members are, however, potential skilled workers, and the interests of skilled workers therefore predominate. It is for this reason that we prefer the term 'Skilled union' to the narrower 'craft union'.

Many of our respondents in the Skilled union group belonged to building unions. In some respects these respondents revealed closely similar characteristics, which were also shared by those from the one building union which we have classified as an Ex-Craft union, the Amalgamated Union of Building Trade Workers. Consequently we have shown separate figures for the building unions in several tables.

[1] Most 'allied process' workers are engaged on machine operations in woodworking factories.

Ex-Craft Unions

The decline of the craft unions has resulted in the development of a new type of union whose characteristics seem to us to have received insufficient attention. They are craft unions which have altered the basis of their membership either by change of rule or by amalgamation, or both, to embrace semi-skilled and unskilled workers (including women workers) but which have maintained the constitutional provisions customary to craft unions (such as the periodic re-election of officers) and whose councils, committees and full-time officer forces are still dominated by apprenticed craftsmen.

The Amalgamated Engineering Union is the most prominent example, closely followed by the Electrical Trades Union. Although both these unions have on occasion laid claim to the title 'industrial', they straddle a great variety of industries. Their opponents some-times accuse them of 'general unionism', but this is incorrect, for all their members are in some sense either engineering or electrical workers, and they have traditions and characteristics quite different from the accepted general unions. Others which we have included in this group, such as the National Union of Printing, Bookbinding and Paper Workers, the National Union of Foundry Workers and the National Union of Vehicle Builders, might well have been placed amongst the single-industry unions. We prefer to use this new classification for them to reflect the domination of craftsmen and craft methods in their affairs.

After some hesitation we have added the Amalgamated Union of Building Trade Workers on the grounds that it has gone further away from strict craft unionism than the Amalgamated Society of Woodworkers. But this is one of the least confident of our decisions.

White Collar Unions

Most students of trade unionism have thought that the difference between unions of clerical, supervisory, administrative and technical workers and other unions are so sharp as to dwarf the difference between these 'White Collar' unions (which may, for instance, be Single-Industry or General), and we have followed this tradition.

It is not easy to find a satisfactory title for this group. Most of them are salaried workers, but not all. The term 'non-manual' is often used, but probably as many of them work with their hands (as typists or technicians) as wear other than white collars. We have therefore retained the older description, which is at least fairly well understood.

Amongst the unions in this group are the National and Local Government Officers' Association, the Civil Service Clerical Association, the Transport Salaried Staffs' Association, and the Clerical and Administrative Workers' Union. The National Union of Teachers is amongst the most important, but has not been included in any of our investigations. The major difficulty was to decide whether the powerful Association of Engineering and Ship-building Draughtsmen[1] was a craft union or 'White Collar', but after some deliberation we placed it in the latter group.

[1] This union is proposing to change its name to the 'Draughtsmen's and Allied Technicians' Association'.

CHAPTER 3

TYPES OF UNION OFFICER

FULL-TIME OFFICERS AND STAFF

THE first stage of our investigation was to seek access to the head office records of a number of unions on the age of entry, period of service, promotion and reasons for ceasing to serve as full-time officers. These records are almost invariably kept only as part of superannuation schemes, and few unions had worthwhile information before the introduction of such a scheme. This determined our starting dates. Many unions introduced a superannuation scheme for staff at a later date than that for full-time officers; some have only partial schemes for staff (or voluntary schemes) whereas schemes for full-time officers are universal and compulsory. Accordingly our attention was directed to the dividing line between officers and staff.

In unions which elect officers the distinction is clear. It is between elected officers and staff. No one who has not won an election can have the full title and privileges of an elected officer. This applies in a union such as the Amalgamated Engineering Union which demands periodic re-election, the National Unions of Miners and of Railwaymen which elect once and for all, and the National Union of General and Municipal Workers, in which election is hardly more than a confirmation of appointment.

In unions which appoint, however, distinctions must be drawn by type of work, responsibility, salary or something else of this kind. At higher stages in the staff hierarchy such distinctions become extremely tenuous. The chief officers of the head office staff of a major union, for example, and its full-time national officers are both primarily administrative and may well have similar salaries and conditions. They both report direct to the general secretary. The remaining distinction is that the former deal mainly with internal union affairs, and the latter with negotiations with employers. This is hardly enough to justify the distinction which still persists in other unions between the 'elected officer' and the 'clerk', so that both in the Transport and General Workers' Union and in the Union of Shop, Distributive and Allied Workers the senior 'staff' posts are graded along with the senior organizing and negotiating posts. The extreme case is that of the National and Local Government Officers' Association, which makes no distinction between officers and staff and uses a single grading system to determine salaries and conditions of work.

It follows that there are difficulties in making comparisons between unions. In one union the research officer, the education officer, or the senior administrative officer may be a full-time officer, and in another a member of the staff. Similar troubles arise even within a single union. In some Areas of the National Union of Mineworkers, for instance, one of the elected full-time officers is the 'Compensation Secretary' and in others 'compensation' cases are handled by a senior member of the staff. In some districts of the National Union of General and Municipal Workers a member of the staff handles legal and industrial injury cases, whereas in others these come within the province of one of the full-time officers. In these circumstances comparisons between unions and sections of unions may be misleading. Apparent difference in staffing can be the consequence of different ways of grading the same post.

One solution would be for us to include all staff as trade union officers. But there are two objections. The first is that when we speak of trade union officers we do not mean to include clerks, typists and telephonists. The second is the insuperable difficulty that many unions have not kept adequate records of their staff.

Another solution would be to classify posts by our own standards, treating all staff doing more than routine office work as officers. This course is also vitiated, however, by the absence of records of staff in some unions.

In the end we decided that we had no alternative but to follow each union's definition of 'full-time officer' for the purpose of extracting information from union records,[1] at the same time collecting figures of staff and of grading systems so that we could detect those instances in which reliance on an individual union's definition might otherwise lead us seriously astray.

[1] In the National and Local Government Officers' Association, we have taken Grade 3 and above as 'officers', and Grade 2 and below as 'staff'. District Organizers, who are roughly equivalent to local organizers in other unions, are included in Grade 3.

Full-Time Branch Secretaries

A similar problem arises over full-time branch secretaries.

In some unions all branches are administered by voluntary or part-time officers, and full-time officers are to be found only at national, regional or district offices. Here there is no difficulty. In others, for instance the National Union of Seamen or the National Union of Boot and Shoe Operatives, full-time branch secretaries belonged to a recognized grade of the hierarchy of officers with exactly the same privileges and obligations as any other full-time officer. Here again no problem arises.

There are other unions, however, in which full-time branch secretaries are distinguished from other full-time officers. The distinction originated in this way. In a union with no formal provision for full-time branch secretaries a large branch which decided that it needed the full-time services of its secretary, and had sufficient funds to pay for them, might act on the decision without consulting its head office. If so the branch secretary would become a full-time employee of the branch without incurring the disabilities which many unions impose on their full-time officers, such as ineligibility for election to the union's national executive committee and annual conference. With continued growth there could develop a group of full-time branch secretaries with a strong interest in preserving their anomalous position.

In a union such as the National Union of Printing, Bookbinding and Paper Workers, which treats its full-time branch secretaries exactly as full-time officers for superannuation purposes, even though not in all other ways, this causes no difficulty. Since it is only an oddity of union rules that distinguishes them from the other, we could add their records in with the rest.

In the National Union of General and Municipal Workers, however, this remedy cannot be fully applied. Their districts have the power, in approved cases, to sanction full-time branch secretaries and, if necessary, to supplement the income derived from the $12\frac{1}{2}$ % commission on contributions received by the branch secretary in order to yield a satisfactory salary. The districts may also recommend such secretaries for membership of the union's superannuation fund. There are instances, however, in which, because of his age or for some other reason, the secretary is not proposed to the fund, or is not accepted by it. In these instances his records are not kept by the union's head office. There are other instances in which branch secretaries decide that their commissions are sufficient to support them without seeking or receiving official sanction, so that no question of superannuation arises. Complete records of the union's full-time branch secretaries are consequently not available, and the union can give only an approximate figure of the current total of such secretaries.

The National Union of Mineworkers presents much more formidable problems. It makes no provision for the superannuation of full-time branch secretaries,[1] and its head office has no official cognizance of them, and maintains no records concerning them. Nevertheless, there are many of them, probably more than the number of full-time officers as defined by rule.

The most simple instance is where a branch (or lodge) decides to support its secretary full-time and pays him out of branch funds (perhaps raising an additional levy for the purpose). This is common, for example, in South Wales. In Yorkshire it frequently happens that a branch secretary draws loss of work allowance (to which he is entitled when on union business) for each working day of the week throughout the year and thus becomes in all but name a full-time employee of the union although he remains on the colliery books. In some Areas it is not uncommon for the branch secretary's employment in the pit to be a paid sinecure so that he can devote his whole time to union business and to negotiations with management.

These practices have undoubtedly been encouraged by the disappearance of checkweighmen as the practice of payment by weight has been replaced by payment by yardage. In the past the checkweighman was stationed at a convenient point in the pit to deal with the men's problems, and could usually find time from his statutory duties to attend to them. The post was filled by vote of the face-workers and paid by a levy on their earnings, and it was natural that the men should find it convenient to elect their branch secretary, although in other instances they chose another branch officer or perhaps a deserving 'compensation case' who needed the money. Some Divisional Coal Boards have argued that the statutory obligation applies only where coal is weighed. In other coalfields the miners themselves have been glad to see the end of the levy when the system of measurement has changed. But the Derbyshire Area of the union, for instance, has insisted that when the check-

---

[1] In 1959 the National Coal Board conceded that full-time branch secretaries of the National Union of Mineworkers could be admitted into the Mineworkers' Pension Scheme.

weighman goes he shall be replaced by a check measurer. The duties of this post are more easily performed even than those of the checkweighman, and if the men choose to elect their branch secretary it can provide him with a paid post which allows him to give most of his time to union business.

Practice varies widely from Area to Area. Some Areas of the union can give the exact number of full-time branch secretaries. Others—including those with most full-time secretaries—regard it as none of their business and can give only rough approximations. In one instance an Area Secretary's guess was not within ten of the figure which subsequent investigation suggested. The Nottinghamshire Area, on the other hand, regards the appointment of full-time branch secretaries by the branches as contrary to the rules of the national union. In any event the distinction between full-time and part-time secretaries is no easy matter, and no Area has kept records of its full-time secretaries in any of the categories which have been mentioned.

Consequently we found once more that we had no alternative but to follow the practice of union rules. We have included full-time branch secretaries along with other full-time officers in those unions which adopt this method, and excluded them elsewhere. We have, however, collected as much information as possible about full-time branch secretaries in this second group of unions so as to correct any false conclusions into which we might otherwise have fallen.

BRANCH SECRETARIES

So far as we know all trade unions have branches (or lodges) except for a few tiny unions so small as to find subdivision unnecessary. Apart from two exceptions the chief administrative officer of these branches (or lodges) are part-time or voluntary branch (or lodge) secretaries. These two exceptions are the full-time branch secretaries which have already been mentioned, and those other full-time officers of trade unions who have to administer the affairs of one or more branches (temporarily or permanently), usually because no one in the branch is both willing and able to do the job.

In general the branch secretaries as a group raised fewer problems of definition and delimitation than the others which we have included in this study.

Shop Stewards and Others

The shop steward is elected by his fellow trade unionists in his shop to represent them to management. Often the stewards of the same union in a works come together as a shop stewards' committee and choose one of their number to be 'convenor' or 'chief shop steward'. In large shops there may be 'shop convenors' who in turn choose the 'works convenor'. In many instances the stewards of different unions form joint committees with their own officers.

Very generally this description applies to the engineering industry and to a wide range of manufacturing industries. But there are many complications.

Nomenclature varies. The printing industry has 'Fathers of the Chapel' and 'Imperial Fathers' (or 'Mothers') with much the same kind of functions. Some unions have 'collecting stewards' who draw a commission for collecting subscriptions and passing them on to the branch secretary (or treasurer). Sometimes collecting stewards act as shop stewards; frequently one man or woman is elected to both posts. In other unions which have no prescribed collecting stewards, many shop stewards in fact collect.

A considerable number of firms and undertakings have joint committees of management and workers under a wide range of title, the most common of which, perhaps, is Works Council. Some of these committees are to be found in undertakings which have no stewards. Where stewards are elected they may constitute the workers' side of these committees. In other works there are separate elections and frequently different electorates (with *all* workers entitled to vote for committee members, regardless of their standing with the unions). If so, there will probably be a considerable overlap. There are thus a number of union members who are works councillors but not shop stewards and who perform very much the kind of functions which shop stewards normally perform.

Then there are unions, such as the National Union of Mineworkers, who expect their branch officers to negotiate with management. In some Areas the branch secretary does the work; in others the president. The third major officer of the branch is the 'delegate' who represents it in the higher counsels of the union. It is unusual, but not unknown, for him to do the job. Branch officers commonly negotiate with employers in civil service unions. In these instances, however, the branch officers negotiate for a very much larger number than the average shop steward—sometimes more than a thousand members. Consequently they may arrange for some assistance in the different departments of the undertaking. Some miners' Lodges arrange for one member of the committee to come from each face so that he can deal with easier problems on the spot.

Our solution to these various problems of definition is to include along with shop stewards all those officers (such as 'Chapel Fathers') who do the same job as shop stewards, collecting stewards who negotiate with management, works councillors (under whatever title) who are trade union members and negotiate with management, and 'branch negotiators' (except branch secretaries). Where branch secretaries are also elected shop stewards or works councillors their functions are separately considered under each heading.

One difficulty remains. Shop stewards normally receive no payment from their union except for such branch offices as they may hold. They customarily negotiate with management during working hours, and may be allowed to meet in committee during their 'employer's time', receiving either their agreed time rate or their average piece-work earnings for time spent away from their jobs. Some convenors spend far more time on union business than working at their employment—or, indeed, all of it. There are firms which recognize this, appoint the convenor or chief steward to a sinecure, and even allow him an office and a telephone. The post of secretary of the workers' side of the Works Council may be full-time, paid by the firm. There is at least one instance in which a branch has levied itself to pay a full-time salary to the chief shop steward at the works at which its members are employed. There are several instances in which a part-time branch secretaryship and a convenorship together provide full-time work and a full-time income.

In the Civil Service branch officers are allowed some freedom to negotiate with management during working hours. Some Areas of the National Union of Mineworkers pay a 'delegation fee' to the branch officer who spends a day on union business, and it thus happens that a large miners' lodge may have a full-time President in addition to or instead of a full-time secretary.

Once more we face the problem of the union officer who is paid to spend his whole time on union work, but is not regarded as a full-time union officer. This time the problem is even more intractable than that of the full-time branch secretary, for no unions keep any records whatsoever. All that can be said is that we have collected what information we could.

OTHER UNION OFFICERS

There are other groups of union officers which have not been the object of a separate inquiry in this study. There are executive members (other than full-time executives), conference delegates, district, area and regional committee members, and branch officers other than secretaries and branch negotiators. The main reason for this exclusion is the common problem of the social investigator: 'You have to stop somewhere'; but there are also specific excuses.

We have looked into the other offices held by branch secretaries and shop stewards. They include such a large number of members of higher union committees, councils and conferences that we feel confident that what we can say about secretaries and stewards will also reveal something about them. So far as other branch posts are concerned, we felt that they were generally less important than the groups we have included and were therefore the most obvious candidates for exclusion.

CHAPTER 4

THE METHODS

UNION RECORDS

AS we have said, we began our study by collecting information concerning 'full-time' trade union officers (and certain full-time branch secretaries) from the records of union superannuation schemes, supplemented by journals and minute books. In most instances it was not possible to obtain information relating to periods before the inauguration of superannuation schemes.

Altogether eighteen unions were included in this part of the study. They included the eight largest unions, and ten out of the next twenty-one. Their records are complete since 1947,[1] so that since then our data covers the full-time officers of unions with about 60% of total trade union membership. The earliest records begin in 1921, but it is not until 1927 that the number has increased to cover trade unions with about a quarter of total membership.

None of these unions can be regarded as small. We considered seeking information from small unions, but there were three reasons for deciding against it. Firstly, the number of 'full-time officers' in most small unions is so few that very little can be deduced about length of service, turnover and the like. The retirement or death of one officer can radically change the figures from one year to the next. Indeed, some of the unions we did include had too few 'full-time officers' to allow firm conclusions on these points. Secondly, two or three small unions might be unrepresentative of their kind, and it would have involved a great deal of effort to collect information from a large number. Finally, whatever figures we collected from small unions would be swamped in a total. Accordingly we decided to find out something about small unions in other ways.

The eighteen unions include the three general unions, seven Single-Industry unions, one Skilled union, four Ex-Craft unions and three White Collar unions. Skilled unions are, of course, mostly small. We also collected figures from the one trade union federation which employs a number of full-time officers—the National

---

[1] Except for some gaps in the records of the Amalgamated Society of Woodworkers.

Federation of Building Trade Operatives.[1] We did not, however, include the staff of the Trades Union Congress.

From most of these unions we also collected figures of the *current* numbers of staff, and the grading system and departmental systems into which they are organized. In addition, either from records or by interview, we have collected information about methods of recruitment, about the salaries of officers and staff and the methods by which they are settled, and about a number of other matters from most but not all of the eighteen unions.

The information was collected over a period of about two years, but was all brought up to date at 31st December, 1958.

LOCAL SURVEYS

The next major stage was a local survey of union officers, part-time and full-time, in Oxford. During the survey we interviewed all the full-time officers in Oxford, all but 4 of the 62 branch secretaries, and 14 shop stewards, of whom 7 were convenors. Although we found the information interesting and useful, we make relatively little use of it in the subsequent pages, for several reasons. A single area presents a very biased sample. Secondly, it would not be easy to avoid all danger of the identification of individuals in giving details of officers and branches from a single area. Thirdly, the most important result of the survey was to allow us to prepare questionnaires for national distribution. We shall, however, refer to the survey from time to time, trying to avoid clues to identification, and drawing attention to dangers of bias.

Several other local inquiries were also undertaken, primarily to discover information about the National Union of Mineworkers which was not available at headquarters, and to attempt to find some information on the number of full-time convenors of shop stewards.

QUESTIONNAIRES

From the beginning we realized that a great deal of information which we required could be had only from trade union officers themselves, and we constructed several questionnaires, one of which (for voluntary and part-time officers) was widely used at the summer schools of several unions. After some time we decided against both

---

[1] Unlike the other two major federations (the Confederation of Shipbuilding and Engineering Unions and the Printing and Kindred Trades' Federation) the Federation employs regional officers as well as a headquarters staff.

the questionnaire and the method of distribution. The questionnaires have been analysed,[1] and occasional use made of the results, but we decided that the job must be done again.

Accordingly we designed a new set of questionnaires[2] based on the work we had already done. There were four questionnaires: one for shop stewards, one for branch secretaries (other than full-time), one for full-time officers (aimed primarily at the lower levels of the union hierarchies) and one for full-time branch secretaries which combined most of the questions of the second and the third.

To obtain satisfactory results it was clear that we required a wide distribution both by area and by union, and we decided to achieve this by asking students of Ruskin College (who might be expected to have good contacts in the Labour Movement) to handle it in their home districts during their Easter vacation, 1959. Happily there was a good response and we were able to cover every important industrial area in the country.

The shop stewards' questionnaire was filled in by 226 respondents, including 13 women. The union distribution (Table 1) shows almost half the shop stewards in three unions.

TABLE 1

DISTRIBUTION OF SAMPLE OF SHOP STEWARDS BY UNION

Union	Actual Numbers	Proportion
Transport and General Workers' Union	33	15
Amalgamated Engineering Union	50	22
National Union of General and Municipal Workers	23	10
Others	120	53
TOTAL	226	100

In terms of membership, the Amalgamated Engineering Union is grossly over-represented, but this may be justifiable. Many unions have no shop stewards, and the branch negotiators of other

[1] The sample was heavily biased in several respects. Of the 284 usable answers, 81% were from members of the Transport and General Workers, and almost half of those who gave their occupations were road transport workers.
[2] Reproduced in Appendix 1.

unions cover far more members than do shop stewards. There are some sections of both the Transport and General Workers and the National Union of General and Municipal Workers which do without stewards. Consequently our union distribution may in fact be roughly representative. A distribution exactly proportionate to union membership would certainly be unrepresentative.

The branch secretaries' (other than full-time) questionnaire was filled in by 211 respondents, including 6 women.

The union distribution is checked against the figures for numbers of branches returned to the Registrar-General in Table 2.

TABLE 2

DISTRIBUTION OF SAMPLE OF BRANCH SECRETARIES BY UNION

Union	Actual Numbers	Proportion of major unions in total sample	Proportion of major unions in total trade union branches
Transport and General Workers' Union	22	10	12
Amalgamated Engineering Union	23	11	6
National Union of General and Municipal Workers	14	7	6
National Union of Mineworkers	12	6	2
National Union of Railwaymen	14	7	3
Union of Shop, Distributive and Allied Workers	14	7	4
Building Unions	20	10⎫	67
Others	92	42⎭	
TOTAL	211	100	100

The average size of branch covered by the questionnaire (464) compares with an average for all unions of 230. This bias was inevitable given the method of distribution. The secretaries of large branches are likely to be more prominent in local trade union affairs and therefore better known to our assistants and more accessible. This also helps to explain the over-representation of all the 'Big Six' except the Transport and General Workers' Union. Their average branch sizes (except for the Shop, Distributive and Allied Workers) exceed the average for all unions (see Table 30A).

The characteristics of the group of 190 'full-time trade union officers' (four of them women) who answered the third questionnaire are checked against the results of our study of head office records in Table 3.

TABLE 3

DISTRIBUTION OF SAMPLE OF UNION OFFICERS BY UNION

Union	Actual Numbers	Proportion of major unions in total sample	Proportion of major unions in total officers of all unions
Transport and General Workers' Union	33	17	23
Amalgamated Engineering Union	11	6	6
National Union of General and Municipal Workers	15	8	6
National Union of Mineworkers	6	3	4
National Union of Railwaymen	0	0	1
Union of Shop, Distributive and Allied Workers	14	7	6
Building Unions	30	16 ⎫	54
Others	81	43 ⎭	
TOTAL	190	100	100

This is as satisfactory a spread as we could have hoped. The whole group contains too many officers from small unions, but in this respect it tends to balance the concentration on large unions in our survey of records.

The analysis of union records showed an average age of 50·5 years for all 'full-time' officers of the unions covered. The average of the questionnaire respondents (50·6) is remarkably close.

The questionnaire was designed for local and regional union officers and we have excluded the replies of the several national officers who filled it in.

The questionnaire for full-time branch secretaries found thirty respondents (including one woman) from unions in which such secretaries are not recognized as 'full-time officers'. Where full-time branch secretaries in other unions had filled in this questionnaire, their replies were transferred to the 'full-time officer' group. The small number may well bear a roughly correct relationship to the total of 190 'full-time officers'. Eight of the thirty respondents were from the National Union of General and Municipal Workers and eight from the National Union of Mineworkers. No other union had more than two respondents. Their average age was 51·1 years, which may be compared with an average of 52 (at the end of 1958) for all full-time branch secretaries included in the superannuation schemes of the National Union of General and Municipal Workers and the National Union of Printing, Book-binding and Paper Workers.

Table 4 shows the percentage geographical distribution of the four samples.

TABLE 4

GEOGRAPHICAL DISTRIBUTION OF SAMPLES

Region	Shop Stewards	Branch Secretaries	Full-Time Officers	Full-Time Branch Secretaries
London ..	10	7	10	10
South ..	18	25	19	7
Midlands ..	19	11	21	7
North ..	29	40	36	43
Scotland ..	11	6	3	23
Wales ..	12	11	8	3
N. Ireland	1	—	3	7
TOTAL ..	100	100	100	100

This certainly does not correspond with the distribution of population nor would we suppose that it corresponds with the distribution of trade union membership (whatever that may be). The North is strongly over-represented in three samples, and possibly in the fourth (shop stewards); London is generally under-represented; and not much more could be claimed for the sample of full-time branch secretaries than that they do not all come from one part of the country. For the other three groups, however, the table does show at least a fair spread.

The distribution by union group is given in the next table:

TABLE 5

DISTRIBUTION OF SAMPLES BY UNION GROUP

Union Group	Shop Stewards	Branch Secretaries	Full-Time Officers	Full-Time Branch Secretaries
Skilled ..	37 (17%)	37 (18%)	34 (18%)	7 (23%)
Ex-Craft ..	70 (31%)	43 (20%)	21 (11%)	3 (10%)
Single-Industry	45 (20%)	55 (26%)	64 (34%)	10 (33%)
General ..	61 (27%)	51 (24%)	62 (33%)	10 (33%)
White Collar	12 (5%)	25 (12%)	8 (4%)	—
Other	1 (—)	—	1[1] (1%)	—
TOTAL ..	226 (100%)	211 (100%)	190 (101%)	30 (99%)

White Collar unions are under-represented except for the branch secretary group, and their numbers are so small in the shop stewards and full-time officers group that little can be based on their replies. Apart from that, however, there seems to be a fair representation. The Skilled unions have the smallest membership of the remaining four groups and this is reflected in the samples of shop stewards and branch secretaries. Ex-Craft unions appear to be under-represented on full-time officers and full-time branch secretaries, but this is at least in part because the major union in the group, the Amalgamated Engineering Union, has a high ratio of members to officers, and no full-time secretaries.

The proportion of women in each group is, of course, far below the share of women in total trade union membership but perhaps not so far below the proportion of women in these four groups of trade union officers.

For some time we were at a loss to discover any means of eliciting evidence on the comparative quality of officers from different unions. In the end it occurred to us that personnel officers were the largest group who come into frequent contact with union officers, and that many of the personnel officers of major firms deal with a wide range of unions. We therefore constructed a brief questionnaire to elicit their views. A number of major undertakings agreed

[1] This respondent was an officer of the National Federation of Building Trades' Operatives, which includes unions from three different groups.

to co-operate, and the questionnaires were sent to them for distribution to their personnel officers. Seventy-two replies were received.

Each questionnaire was answered by only a small proportion of the total number in the class concerned. This is inevitable in any practical inquiry into the characteristics of large groups of people, but it raises the question of how far the results can be taken as representative. Some assurance is given by the structure of the samples which has just been set out. We have not gone further and submitted our figures to significant testing analyses. Having taken the advice of statisticians, we decided that common sense was the best guide in this instance.

Comparisons between the answers to our three main questionnaires provide fairly firm conclusions, since there were about two hundred respondents for each of them. We have also made considerable use of breakdowns within each of these three classes of trade union officer, by union groups or by actual unions. The numbers vary between seventy and twenty, and in one or two instances we have used even smaller sub-groups. Here we draw attention only to large variations between sub-groups, and confine ourselves to general comments upon them. We do, however, regard all the figures we have used as significant, as yielding reliable information about the groups from which the samples are drawn. The answers to the great majority of our questions are consistent not only with the answers to other questions but also with the information which we have obtained by other methods.

OTHER METHODS

It has always been the practice of Nuffield College to hold conferences at which academic students and men of affairs can discuss matters of common interest. Papers covering the preliminary results of several aspects of this study have been discussed at conferences of trade union officers and at a conference of personnel officers and officers of employers' federations. We have also taken the opportunity of discussing our problems with trade union officers and others whenever the opportunity arose.

PART II

RESULTS

CHAPTER 5

FULL-TIME OFFICERS[1]

TOTAL NUMBERS

ASSUMING that the ratio of officers to members is the same for all unions as in the eighteen unions for which we have records,[2] it is possible to make an estimate of the total number of trade union officers in Britain. Table 6 shows the estimated figure for several representative years since 1921. The years are chosen to give six-year periods from 1921 onwards (with 1947 and 1953 included to permit two further six-year periods ending in the last year for which we have figures). The advantages of these dates are that 1921 was the membership peak after the First World War; 1933 was the trough; 1939 and 1945 show pre-war and wartime growth; and subsequent years the slow levelling off of post-war growth.

The most interesting column is the last, which shows the ratio of members to officers. Not much reliance can be placed on the estimate for 1921, since the coverage of our data is too small. Probably, however, the ratio of members to officers was high in most unions in that year owing to recent rapid growth to which the unions had not adjusted themselves. Otherwise the figures show a decline during the inter-war years of heavy unemployment and then an increase to 4,000 in 1939, which has been roughly maintained since then. This change is not the consequence of the inclusion of new unions in the 1939 figures, but represents a permanent shift affecting most of the unions included.

We have not included the National Federation of Building Trades' Operatives in these figures since their membership arises

---

[1] This chapter is concerned only with 'full-time officers' as defined by union rules. Accordingly, the quotation marks which we have hitherto used to denote this are no longer necessary.

[2] Since these unions are relatively large, and most of the 657 unions in the country are small, this assumption requires justification. We suggest three reasons for supposing that it is not too wide of the mark. First, our unions already cover a wide range of size, and show no tendency for the ratio of members to officers to vary with size of union. Second, although we suspect that some of the unions of 5,000 to 50,000 members have a lower ratio than our unions, this should be balanced by the consideration that very few of the 304 unions with less than 500 members, and few of the 161 unions between 500 and 2,500 have a full-time officer at all. Third, the membership of all the 621 unions with less than 50,000 members accounts for less than 20 per cent of total trade union membership. (*Ministry of Labour Gazette*, December 1959.)

TABLE 6

Estimates of Total Numbers of Full-Time Officers

Year (Beginning)	Total Membership of Unions supplying data (A)	Total Officer-Force of these Unions (B)	Total T.U. Membership[1] (C)	(A) as a % of (C) (D)	Estimated total number of Officers (E)	Members per Officer (F)
1921	1,225,512	205	8,348,000	14·7	1,395	5,978
1927	1,214,482	387	4,919,000	24·7	1,567	3,138
1933	1,102,438	412	4,444,000	24·8	1,661	2,676
1939	1,902,301	476	6,053,000	31·4	1,516	3,996
1945	4,617,249	1,188	8,087,000	57·1	2,081	3,887
1947	5,237,470	1,312	8,875,000	59·0	2,224	3,992
1951	5,493,355	1,508	9,242,000	59·4	2,539	3,643
1953	5,743,565	1,537	9,524,000	60·3	2,549	3,737
1957	5,874,523	1,530	9,704,000	60·5	2,529	3,840
1959	5,813,634	1,533	9,616,000	60·5	2,534	3,792

[1] Source: *Ministry of Labour Gazette.*

from the affiliation of other unions. The total officer force of all federations (including the Trades Union Congress) is probably rather more than sixty, making perhaps 2,600 in all. The comparable pre-war figure would have been much smaller. A revision of the figures to include them would consequently give a fractionally smaller ratio of members to officers, but would make no appreciable difference to the change from one year to another.

DIFFERENCES BETWEEN UNIONS

Table 7 sets out the ratios of members to officers in individual unions since 1921 together with their total officer-forces at the present time.[1]

The first thing to be said about these figures is that the exclusion of full-time branch secretaries (where not defined as union officers by rule) has a marked effect on several of the unions. The National Union of Printing, Bookbinding and Paper Workers is the most obviously affected. Since we have exact figures of this union's full-time secretaries it is possible to calculate that their inclusion would reduce the 1959 ratio to 2,773. The effect on the National Union of Mineworkers is probably not so great as this, and on the National Union of General and Municipal Workers certainly much smaller, but still considerable. The ratio of staff to officers also affects the comparison. The National Union of Railwaymen, for example, has a staff five times larger than its corps of officers. Numbers of full-time convenors and staff side secretaries must also be taken into account. These corrections can only be applied, however, after we have presented our findings on this type of union officer; for the moment we must confine ourselves within the definitions of the rule books.

Fluctuations over the years divide the unions into five groups. The largest includes six unions (the General and Municipal Workers, the Shop, Distributive and Allied Workers, the Electricians, the Agricultural Workers, the Iron and Steel Trades Confederation and the Transport Salaried Staffs) whose ratio rose before and during the war and has since remained fairly constant. In each case this was

[1] The ratio for each union may, of course, hide wide variations in different sections of the union, as, for example, between the various Areas and sections of the Mineworkers. Amalgamations may also affect the ratio. For example, the increase in members to officers in the Union of Shop, Distributive and Allied Workers between 1947 and 1951 may have been due to a redeployment of staff due to the amalgamation of the two constituent unions (the National Union of Distributive and Allied Workers and the Shop Assistants' Union) which became effective in 1947, and not to any reduction in service to members.

TABLE 7.   Member/Officer Ratios (Number of members per officer at beginning of year)

	1921	1927	1933	1939	1945	1947	1951	1953	1957	1959	Total Officer-Force 1959
T. & G.W.U.	—	—	—	2,303[3]	2,124	2,304	2,168	2,255	2,265	2,222	551
A.E.U.	11,833	5,286	6,000	11,887	8,537	6,633	5,188	5,851	6,235	6,345	140
N.U.G.M.W.	—	2,430	2,118	3,480	4,762	5,847	5.199	5,317	5,468	5,236	148
N.U.M.	—	—	—	—	7,687	6,108	6,618	6,891	7,253	7,248	93
N.U.R.	32,793	22,796	18,120	19,298	21,282	22,637	17,035	17,267	16,060	16,152	22
U.S.D.A.W.[2]	1,130	862	1,076	1,500	2,386	1,855	2,521	2,247	2,373	2,407	147
N.A.L.G.O.	—	—	—	—	—	2,705	3,284	3,528	4,045	3,680	67
E.T.U.	—	—	1,727[1]	2,904	4,416	5,061	4,580	4,621	5,070	4,897[4]	47
N.U.A.W.	—	—	1,322	1,806	2,765	3,475	3,639	3,219	3,051	3,002	50
A.W.A.	—	—	—	—	—	1,705	2,173	2,140	1,577	1,690	39
N.U.B.S.O.	—	1,614	1,333	1,474	1,667	1,477	1,519	1,500	1,594	1,679	46
N.U.P.E.	—	—	4,141[1]	2,518	3,090	3,430	3,785	4,242	3,915	4,004[4]	46
I.S.T.C.	4,793	2,382	2,618	4,497	5,213	5,836	5,366	5,874	6,298	5,813	22
A.U.B.T.W.	—	—	—	—	1,371	1,557	1,451	1,362	1,313	1,115	74
C.S.C.A.	—	—	—	9,342	11,531	10,258	12,250	11,507	11,447	10,627	13
T.S.S.A.	6,218	3,914	4,212	5,810	6,832	6,240	6,087	6,537	6,751	6,717	13
N.U.P.B.P.W.	—	—	—	6,488	6,743	6,486	8,248	9,164	10,986	10,109	15

[1] 1934.

[2] There is probably some error in the pre-war figures of the Union of Shop, Distributive and Allied Workers. This is due to uncertainty about the exact number of officers.

[3] 1943.

[4] In 1959 both the Electrical Trades' Union and the National Union of Public Employees were planning substantial

due to the failure to increase the corps of officers with rising membership. One union, however, the National Union of Railwaymen, has failed to decrease its corps with falling membership and its ratio has thus fallen.

Four unions (the Transport and General Workers, the Miners, the Boot and Shoe Operatives and the Civil Service Clerks) have remained roughly constant, although the absence of pre-war figures for the first two may be the explanation.

Sharp fluctuations in the Amalgamated Engineering Union and the National Union of Public Employees are at least in part due to major expansions in their officer corps after periods of rising membership. The same may perhaps be to some extent true in the remaining unions (National and Local Government Officers, Weavers,[1] Building Workers and Printing, Bookbinding and Paper Workers) whose ratios show erratic but not very large fluctuations.

Table 8 gives the ranking of the thirteen unions for which we have ratios both in 1939 and 1959. It reveals an almost incredible stability.

TABLE 8

FULL-TIME OFFICERS: RANKING OF MEMBER/OFFICER RATIOS

Union	Ranking of Member/Officer ratios from lowest to highest	
	1939	1959
N.U.B.S.O. ..	1	1
U.S.D.A.W. ..	2	3
N.U.A.W. ..	3	4
T. & G.W.U.	4[2]	2
N.U.P.E. ..	5	5[3]
E.T.U.	6	6[3]
N.U.G.M.W.	7	7
I.S.T.C. ..	8	8
T.S.S.A. ..	9	10
N.U.P.B.P.W.	10	11
C.S.C.A. ..	11	12
A.E.U.	12	9
N.U.R. ..	13	13

[1] In the Weavers it would be reorganization to meet *falling* membership, due to the contraction of the cotton industry.   [2] 1943 figure.
[3] The subsequent expansion of the Public Employees' and the Electricians' officer forces does not affect their ranking.

The table shows that unions which grow rapidly are prepared to add new officers to suit. All the thirteen unions except the National Union of Railwaymen and the National Union of Boot and Shoe Operatives have expanded since 1939, but at very different rates. None of them has increased its officer-force at the same rate as its rise in membership, but in each case the lag[1] has been much the same. Otherwise there would have been far greater changes in ranking. The four unions with the greatest rate of expansion of membership were the Engineers, the Electricians, the Agricultural Workers and the Public Employees. Their officer forces increased, respectively, from 31 to 140, from 22 to 47, from 26 to 50, and from 19 to 46.[2] With moderate expansion the General and Municipal Workers increased from 130 to 148, the Shop, Distributive and Allied Workers from 134 to 147 and the Iron and Steel Trades' Confederation from 19 to 22. In the National Union of Railwaymen a slight fall in membership was also accompanied by an increase of officers from 19 to 22, but in the National Union of Boot and Shoe Operatives there was a decline from 59 officers to 46.

Two consequences seem to follow. The first is not surprising—that change in membership is the main cause of fluctuation in the size of trade union officer forces. The second is perhaps more interesting—that each union has long developed its own system of administration and activity which requires a certain number of full-time officers. The systems of administration must be very different from each other, because they permit vastly different ratios of members to officers, but they change very little because the ranking of the ratios remains roughly the same. Accordingly the differences are not likely to be explained except by an examination of the unions' practices in administration and negotiation, and the first step towards this is to say something about the nature of the job of a full-time officer.

MAJOR DUTIES

Respondents were asked to pick out from a list the four aspects of their work (in order of priority) which took up most of their time. By allotting marks (4, 3, 2, 1) to the items in each answer, totals could be added up for the whole sample and for sections of it, and converted into percentages, which cannot, of course, be

---

[1] The lag itself may be partly explained by economies of scale.
[2] See Appendix 4.

taken as the proportion of total working time devoted to that item, but give a fair indication of the order of magnitude. Table 9 gives the percentages for all unions, for the four main union groups,[1] and for unions with low and high ratios of members to officers. The first of these groups includes the officers of all those unions (principally the Transport and General Workers, the Shop, Distributive and Allied Workers, and the major building unions) which we know to have less than 3,500 members to each officer; the second includes the officers of those unions (principally the Engineers, the General and Municipal Workers, and the Mineworkers) which we know to have more than 4,500 members to each officer. There were 78 respondents in the first group and 42 in the second.

From the table it would seem that the total working time of trade union officers is divided into four roughly equal parts which are spent on negotiating, on various types of office work, on various kinds of meetings and on recruiting new members or helping existing members with their problems.[2] There are, however, considerable differences between union groups.

We suggest that the first step towards an explanation of the differences, however, is not to be found in the nature of the union groups, but in the differences in the ratios of members to officers.

It would seem to be a reasonable assumption that the volume of negotiations in an industry is even more dependent upon the structure of the industry, its technology and its methods of wage payment than upon the trade unions within it; and that these same factors will limit the possibility of transferring negotiating duties from full-time to other officers. It follows that, within any given industry, large variations in the ratio of members to full-time officers will entail variations in the proportion of time given to negotiations by full-time officers. It should also follow that, if we take unions negotiating in a wide variety of industries, officers in unions with high ratios of members to officers give more of their time to negotiations than do the others; the last two columns of Table 9 show that this is so. Much correspondence arises from

[1] In this and subsequent tables in this chapter, and in Chapter 9, no separate figures are given for the White Collar group because of the small number of officers in these unions who answered the relevant questionnaire. Consequently the figures in the union group column are not the sum of the union group figures.

[2] Personal problems of members include industrial injury cases and other claims for benefits under social service legislation, the preliminary stages of claims for damages at common law and other legal proceedings; sometimes tax assessments and housing problems; and in some instances almost any other personal or family matter imaginable. They also border on collective bargaining in instances where issues of discipline or personal grievances have to be raised with the employers.

TABLE 9

FULL-TIME OFFICERS: IMPORTANCE OF MAIN DUTIES

Duty	All Unions	Skilled	Ex-Craft	Single-Industry	General	Unions with low Member/Officer ratio	Unions with high Member/Officer ratio
Negotiating ..	24	19	27	26	24	21	33
Correspondence ..	18	26	20	17	15	15	20
Helping Members with individual problems ..	17	14	16	17	18	18	14
Branch Meetings	13	8	10	13	18	16	13
Recruiting New Members ..	12	15	8	10	14	15	6
Other Meetings ..	8	6	15	7	7	6	12
Other Office Work	5	8	3	6	3	5	2
Financial Work ..	3	4	1	4	1	4	—
TOTAL ..	100	100	100	100	100	100	100

negotiations, and we should therefore expect correspondence to vary with negotiations, as in fact it does.

Officers in unions with low ratios transfer the time saved to other office work and financial business, to recruitment, and to helping individual members with their problems. It is also worth noting that these last two duties varied most clearly with the number of hours worked in the sample as a whole. Officers working over 60 hours gave recruiting a 34% higher rating than those working less than 50 hours, and helping individual members a 25% higher rating. It seems fair to conclude that most full-time officers can find time for this type of work only when other more urgent work has been completed.

This, however, does not finish with Table 9, for it does not explain variations in branch and other meetings, nor the very high score of correspondence, other office work and financial work in the Skilled unions. For this purpose we need certain additional information.

Sometimes no successor can be found to a branch secretary who has resigned or died in office, and a full-time officer takes over the affairs of the branch until a replacement is discovered. Our survey seems to show, however, that this is a common practice only in certain unions. Excluding these full-time branch secretaries who rank as full-time officers, 35% of the sample were acting as secretaries for one or more branches. The distribution between union groups was not very significant, except that the Ex-Craft group came very low and the General group rather high, but the variation between unions was more interesting. Fifteen out of 33 officers of the Transport and General Workers' Union acted as branch secretaries, but only two of them for more than two branches. The Shop, Distributive and Allied Workers' score was 10 out of 14, with four taking care of four or more branches.[1] All three officers of the National Union of Agricultural Workers who answered the

[1] The Shop, Distributive and Allied Workers have taken a full check on this point, and found that the information supplied by our sample is substantially correct, except that it rather exaggerates the number of officers who are responsible for four or more branches.

It must also be pointed out that, since the union does not employ full-time branch secretaries, the Executive Council has directed full-time officers to look after a number of the larger branches in the union which, they consider, constitute too heavy a task for part-time secretaries. This accounts for about 14% of the total number of branches administered by full-time officers, but almost two-thirds of the total membership of these branches. The remaining branches are about the average size for the union as a whole. In a number of branches the responsibility of the full-time officer is transitional, until a volunteer can be found; but in about half the total, including all the branches where this responsibility is by direction of the Executive Council, it has lasted for five years or more.

questionnaire looked after branches, two of them covering seven branches each, and all three returned a working week of over eighty hours. At the other extreme a number of unions, including the Engineers and the General and Municipal Workers, returned no examples of the practice at all.

In those unions in which this practice is common, full-time officers give more time than elsewhere to branch meetings. Since amongst major unions these unions are the Transport and General Workers' Union and the Shop, Distributive and Allied Workers, this explains the high score of the General union group under this heading.

Other questions concerned secretarial assistance and the provision of office equipment. The first of these questions was perhaps misleading, for we asked: 'Does the union employ a secretary to help you?' It is apparent that some officers who had access to typing pools in union offices answered 'yes' to this question, whereas others answered 'no'. Even so, it is significant that the score of the Skilled unions (59% with assistance) was the lowest of any union group. Amongst the whole sample, 75% were supplied with all four pieces of equipment covered by our question (typewriter, duplicator, telephone and filing cabinet); amongst Skilled unions the score was again 59%. As usual, these figures are almost identical with the figures for the Building unions.

It would seem sensible to conclude that officers in the Skilled group, and therefore in the building unions, have to give more time to office work because they lack adequate assistance and equipment.[1] This explanation, however, cannot apply to the Shop, Distributive and Allied Workers' score for correspondence (28%), which is the highest of all. Unless this is due to a sampling error, it can only be explained as arising out of the branch business for which so many of their officers are responsible, or some other peculiarity in the structure of the union.

Finally the high score of the Ex-Craft group for 'other meetings' is due entirely to the Engineers. If this is not a sampling error, it may be due to the fact that most of the respondents from that union were District Secretaries, and had to attend a considerable number of meetings in that capacity.

[1] The Building Trade Workers, for example, provide only a typewriter for their Divisional Organizers, or the opportunity to have work done by the clerical staff at the nearest Divisional Office. We have, in fact, come across Organizers who enjoyed neither of these facilities. Their duties of negotiation, recruiting and servicing branches clearly entail correspondence and the maintenance of records. And some of them have also to act as branch secretaries.

ORIGINS

We can comment on four aspects of the origin of trade union officers: their age, their educational experience, their previous occupation, and the previous union offices held.

We have full information on age for all the unions whose records we studied except for the Amalgamated Society of Woodworkers. Table 10 sets out the details for various periods.

TABLE 10

FULL-TIME OFFICERS: AVERAGE AGES ON ENTRY

Union	Figures available from	Overall Average	Average since 1945
T. & G.W.U.	1943	41·3	41·0
A.E.U.	1921	44·3	45·4
N.U.G.M.W. ..	1921	39·0	38·5
N.U.M. ..	1945	47·4	47·4
N.U.R. ..	1921	43·6	44·4
U.S.D.A.W. ..	1921	36·0	35·8
N.A.L.G.O. ..	1947	34·4	34·4[1]
E.T.U.	1934	45·0	46·3
N.U.A.W. ..	1933	36·6	35·2
A.W.A. ..	1941	42·3	42·3
N.U.B.S.O. ..	1927	43·0	40·5
N.U.P.E. ..	1934	33·9	33·5
N.F.B.T.O. ..	1921	44·3	43·6
I.S.T.C. ..	1921	41·6	38·2
A.U.B.T.W. ..	1945	40·7	40·7
C.S.C.A. ..	1939	29·2	30·5
T.S.S.A. ..	1921	40·3	39·5
N.U.P.B.P.W.	1939	40·6	41·4

Eight of the eighteen unions have an average age of entry into office of under forty years of age since the war, although two of these (the Iron and Steel Trades' Confederation and the Transport Salaried Staffs) have an overall average of rather more than forty years. All eight appoint their officers, except the General and Municipal Workers, and their elections are no more than confirmation of previous appointments.[2]

[1] Since 1947.   [2] See p. 11.

Of the ten other unions, seven elect their officers and two (the Transport and General Workers' Union and the National Federation of Building Trades' Operatives) appoint. In the tenth union, the Amalgamated Weavers' Association, some local associations elect their officers and others appoint. It therefore seems to be a firm conclusion that the age of entry is largely determined by the method of selection.

The customary explanation for this is that a man has to reveal his abilities and make himself known to a far larger number of people to win an election than to impress a committee, and that this process takes time. It does not necessarily conflict with the rather cynical view that trade union members are more conservative than their leaders and would not want to give a chance to a bright young man.

There have been slight variations over time in some unions, but the main impression is one of stability. Most unions stick closely to their own pattern, and given the small numbers involved in most unions in any one period, the variations are remarkably small.

The method of appointment seems to determine the differences between union groups. All three general unions effectively appoint. In one the age of entry is well below average, the second somewhat below, and the third fractionally above. All three White Collar unions appoint and all three are below average, two well below. Most Ex-Craft unions elect. Two of them come about the average for age of entry, and the other two are amongst the highest. The practices of Single-Industry unions vary and so do average ages of entry. They range from the highest of all, the Mineworkers (which elects), to the next to lowest, the Public Employees (which appoints).

This table does not tell us anything about Skilled unions, most of which elect their officers, but we know from our questionnaire answers that the *average* age of officers of Skilled unions is high. Their group had the smallest proportion under 40 (6%) of all five groups, and the highest proportion (18%) over 60.

All but 10% of the officers who answered our questionnaire had left school at 15 years of age or earlier.[1] The remainder subdivides into 8% who left at 16 and 2% at 17 years of age. The last school attended for the whole sample and for union groups is shown in Table 11.

Although the average of the sample was 50·6 years, 71% of the Grammar School boys were under 50 years old, and 36% of them under 40. All seven Technical School boys were under 50, although

[1] 22% at 13 or earlier, 58% at 14, and 10% at 15.

TABLE 11

FULL-TIME OFFICERS: LAST SCHOOL ATTENDED

Union Group	Type of School				Total
	Elementary	Technical	Grammar	Other[2]	
Skilled	82	3	12	3	100
Ex-Craft ..	71	–	24	5	100
Single-Industry	77	6	6	11	100
General ..	72	5	18	5	100
White Collar[1] ..	37	–	50	13	100
All Groups ..	74	4	15	7	100

only one was under 40. In other words, although the proportion of Grammar and Technical School boys in the total sample is 19%, it rises to 32% of officers under the age of 50, and 44% of officers under 40. It seems to be a fairly safe deduction that the number of Grammar and Technical School boys amongst full-time officers is rising and may continue to rise. This conclusion is hardly affected by the exclusion of the White Collar unions. The proportion of general union officers under 40 with a grammar or technical school education is 50%.

The analysis by groups has some mild surprises. It is only to be expected that the officers of White Collar unions should include many Grammar School boys, but it is surprising that both Ex-Craft unions and still more that General unions should rank so high in this respect, and also surprising (although the numbers are not large enough to bear much weight) that nearly all the Technical School boys should be in the Single-Industry and General groups.

Previous occupations are analysed in Table 12.

Part of the explanation of the relatively high proportion of Ex-Craft union officers who have attended Grammar Schools may be that virtually all of them (as in skilled unions) are drawn from skilled occupations. Single-Industry unions reveal a fairly wide spread of occupations which contains no surprises. The General

[1] In this instance it seemed worthwhile to include the White Collar group separately, despite its small number.
[2] These include Central Schools and Scottish schools which do not fit into the English categories. Most of them appear to be the equivalents of Elementary rather than Technical or Grammar Schools.

TABLE 12

Full-Time Officers: Previous Occupation

Union Group	Un-Skilled	Semi-Skilled	Skilled	Clerical	Supervisory and Admin-istrative	Other	Total
Skilled ..	–	3	94	–	–	3	100
Ex-Craft ..	–	–	95	–	–	5	100
Single-Industry	5	34	41	8	1	11	100
General ..	5	48	14	18	8	7	100
All Groups ..	3	28	47	11	4	7	100

unions, however, are more interesting. They have few unskilled workers, and a surprising number of both clerical and supervisory, and of administrative employees (the latter from the retail trades). It is the practice in all three General unions to allow members of the union staff to apply for posts as organizers, and (from inspection of records and from interviews) we know that a number of applications of this kind are successful.[1] This does not appear to be more than a minor part of the explanation here, however, for only 1% of the total sample stated that they had previously been employed as members of trade union staffs. Most of this group of officers must, therefore, come from clerical, supervisory and administrative posts organized by the General unions. It should be noted that the Transport and General Workers has a special clerical and supervisory section, and the Shop, Distributive and Allied Workers include shop managers as well as assistants.

Most of them had showed an interest in trade unions from an early age—far earlier than we believe is customary. Over half held their first voluntary office by the age of 25 (13% under the age of 20); and over three-quarters by the age of 30.

Table 13 shows two things: that, although most full-time officers have previously held only branch or workshop posts, a fair proportion have had district or regional offices, and a number have served on national executive councils or committees;[2] and that prospective

[1] This practice is also common in the White Collar group. In the Transport Salaried Staffs, for instance, eight of the thirteen full-time officers in 1958 had been promoted from the union's clerical staff.

[2] Details for the Transport and General Workers from 1922 to 1952 are given in V. L. Allen, *Power in Trade Unions*, 1954, p. 161.

TABLE 13

FULL-TIME OFFICERS: VOLUNTARY POSTS HELD
IMMEDIATELY PRIOR TO FULL-TIME WORK

Office	Percentage holding office
Shop Steward, etc.	35
Branch Secretary	38
Branch Chairman	27
Other Branch Office	12
District Office	14
District or Regional Committee	16
National Executive Council ..	9
Other National Office	4
Others	7
None	5
No information	7

full-time officers (and probably other prominent lay members) are likely to hold more than one office. The total number of offices held work out at more than 1·7 for each respondent who had held a voluntary position in the union immediately prior to full-time office.

SELECTION

The division between unions which elect their officers and those which appoint has already been noted. We have made no investigation into the electoral procedures of those unions which adopt this method. A number of unions, however, only accept the credentials of a candidate for full-time office if, in addition to showing the requisite period of membership in the union and so forth, he had passed a prescribed examination. The procedures of the cotton unions in this respect were made famous by the Webbs;[1] candidates for the posts of General Secretary and Assistant General Secretary in the Amalgamated Society of Woodworkers have to pass certain elementary tests and undergo an oral examination; and the National Union of Railwaymen has perhaps applied the examination technique more rigorously than any other union.

[1] Sidney and Beatrice Webb, *The History of Trade Unionism*, 1920 edition, pp. 308–309; *Industrial Democracy*, 1920 edition, pp. 196–199. The examination system is still customary for selecting candidates for office in the Weavers' Amalgamation, but the constituent associations, particularly those paying the lowest salaries, do not always insist on it.

E

The National Union of Railwaymen requires candidates for the posts of Organizer and of Assistant General Secretary to sit a written examination, which is held in an hotel adjacent to the union's Head Office. So far as Organizers are concerned, two papers are set by the senior Assistant General Secretary, one in finance,[1] which they answer in the morning, and one in other duties, which they answer in the afternoon. In the first period they are given a set of branch books into which a number of errors have been introduced and they are judged on the discovery of the errors and on the recommendations which they make in the report they have to write on what action should be taken. In the second period they are asked to answer twenty questions on other aspects of administration, on legal work and on rates of pay and conditions of service. Once candidates have passed the examination their names can go forward in elections so long as they remain otherwise eligible and are willing to offer themselves.

Unions which appoint do so through selection by a national, regional or district committee as the case may be. The composition of the committee varies. In the National Union of General and Municipal Workers, for example, district appointments are normally district affairs, and the District Committee interview the candidates and make the appointments. In the Transport and General Workers, however, the General Executive Council is ultimately responsible for all appointments, and the 'examining sub-committee', to which it delegates responsibility for junior posts, includes two representatives of the Executive Council from regions not concerned in the appointment. In both these unions, and in several others, the Education Department helps in this process by encouraging likely candidates to take courses arranged by the union, thus improving their potential.

The Shop, Distributive and Allied Workers have a more elaborate scheme. In 1951 its Executive Council decided that the advertising of posts as they became available was not an efficient method of discovering and encouraging potential full-time officers. The union journal announced that future appointments to full-time posts would be made from a pre-selected panel, and asked members who wished to be considered for inclusion in the panel to submit applications. These candidates were then interviewed by a sub-committee

---

[1] Contrary to the practice of most unions, the National Union of Railwaymen requires its organizers to exercise considerable supervision over the financial work of branch secretaries who otherwise make their returns direct to the union's headquarters.

in their own Divisions, consisting of Executive Council members from other Divisions, the President, either the General Secretary or the Assistant General Secretary and the Divisional Officer. After interview each candidate was placed in one of three grades—'short list', 'next time', or 'unsuitable'. Subsequently, as posts became vacant the Executive Council interviewed a selection of candidates chosen from the short list who were thought most suitable for the particular post. The process has been repeated at intervals of two years so that the panel might be replenished. Candidates graded 'next time' are sometimes advised how to improve their chances in the next round. Unsuitable candidates are discouraged from re-applying, but they cannot be debarred from their rights as union members merely because of a sub-committee's opinion of their abilities. One of them has, in fact, succeeded in winning his way through to the final panel.

The selection methods employed by the Railwaymen and the Shop, Distributive and Allied Workers serve to give some idea of the pool of capable and willing potential officers in the two unions, and the details are set out in Tables 14A and B.

TABLE 14A

NATIONAL UNION OF RAILWAYMEN: CANDIDATES FOR THE POST OF ORGANIZER 1948–1959[1]

	1948	1949	1950	1954	1958	1959
Eligible Candidates[2]	47	44	30	29	28	20
Submitted to Test	39	31	18	19	22	12
Passed	9	4	5	1	5	3
Available from those who have passed previous tests	8	13	12	10	6	8
Submitted to ballot	17	17	17	11	11	11
Elected immediately after passing tests	1	–	–	–	–	–
Subsequently elected	3	4	2	2	2	2

[1] Examinations are held only in years in which vacancies occur.
[2] Candidates must be nominated by ten or more branches.

TABLE 14B

UNION OF SHOP, DISTRIBUTIVE AND ALLIED WORKERS: CANDIDATES FOR INCLUSION IN PANEL OF PROSPECTIVE OFFICERS

	1951	1953	1955	1957	1959
New Applicants	195	114	93	79	114
Applicants previously 'short-list' ..		39	27		
Applicants previously 'next time' ..		13	7	35	35
Applicants previously 'unsuitable' ..		1	1		
Total Applicants	195	168	128	114	149
Total Interviewed[1]	167	132	107	93	131
'Short-list'	70	50	64	47	49
'Next time'	22	29	8	14	20
'Unsuitable'	75	53	35	32	62
Appointments during subsequent two years	9	7	11	8	–

Although the Railwaymen's standards of marking might appear to be affected by what they regard as the appropriate number of candidates for a ballot paper,[2] these two tables reveal the number of those that the Executives of the two unions are willing to certify as suitable for full-time posts as well in excess of the demand. It may be that the considerable leakage of approved candidates from the Shop, Distributive and Allied Workers' panel is to be explained in terms of disappointment sustained by candidates included on a panel so large that many of them cannot expect an appointment for many years, if ever. On the other hand, some may lose interest as a result of a change of occupation or promotion in their employment. In the National Union of Railwaymen successful examinees

[1] This excludes candidates withdrawing before interview, candidates failing to attend and candidates actually appointed between original application and interview.

[2] The union denies that this is so, and claims that every effort is made to ensure a consistent standard.

seem willing to continue chancing their electoral luck. One candidate in the 1959 ballot had passed the examination before 1947.

SALARIES

The remuneration of full-time trade union officers has always
been a problem. On 10th September, 1876, the four agents of the
Durham miners wrote to the Durham Miners' Association in these
words:[1]

Let fair hours be fixed for us to work, whether the work be done in the office
or in the County. Every hour we lose out of this time for any cause whatsoever,
for purposes apart from your legitimate work, let a proportionate amount of our
wages be kept back; and on the other hand, for every hour worked beyond this
time, either in office, or in the County, let us be paid a proportionate amount of
overtime. . . .
We are well aware, that in accordance with our recognized principles, if you
demand arbitration in this or in other matters, either in regard to our wages or
practices, we cannot refuse you, neither will we complain. But it must be clearly
understood, that arbitration must be an open one, so that our wages can be reduced
or advanced to any amount which the Arbitrators or Umpire may deem necessary....
But just as you refuse to take reductions at the mere bidding of the employers—
and we think rightly so, so we shall refuse to take the slightest reduction at your
mere bidding, without full and open inquiry, as a matter of right and justice.
Don't force upon others, burdens that you refuse to carry yourselves. The
privileges we have sought for you, we shall assuredly claim *from you*, for ourselves

This is an evergreen problem. Most trade union officers to-day
would give heartfelt support to a demand for the same rights from
the union as they demand from employers for union members.
But there is a real problem. So long as the officers of trade unions
are treated both as the servants of a movement and as the practitioners of their profession, their remuneration cannot be treated on
the same terms as the payment of trade union members by outside
employers. New criteria apply. It may be thought impossible, for
example, for a man to represent the interests of workers if he is
paid to live on a scale which they cannot afford. There is also a
problem concerning the method of settling his salary. Trade unions
believe in collective bargaining, but officers are paid out of the
members' contributions. If the salaries and conditions of officers
are settled by a conference or a ballot vote, collective bargaining
becomes impossible. Collective bargaining is only possible if

[1] The occasion was a resolution submitted to the Council of the Association proposing
that the agents' pay should be stopped when receiving pay elsewhere for attending arbitration
meetings in other counties, or performing similar paid work.

workers are collectively organized. Should the officers of a trade union be permitted to form their own union?

Many unions have responded to these problems by removing the topic to their secret counsels and imposing a ban on all publicity. Consequently, although we have collected fairly full information from a number of unions, we publish the details only of those unions who have not succumbed to secrecy and still broadcast their officers' salaries in their union rule book. Four of these are the Amalgamated Engineering Union, the National Union of Railwaymen, the Electrical Trades Union and the Amalgamated Union of Building Trade Workers; and Table 15 sets out the details.

TABLE 15

FULL-TIME OFFICERS: SALARIES IN CERTAIN UNIONS

Percentage Increase in Retail Prices 1938–58[1]	..	..	..	..	.. 175
Percentage Increase in Wage Rates 1938–58[1]	..	..	..	..	.. 205
Percentage Increase in Earnings of Male Adults 1938–58[2]		..	..	.. 280

Union	Grade	1938 Salary	1958 Salary	% increase
A.E.U.	President and Gen. Secretary	£450	£1,180[3]	162
	Executive Committee Member	£350	£940[3]	169
	Assistant Gen. Secretary	£365	£910[3]	149
	National Organizer ..	£340	£910[3]	168
	Regional Officer[4] ..	—	£880[3]	—
	Divisional Organizer ..	£340	£880[3]	159
	District Secretaries: Over 20,000 members	£208–340	£880[3]	309 (at minimum)
	Less than 20,000 members		£850[3]	159 (at maximum)

[1] London and Cambridge Economic Service. [2] *Ministry of Labour Gazette.*
[3] Excludes £100 personal allowance. [4] Post created since 1938.

Union	Grade	1938 Salary	1958 Salary	% increase
N.U.R.	General Secretary ..	£800–1,000	£2,045	156 (at minimum) 105 (at maximum)
	Assistant Gen. Secretary	£700	£1,545	121
	Head Office Organizer[1]	—	£1,300	—
	Organizer	£550	£1,160	111
E.T.U.	General Secretary ..	£500	£1,158	132
	President[1]	—	£1,158	—
	Assistant Gen. Secretary	£400	£1,068	165
	National Officers ..	£400	£978	145
	Area Officers	£300–338	£858	186 (at minimum) 154 (at maximum)
A.U.B.T.W.	General Secretary ..	£400	£1,197	199
	President	£350	£1,147	228
	Assistant Gen. Secretary[1]	—	£988	—
	Divisional Organizer ..	£208	£845	306
	District Organizer[1] ..	—	£767	—

The range of these figures allows us to say that only two other of the nearly 100 rates that we have collected have risen by less than the lowest increase amongst the printed salaries (111%), and none have risen by more than the largest increase (309%). So far as the 1958 figures are concerned, the only rates higher than the highest shown in the table are those of the senior officers of one or two White Collar unions,[2] and the only lower rates are one or two starting rates for junior officers.

[1] Post created since 1938.
[2] The salary of the General Secretary of the National and Local Government Officers, which was advertised in the press last time it fell vacant, is £3,250–£4,000.

The salaries of the National Union of Railwaymen were well above the average in 1938, and, although they have risen by less than the others, they are still the highest of those included in the table. Otherwise it seems that most union salaries have risen by almost as much as the cost of living since 1938; that a minority (and mostly those of the lower paid) have risen as fast as the wage index; and that only a few exceptional rates have risen by so much as the earnings index.

By these standards trade union officers have done badly. If their salaries were compared with other *salaries*, however, a different tale would emerge. There is no index of salaries since 1938, but all the evidence shows that they have risen by considerably less than wage rates, and certainly no faster than the cost of living.[1] Consequently the experience of the trade union officer is probably about the same as that of the general run of salary-earners.[2]

We have tried to discover from trade union leaders the criteria which they think should apply to union salaries, and have found them most reluctant to give a clear opinion. The only one who had a firm and consistent view held that the important salary is the first year's salary for junior officers. This must be clearly above the incomes of the workers from whom the union recruits, both to make the post attractive, and to give the occupant some dignity. The required margin should be something between 25–50%. Other salaries are of less importance. They must give some recognition for promotion and for increased responsibility, but the main incentives for an existing offer to accept promotion are ambition, or a desire to increase his scope for service to his fellows.

This is at least a coherent approach. The second part receives some support from the very wide spread of top salaries. Whatever the motive for withdrawing salary figures from union rule books, most of the large unions which do not publish their salaries pay considerably higher salaries at the top than do the Engineers, the Electricians and the Building Workers, but it does not follow that starting salaries are also higher.

If this approach is accepted it follows that the decline in trade union salaries since 1938 is becoming dangerous. This is not because

---

[1] The adjudication of Mr. Justice Danckwerts on the incomes of medical practitioners in 1952 seems to have been based on the assumption that professional salaries had risen by about 100% between 1938 and 1950 (*Royal Commission on Doctors' and Dentists' Remuneration*, 1957–1960, Cmnd. 939 of 1960, p. 163). Between 1950 and 1958 average salaries per head in manufacturing industry rose by 55%.

[2] In civil service unions the salaries of full-time officers are directly linked with civil service salaries.

the starting rates of trade union officers have ceased to show a comfortable margin over the rates of, say, skilled engineers, electricians or bricklayers. In December 1958, few skilled workers had a national time rate of more than 5s. an hour or £11 for a 44-hour week. Most of them, however, received considerably more than that, due to overtime, piece-work, or local allowances and plus rates. In October 1958 the *average* weekly earnings of adult males were just under £13 a week, or £650-£700 a year. It is well known that earnings vary considerably from industry to industry, from firm to firm, and even more from man to man. Face-workers in the coalmining industry, for example, were at this time *averaging* nearly £18 a week (including allowances in kind); even in 1957, 16% of boilermakers working for federated shipbuilding firms earned over £20 a week, and there is good reason to suppose that many engineering workers were offering them strong competition.

In 1938 there were probably some engineers who would have lost money if elected to a district secretaryship at £4 a week, and bricklayers who would have lost money on election to the post of divisional organizer at the same figure. There could, however, have been very few electricians who would not have gained handsomely from posts as area officers at £6 a week (average adult male earnings were then £3 9s. a week) and fewer engineers who would not have gained from a divisional organizer's post at £340. To-day there are not inconsiderable minorities of engineers, electricians and bricklayers who would lose (at least, so far as the salary is concerned) by accepting any post in their trade unions.

It is true, of course, that these earnings are not guaranteed. The workers who receive them might fall to their plain time rates next week if circumstances change, and a steady salary at a lower annual figure may have very great advantages for them. Even if this is admitted, however, it cannot be denied that the margins have declined considerably since 1938.

It does not seem, however, that all unions have related starting salaries to their members' earnings in the past. If they had, the salaries should vary with the average incomes of the members of the unions concerned. Amongst those included in Table 15, the Railwaymen are clearly out of line. The average earnings of members of the National Union of Railwaymen are below those of the members of the Amalgamated Engineering Union, and this was probably true also in 1938, but all grades of Railwaymen's officers are paid well above the salaries of officers of the Engineers.[1] Amongst unions not included in Table 15, the officers of the country's lowest-paid industry, agriculture, receive rather lower salaries than officers of most other large unions, but the mine-workers, the country's highest paid workers, do not have the highest paid union officers.

The Amalgamated Weavers' Association has a special problem. Most of its officers are appointed and paid as the Secretaries or Assistant Secretaries of its constituent associations. Because of the decline in the union's membership (it has now only a quarter of its 1921 membership and has lost a third of its 1955 membership over the last three years) some of the local associations cannot properly support a full-time officer. On the other hand, being independent trade unions and not mere branches of the Amalgamation they have in the past offered resistance to suggested mergers. In the mean-time, full-time officers continue to receive obviously inadequate salaries. The Amalgamated Association of Card, Blowing and Ring Room Operatives (the main spinning union) has not the same salary problem, although it is equally affected by the decline of the industry. The salaries of its officers have been traditionally related to the minority of male members in the Amalgamation, who are almost all skilled craftsmen, and are therefore higher than the salaries of officers of the Amalgamated Weavers. Weaving has customarily paid the same rate to men as to women, and weaving is therefore not a high-paid occupation for men.

Some unions have adopted scales for the payment of their junior officers. In one or two unions the scales have as many as five or six annual increments. There is no obvious justification of this arrange-ment. Trade union officers are usually required to undertake the full duties from the day of entering office. In other instances there are probationary periods of up to one or two years, which would justify one or two increments. Most trade union officers enter their career in their thirties or forties so that there is no place for a 'wage-by-age' scale. Since the maximum of the junior grade salary scale is usually fairly closely determined by the rate of the next grade the main con-sequence of the practice seems to be that starting rates are needlessly depressed, and, in so far as recruitment is affected by salaries, the likelihood of securing competent candidates for office is reduced.

[1] It is not easy to reconcile the rates paid to officers of the National Union of Railwaymen with the common opinion that salaries ought to be removed from the rule book because union members are so mean-minded on such issues.

COLLECTIVE ACTION

In order to have any share in the settlement of their salaries, union officers must be organized, and it is not only their interests in major questions of salary that may require representation. Men accumulate all manner of grievances against their employers, both large and small. If it were not so trade unions would lose their *raison d'être*, and trade unions always demand that there should be proper channels for voicing these grievances and seeking to remedy them. Should the officers of trade unions not have the same rights?

There are many unions which make no formal recognition of the rights of their officers in these respects. In the Amalgamated Engineering Union, for example, salaries are settled along with other union rules, and must be altered through the process of rule amendment. Officers are members of the union, and should they be aggrieved by a decision of the union they have the same right as other members to appeal against it to the National Executive Council, and to the Final Appeal Court of the union. Officers of the National Union of General and Municipal Workers have the same right of appeal (except that the union has no Appeal Court). Their salaries are reviewed by the Salaries Sub-Committee of the National Executive Committee, which consists of the five members of the committee who are not full-time officers, subject to the decision of the fourteen lay members of the General Council.

In both these unions (and in many others, including the Mine-workers and the Railwaymen), these formal provisions are modified by informal organization. The officers have opportunities to meet and discuss their affairs and can decide to approach their General Secretary with a proposal for revision of salaries and a request that it should be brought to the notice of the appropriate body. Minor grievances are usually settled directly between the General Secretary and the officer concerned, except that district officers in the General and Municipal Workers approach their district secretary in the first instance. In at least one of the ten districts one of the officers is recognized as the 'shop steward' to speak for himself and his colleagues.

In other unions the officers are recognized as a separate section of the union with certain rights to approach the governing committee as a body. The officers of the Transport and General Workers' Union have a committee for this purpose, and there is a separate officers' 'chapel' in the National Union of Printing, Bookbinding

and Paper Workers. In other unions the officers' organization is
a separate association, as in the Shop, Distributive and Allied
Workers and the National Union of Public Employees. In these
instances the officers belong to two separate organizations, the
unions in which they are officers, and the associations of which they
are members. In one or two instances these associations have
established their position at law. The staff association of the National
and Local Government Officers' Association (which include 'officers'
and 'staff') is a certified trade union,[1] and the field organizers of the
National Union of Agricultural Workers have their own registered
union. Should they be promoted to posts at their Head Office,
however, these organizers join the Clerical and Administrative
Workers' Union along with the rest of the Head Office staff (excluding the general secretary). This seems to be one of the few
instances where membership of *two* unions (since all of them must
hold Agricultural Workers' cards) is a condition of employment.

So far as we know there has only been one attempt to establish
a trade union for trade union officers from different unions. This
was the National Trade Union Organizers' Mutual Association,
promoted by an officer of the Birmingham district of the General
and Municipal Workers. It was seen as an attempt to build up a
position of power in the trade union world, and when he refused
to disband it, the officer concerned was dismissed.[2] It can be seen
that such an organization might be thought to entail awkward
problems of dual loyalty.

The evidence seems to show that no unions which elect officers
have any formal organization for dealing with salaries and grievances. Perhaps there is an appearance of incongruity in the notion
of a body of elected officers forming themselves into a trade union,
since they are clearly not employees in the usual sense; although
that does not destroy their need for protection. Many appointing
unions have, however, come to accept organizations and grievance
procedures. Apart from the incident of the Organizers' Mutual
Association, none of them seem to have suffered any disadvantage
thereby, and there seems to be no reason to suppose that other
unions would lose by imitating them. Perhaps this would allow
grievances a more thorough airing than do less formal arrangements. On the other hand there is little reason to suppose that it

[1] Some unions which are not registered under the appropriate Trade Union Acts are
nevertheless certified to be trade unions by the Registrar of Friendly Societies (N. A. Citrine,
Trade Union Law, 1950, pp. 311–314).
[2] H. A. Clegg, *General Union*, 1954, p. 82.

would result in general increases in trade union salaries, for by no means all of the unions which recognize officers' organizations are amongst those with the highest salaries.

HOURS OF WORK

Precise information on the average hours spent at work each week was given by 159 of the 190 respondents. One or two explained that they were able to make use of records which they had kept; others must have made rougher estimates. The overall average was 57·2 hours a week, well above the average weekly hours of British male workers, which stood at 48·0 in April 1959.

The average disguises a very considerable spread revealed in Table 16.

TABLE 16

HOURS WORKED BY FULL-TIME OFFICERS

Hours	Skilled	Ex-Craft	Single-Industry	General	All Groups
No precise answer	9	15	17	13	14
−40	–	–	6	3	3
41–45	6	5	8	3	6
46–50	32	14	22	11	20
51–55	15	19	19	13	16
56–60	32	19	11	34	24
61–65	3	14	5	8	6
66–70	3	14	3	5	5
71–	–	–	9	10	6
TOTAL	100	100	100	100	100

Most trade union officers work between 46 and 60 hours a week, but a number work either longer or shorter hours.[1] This goes for

[1] Ernest Bevin once described how he spent '115 hours working and travelling for the Union' in what he described as a 'fairly typical week'. (Alan Bullock, *The Life and Times of Ernest Bevin*, Vol. 1, 1960, p. 93.)

each of the four groups included in the table (and for the White Collar group which is excluded since the total number is so small). The only deviation from the norm is that the officers of General unions seem to work slightly longer than others. The same wide range can be found in the four individual unions (the Transport and General Workers, the Engineers, the General and Municipal Workers and the Shop, Distributive and Allied Workers) with more than 10 officers in the sample except that no General and Municipal officer worked less than 46 hours. Many other unions showed considerable spreads.

Most full-time officers, therefore, work long hours, but there are large variations from one officer to another, and these variations are to be found in all union groups and, probably, in all major unions. Variation in hours, in other words, is not a consequence of differences between union administrative systems.

The nature of their work involves most officers in absence from home during evenings and at week-ends, and questions on this point were included. The replies are given in Tables 17A and B.

Thus it appears that most officers spend, on average, three evenings a week and one or two week-ends a month on union business. The few who spend all or almost all of their evenings and week-ends on union work cannot be regarded as typical.

TABLE 17A

FULL-TIME OFFICERS: EVENINGS WORKED

Number of Evenings	Proportion of Sample
One a week	8
Two a week	21
Three a week	34
Four a week	19
Five a week	7
Six a week	2
Seven a week	1
Don't know	2
No answer	6
TOTAL	100

TABLE 17B

FULL-TIME OFFICERS: WEEK-ENDS WORKED

Number of Week-ends	Proportion of Sample
None	5
Less than one a month[1]	18
One a month	35
Two a month	20
Three a month	7
Four a month	2
Don't know	2
No answer	11
TOTAL	100

Analysis by union group and by major unions shows (as with hours) that each has wide variations in the incidence of evening and week-end work. Differences between unions and groups are less marked than the similarities. The officers of General unions seem to give rather more week-ends to their work than do officers of other unions, but in all four main groups one week-end a month is the most common experience, and a few give three and four.

It is one of the characteristics of a trade union officer's life that the intensity of work varies considerably. During a strike, during negotiations or at important meetings, and in the period of preparation for them, he can be working at full pressure, and at other times he may be looking for work to fill his time. Anyone who frequents trade union offices will know that there are times when a visitor is most unwelcome and occasions when he is almost a godsend.

Many trade union officers are willing to admit that their jobs are what they choose to make them. If they cared to cut their work down to the bare essentials many of them could enjoy short hours without positively neglecting their work. Our evidence points in the same direction. The two duties which become more important as hours increase are helping members with individual problems and recruiting,[2] and these are duties which are relatively easily cut down

[1] This is made up of 5% 'very rare', 2% 'less than 4 a year', and 11% 'between 4 and 11 a year'.

[2] This is not true of the Building unions.

to taste without much possibility of effective supervision. The extreme variations in hours and in evening and week-end work within individual unions suggests that those who work the longest hours could make their performance more like that of their colleagues, if they chose to do so.

In other words, trade union officers work long and inconvenient hours at least in part because they choose to work them. This general statement, however, must not be taken to apply in all individual cases. Where an officer has had to take over the affairs of several branches, he may find almost all his evenings booked. Where he is involved in a training scheme he may find a large number of week-ends taken up by lectures and classwork at week-end schools. Neither of these instances, however, is typical.

There is another consideration. Trade union officers are not the only people who work long and awkward hours. Doctors, parsons, probation officers and adult tutors are amongst the many professional groups who have the same problem. They also work with relatively little supervision, and experience suggests that they also have at least some elbow room to vary their commitments to suit themselves.

Other Conditions, Cars and Expenses

All the unions about which we have collected information and all but one of those of which we have any knowledge have superannuation schemes. The provisions vary considerably. Most unions make retirement compulsory at 65 years of age. A few allow officers to continue after 65 if the arrangement satisfies both parties. Several enforce retirement at 60, and one, the Civil Service Clerical Association, at 55. (Some of these unions run their pension funds into heavy deficits.) Many of those unions which enforce retirement at 65 permit it at 60. All schemes provide for contributions both from the officers concerned and from the union, but the details of the schemes vary.

Most major unions have schemes to encourage their officers to use cars. Some provide union cars, some offer interest-free loans, and others low-interest loans. In some unions the mileage allowances include an element of depreciation.

Amongst our sample 69% had cars. Over half of these had bought them with union assistance. Most of the remainder used cars owned by the union, but 18% had bought cars without union help. The remaining 3% gave no details. The main differences between union groups were that Single Industry unions showed a surprising number of officers without cars, and direct purchase of cars seemed the most common method of assistance in the Skilled group.

The details of the schemes make clear that, whereas some unions are not over-generous, there are others in which assistance with car ownership, and allowances for the use of cars, amount to a real if marginal addition to the incomes of their officers. This leads on to the extremely difficult field of perquisites and expenses.

The Engineers pay a personal allowance of £100 a year. Other unions pay a weekly 'deputations allowance' in addition to the prescribed expenses for absence from home. As with any scheme of prescribed allowances, there is no way of setting a figure which will adequately cover reasonable expenses and not allow some recipients to save. In many unions the senior officer lives in a house owned by the union. Some unions provide all their officers with houses. In some others the rents are nominal. Heat and light are sometimes provided free.

Some of the areas of the National Union of Mineworkers pay honoraria to their officers as Presidents or Secretaries of the Area in addition to their salaries as officers of the national union. Many trade union officers serve as secretaries of the workers' side of national or regional joint councils or other collective bargaining bodies. Some of them receive honoraria, delegate's fees or special expense allowances for their pains.

This list covers the main perquisites (though by no means all the perquisites) which may go with a trade union officer's job. Although we have collected details of a considerable number of schemes, an estimate of their worth can be no better than a guess. Our guess is that many trade union officers have the opportunity to make between £2 and £4 a week in addition to their salaries (for most of them coming mainly from expenses and car allowances); in a few unions they can make little or nothing; and in some they can make more. It should be added that, even so, many trade union officers would be out of pocket if the money they spend on entertaining their members was included in the balance.

PROMOTION PROSPECTS

Opportunities of promotion for trade union officers vary considerably from one period to another, and even more from union

F

to union. Table 18A sets out the details of promotions for the officers of all unions whose records we have studied for various periods. Table 18B sets out the individual experience of the individual unions since the war.

TABLE 18A

FULL-TIME OFFICERS: PROMOTIONS

Year	Promotions to Total Number of Officers
1921–1926	1 : 8
1927–1932	1 : 19
1933–1938	1 : 8
1939–1944	1 : 9
1945–1950	1 : 7
1951–1956	1 : 10
1953–1958	1 : 10

Explanations are readily available for the main changes in the first table. From 1927–32 trade unions were contracting. Accordingly there were no new posts and some posts were abolished as they fell vacant, so that promotion became less frequent. Expansion commenced again in 1934, new appointments were made, and promotions multiplied. During the war, however, new posts failed to keep pace with growing membership and promotions declined a little; but they rose again after the war. Membership began to flatten out by 1951, and there has been little expansion since then, so that there have been few new posts, and a marked decline in promotions.

The main omission from this table is the National Union of Mineworkers. There are three main grades of officer in this union: national officer (general president and general secretary); area officer; and area agent. In some Areas, however, *all* the officers are classified as area officers. In others some are classified as area officers and some as agents. Some small Areas have an agent only. All

TABLE 18B

FULL-TIME OFFICERS: PROMOTION BY UNION

Union	Promotion Ratio		Number of Grades[1]	Percentage of the total Officer-Force in the lowest Grade
	1947–52	1953–58		
T. & G.W.U.	1 : 7	1 : 9	8	—[2]
A.E.U.	1 : 10	1 : 6	8	53
N.U.G.M.W. ..	1 : 12	1 : 37	4	85
N.U.R. ..	1 : 7	1 : 4	4	82
U.S.D.A.W. ..	1 : 19	1 : 75	4	83
N.A.L.G.O. ..	1 : 4	1 : 9	8	48
E.T.U.	1 : 19	1 : 23	4	83
N.U.A.W. ..	1 : 11	1 : 10	4	76
A.W.A. ..	1 : 5	1 : 5	4	—[2]
N.U.B.S.O. ..	1 : 9	1 : 10	7	—[2]
N.U.P.E. ..	1 : 6	1 : 7	7	72
I.S.T.C. ..	1 : 10	1 : 7	4	59
A.U.B.T.W. ..	1 : 6	1 : 36	6	80
C.S.C.A. ..	1 : 13	1 : 4	4	69
T.S.S.A. ..	1 : 1	1 : 2	5	69
N.U.P.B.P.W.	1 : 3	1 : 15	5	73
Average ..	1 : 7	1 : 10	–	–

these posts are filled by ballot, after permission has been given by the National Executive Committee. Some Areas create additional confusion by shuttling area officers between the posts of Area Secretary, Area President, Area Treasurer, and so on. Consequently there is no adequate measure of promotion in this union.

Table 18B makes it clear that one of the factors affecting the rate of promotion is the number of grades. The eight unions with more than four grades provided five out of the six unions with a promotion ratio of 1 : 6 or better in 1947–52 and five out of the nine with a ratio of better than 1 : 10 in 1953–58. The unions with four grades provided the worst four ratios in the first period and the worst two in the second.

[1] In compiling the figures in this column, we have had to use our own judgment in deciding the number of effective promotion grades in several unions.

[2] These three unions are excluded from column 3 because they do not have one clear 'starting grade' in their systems of promotion.

Another consideration is the proportion of the total officer force in the lowest or 'starting' grade. The greater the number of higher posts, the bigger the chance of promotion. All the unions in which the proportion is less than 70% have promotion ratios of one in ten or better. Four of the five in which it is 80% or more have ratios of one in twenty or worse.

The average age of entry should be another factor. Comparison of Tables 10 and 18B, however, seems to show little connection between a high average age of entry and good promotion prospects. We must therefore assume that the influence of this factor is obscured by that of the two already mentioned.

Finally, the numbers are in most instances too small to exclude the effect of chance. The Transport Salaried Staffs have changed general secretaries four times since the war with consequent reshuffles throughout the ranks. A similar turn-over at the top seems to be the explanation for the one exception amongst the unions with more than 80% of their officer force in the lowest grade—the Railwaymen.

Promotions most closely concern those who want them. We attempted to measure the demand by two questions included in the questionnaire. Out of the total sample 30% said that they would be disappointed if they were not promoted or elected to a higher post in the union before they retired. The remainder (except 3% who gave no answer) claimed that they would not be disappointed. Five-sixths of those who confessed to ambition in this way (25% of the total sample) said that they would like to hold the top post in their unions. In the General unions and White Collar unions 37% confessed they would be disappointed if they were passed over, 31% in the Single Industry group, 19% in the Ex-Craft group, and only 12% in the Skilled group. The percentage for the General group is misleading, since it is compounded of 49% for the Transport and General Workers, 27% for the General and Municipal Workers and 21% for the Shop, Distributive and Allied Workers.

Taken together with Table 18B these last three figures suggest that ambition thrives on the opportunity to satisfy it. On the other hand, the variation in opportunity is far greater than the variation in desire for promotion, and both the General and Municipal Workers and the Shop, Distributive and Allied Workers might well ask themselves whether their grading structures are not the cause of too much thwarted ambition.

The comment of one respondent must be recorded because of its ring of truth:

I have answered Question 12 with the knowledge that it is extremely unlikely that I shall move from my present position due mainly to my age and the age of the present holders of positions above me. But I have competed for these positions and acknowledge a feeling of disappointment in not attaining to them.

ATTITUDES

Several of our questions were intended to discover the attitudes of full-time officers to their work and to their posts.

The first of these related to trade union aims, but the answers were of relatively little interest, and are therefore relegated, along with similar answers from branch secretaries and shop stewards, to Appendix 7.

Respondents were asked whether they would like their sons to become union officials. Out of the total sample 55% said that they would, 22% that they would not, and the remainder gave a variety of answers which included 'doubtful' and 'no son'. The union groups showed very little variation indeed, but on investigating the replies from individual unions this constancy proved deceptive in the General union group. The other major unions shared the general experience, but the Transport and General Workers' officers showed a very high degree of morale in this respect, with 73% in favour of union posts for their sons; and the other two general unions fell behind, with 47% for the General and Municipal Workers and 43% for the Shop, Distributive and Allied Workers.

Respondents were asked to give reasons for their answers. About half of those who answered 'yes' did so, and of these half gave 'idealistic' reasons such as the need to serve humanity or to help fellow-workers. Almost a third mentioned that the work was interesting or satisfying, or both. Only 20% of those who answered 'no' gave any reason. Almost half of them stressed the attitude of union members to their officers. A quarter described their work as frustrating or worrying. Almost as many mentioned poor prospects, and low pay and poor conditions received one specific mention each.

One officer who could not make up his mind said that it was 'difficult to say without seeming pompous. Long hours and very moderate wage, exceptionally worrying at times, but occasional successes bring inner satisfaction as adequate but only reward'.

Naturally enough, it is the reasons for dissatisfaction that make the most interesting reading. One respondent said that 'the hardest taskmaster in the world is a trade union member'. Another wrote at length:

A district organizer . . . is the lowest form of life. In essence, he is a bum. His primary business is to extract cash from unwilling contributors, who, if he was not around, would, without regret or stricken conscience, gladly resign from their obligations. Any man who is interested in Trade Unionism is already a member. . . .

He has no say in the terms of his employment, yet is the most important man in the organization. He is the man who meets the members, all day, every day. Directives come to him from above, but no assistance. . . . If they [members] lapse quicker than they are recruited, as these days, the executive is pained, and point out to the district organizer that if he does not pull up his socks, he will not draw his pension. His material is human nature, his job is to please everyone. He is trying to sell a commodity that is too expensive for too many, who . . . see no earthly reason why they should pay for something they can get for nothing. He is not a good insurance risk, often suffers with ulcers or nervous trouble. Overworked, underpaid, spends his days riding around in a car. . . .

It is not surprising if this officer was amongst those who rated 100% membership as the first aim for trade unions. Having quoted him, however, we must hasten to repeat that the figures seem to show that his opinions and experiences are not typical.

We attempted to measure the feeling of trade union officers towards the social standing of their jobs by asking them to place their own posts and the posts of their general secretary in a list of thirty occupations ranging from medical officer of health to roadsweeper, according to what they thought would be 'the generally accepted view' of their social standing.[1]

At one end of the scale some facetious replies placed the trade union officer below the roadsweeper. At the other end of the scale several officers (particularly in the General unions) thought their general secretaries ranked far above medical officers of health and company directors. This was a serious fault in our list, which was unavoidable if we were to borrow a list that had already been tested instead of inventing our own.

The question was answered by 79% of the sample, and of these 64% placed their general secretary's post as equivalent or superior to that of a medical officer of health or a company director, and

[1] The list (Question 29 in the Questionnaire for Full-Time Officers, Appendix 1) is the Hall-Jones scale, see D. V. Glass (ed.), *Social Mobility in Britain*, 1954, p. 39. The form of the question was prescribed by the consideration that the social standing of a job is settled by what other people think, not by the attitude of the occupant.

36% put it somewhere between a country solicitor and an elementary school teacher. Only 10% rated their own posts equal to or above a civil servant (executive grade); 69% put themselves somewhere between a nonconformist minister and an elementary school teacher; and 21% somewhere below the school teacher. Differences between union groups were small, but the General union officers gave the highest rating to their general secretaries, with 80% of those who replied equal to or above company director, whereas the Ex-Craft unions were the most confident in their own standing, with 16% of those who replied above the civil servant and 74% between the nonconformist minister and the elementary school teacher.

We compared the answers with the replies to the question: 'Would you be disappointed if you were not promoted or elected to a higher post in your union before you retire?' Of those who answered 'yes' and also answered the question on social standing, 70% put their general secretaries' posts equal to or above the company director, and 98% put themselves equal to or below the nonconformist minister; for those who answered 'no' the comparable figures are 62% and 87%. In other words there is a noticeable tendency for those who are interested in promotion to rate their general secretaries' posts higher and their own posts lower than those who are not interested.

The question aroused more comments than any other. A common point of view was expressed in these words by one officer:

There is no such thing as a 'generally accepted view' in such questions. The view of the members of my union (and I believe of most trade unionists) is that the General Secretary, Organizers and other full-time officials have the social standing of a skilled ... worker; that if they 'aspired' to some other 'social standing' they would be betraying the trust put in them by their fellow members.

A number of the respondents seemed hesitant to think of their jobs (or any other union post) in terms of 'social standing', or took the view that the status of all union officers ought to be the same as the workers they represent. On the other hand the great majority rate their own posts equivalent to professional occupations well above all manual or clerical posts, and most of them place their general secretaries near the top of the social scale. Taken together, these two points suggest some confusion in their minds concerning their social position.

During our investigation we heard frequent complaints of the bad effects on domestic life of the long, inconvenient hours and the worries of full-time officers' posts. We therefore asked our respondents to indicate the reaction of their wives or families to the amount of time they spent on union work. Table 19 shows the answers, which seem to indicate that the problem is not so serious as we had been led to believe. It may be that the wives of trade union officers are unusually stoical or unusually willing to make sacrifices for their husbands. Perhaps a more credible explanation is that in answering the question many of our respondents minimized the domestic displeasure caused by their work.

TABLE 19

FULL-TIME OFFICERS: FAMILY REACTION TO UNION WORK

Family Attitude	Proportion of Sample
Quite happy	50
Not at all or only slightly displeased	24
Moderately displeased	16
Very displeased	1
Others (including 'not married' and no answers)	9
TOTAL	100

Even if this is true, there is no reason to doubt the validity of the relative attitudes revealed by their answers. 'Moderately displeased' may be a euphemism for 'almost driven to desperation', but it still betokens a stronger feeling than 'only slightly displeased'. We compared these family attitudes with the number of evenings actually worked, but found no significant relationship between them, or between family reactions and the number of week-ends spent on the job. Other factors must also play their part in determining whether a wife criticizes her husband's post.

TURNOVER

Turnover is defined as the percentage relationship between the average number of officers ceasing to serve the union during each year of a period and the average number of officers during the period. Table 20 shows the rates of turnover during various periods for the unions to whose records we have had access.

TABLE 20

FULL-TIME OFFICERS: TURNOVER

Period	Average Percentage Annual Turnover
1921–26	2·1
1927–32	3·7
1933–38	5·0
1939–44	5·5
1945–50	6·4
1951–56	4·2
1957–58	4·0
1947–52	5·6
1953–58	4·3
1921–58	5·2

The average for the whole group of unions rose steadily through the 'thirties[1] and the war into the immediate post-war period (when the total number of officers was rising), and has since fallen (in a period when the total has been stable). Thus there would seem to be a positive relationship between the numbers leaving and the rate of growth in the total number of trade union officers. In fact, this is the reverse of what one would expect. The immediate effect of an increase in numbers should be to reduce the proportion of those leaving to the total. Subsequently the proportion leaving should rise gradually (according to the average length of service) back to its old figure, unless some other influence supervenes.

Accordingly there should be another influence, and it must be sought in Table 21, which gives reason for leaving by periods.

During the 'twenties trade union membership was falling and the unions were absorbing a large increase in their officer forces due to the rapid increase in membership before 1921. In the 'thirties the unions were slow to respond to expansion in numbers. Consequently the average age of officers rose, and with it the number of

---

[1] It must be remembered that the 1921–26 figure includes so few unions as not to be representative.

TABLE 21

FULL-TIME OFFICERS: REASONS FOR LEAVING

	Average Age at beginning of Period	Normal Retirement	Premature[1] Retirement	Death	Ill-health[1]	Resignation	Defeated	Dismissed	Redundant	Total
1921–26 ..	—	38	2	22	2	16	2	18	—	100
1927–32 ..	48·6	48	3	27	4	2	15	1	—	100
1933–38 ..	51·0	57	11	17	7	6	1	1	—	100
1939–44 ..	48·7	53	4	13	11	13	1	4	1	100
1945–50 ..	47·7	39	6	13	6	25	3	7	1	100
1951–56 ..	48·8	45	6	18	6	17	3	5	—	100
1957–58 ..	50·5	40	9	18	6	20	2	5	—	100
1947–52 ..	—	42	6	13	5	23	3	7	1	100
1953–58 ..	—	44	6	19	6	18	2	5	—	100
All Years ..	—	45	6	16	7	18	3	5	—	100

[1] Some unions allow premature retirement only on health grounds; others use both categories.

retirements. This was reinforced by another influence, the super-annuation schemes and retirement rules which a number of unions introduced during the 'thirties. Normal retirement continued at a high rate during the war, and both resignations and dismissals rose. After the war normal retirements fell off fairly sharply, but resignation and dismissals reached their peak (neglecting the freak dismissal figures of 1921–26 caused by a reorganization in one union). Since 1951 resignations and dismissals have fallen off somewhat but remain at a far higher rate than during the 'thirties. Thus a comparison between 1933–38 and 1953–58 shows that turnover in the second period is rather lower than in the first. Normal retirements have declined considerably with a decline in average age, but this has been partly balanced by a marked increase in resignations and dismissals.

There are considerable differences between the average age of appointment or election in different unions,[1] and not all unions have the same retiring age.[2] Consequently there are differences between the average years of potential service in different unions. A union in which the average age of appointment is 45 must expect a higher turnover than a union which appoints at 35, if retirement in both unions is at the same age. We have made some correction for this by calculating for each union and for each period the years of potential service, defined as the difference between average age at the commencement of the period and the retirement age in force during the period. The turnover rate for the period has been multiplied by the resulting figure. The result is set out in Table 22. No attempt is made to calculate an average for the whole period, since retirement rules have been changed from time to time. The weighted arithmetic averages for the last three periods in the table, however, are 72, 111 and 65 respectively.

Turnovers are therefore well above average in the Transport and General Workers and the Agricultural Workers, and well below in the Railwaymen and the National Federation of Building Trades' Operatives. The General and Municipal Workers, the Electricians, the Boot and Shoe Operatives, and the Iron and Steel Trades Confederation are all somewhat below average.

These results can be explained by the information contained in Table 23. High turnover in the Agricultural Workers is due to the large number of dismissals (which may be partly the result of a more honest classification of what other unions call 'premature

[1] See p. 47.　　　　[2] See p. 66.

TABLE 22

FULL-TIME OFFICERS: TURNOVER CORRECTED FOR POTENTIAL YEARS OF SERVICE

Period	T.G. W.U.	A.E.U.	N.U.G. M.W.	N.U.M.	N.U.R.	U.S.D. A.W.	N.A.L. G.O.	E.T.U.	N.U. A.W.	A.W.A.	N.U.B. S.O.	N.U. P.E.	N.F.B. T.O.	I.S. T.C.	A.I.U.B. T.W.	C.S. C.A.	T.S. S.A.	N.U.P. B.P.W.
1927-32	—	152	—	—	35	—	—	—	—	—	—	—	38	107	—	—	19	—
1933-38	—	70	—	—	21	—	—	—	—	—	77	Nil	25	49	—	—	69	—
1939-44	—	59	107	—	66	48	—	100	—	—	89	Nil	58	75	—	27	36	45
1945-50	138	66	81	—	64	80	—	94	170	—	84	133	72	65	100	101	86	90
1951-56	76	84	50	34	14	69	53	35	94	53	51	43	13	55	81	71	54	74

NOTE: No figures are included for any union in periods prior to the adoption of retirement rules.

	Normal Retirement	Premature Retirement[1]	Death	Ill-health[1]	Resigned	Defeated	Redundant	Dismissed	Total
T. & G.W.U. (1943–58)	35	12	15	8	23	N.Ap.	1	6	100
A.E.U. .. (1921–58)	51	—	14	3	10	21	—	1	100
N.U.G.M.W. (1921–58)	53	—	18	14	10	N.Ap.	—	5	100
N.U.M. .. (1945–58)	55	2	19	5	19	N.Ap.	—	—	100
N.U.R. .. (1921–58)	71	—	16	5	8	N.Ap.	—	—	100
U.S.D.A.W... (1921–58)	34	22	21	2	11	N.Ap.	—	10	100
N.A.L.G.O. (1947–58)	3	6	3	10	78	N.Ap.	—	—	100
E.T.U. .. (1934–58)	37	—	31	6	26	Nil	—	—	100
N.U.A.W. .. (1933–58)	29	2	11	4	25	N.Ap.	—	31	100
A.S.W. .. (1947–58)	51	—	19	—	8	14	—	6	100
A.W.A. .. (1941–58)	65	6	9	—	20	N.Ap.	—	6	100
N.U.B.S.O. (1927–58)	64	—	11	6	10	N.Ap.	—	3	100
N.U.P.E. .. (1934–58)	20	—	5	—	60	N.Ap.	—	15	100
N.F.B.T.O. .. (1921–58)	54	5	41	—	—	N.Ap.	—	—	100
I.S.T.C. .. (1921–58)	65	5	14	5	11	N.Ap.	—	—	100
A.U.B.T.W. (1945–58)	41	—	22	2	20	13	—	2	100
C.S.C.A. .. (1939–58)	38	—	12	—	50	N.Ap.	—	—	100
T.S.S.A. .. (1921–58)	60	—	16	12	12	N.Ap.	—	—	100
N.U.P.B.P.W. (1939–58)	79	—	7	—	7	N.Ap.	—	7	100
All Unions .. —	45	6	16	7	18	3	—	5	100

[1] See note, Table 21.

retirement', 'ill-health' or 'resignation'). In the Transport and General Workers' Union there is no single explanation, but premature retirements, resignations on grounds of health, other resignations, and dismissals are all higher than average.

Low turnover amongst the officers of the National Union of Railwaymen is the consequence of staying on the job until retirement. Normal retirements are also above average in the National Federation of Building Trades' Operatives, in the General and Municipal Workers, in the Iron and Steel Trades Confederation and in the Boot and Shoe Operatives, but not in the Electricians.

If reasons for leaving are considered on their own account, and not merely as an explanation for turnover, several interesting points stand out.

Some 'freak' figures are to be explained by unusual events in single unions. For example, the unusually high rate of dismissals in 1921–26 (Table 21) and the unusually high rate of premature retirements in 1933–38 are both consequences of reorganizations of the staffing and structure of the main constituent of the Shop, Distributive and Allied Workers. The heavy incidence of retirements due to ill-health during the war years was concentrated in the Transport and General Workers and the General and Municipal Workers, who between them accounted for 22 cases out of a total of 24 in all unions. The high rate of electoral defeats in the 1927–32 period is a consequence of the amalgamation which formed the Amalgamated Engineering Union in 1920. The officers of the new union were 'appointed' to their new posts under the amalgamation arrangements (having been elected to their previous positions in the constituent unions) and guaranteed security until 1926. Thereafter the union's rule prescribing re-election every three years (as it then was) came into force, and the members took advantage of their opportunity by defeating thirteen office-holders.

It is sometimes suggested that union members are too lenient in re-electing officers regardless of their competence. This may be true, but it is worth noting that electoral defeats account for 12% of the total number leaving office in those unions which enforce periodic elections. The Electrical Trades Union provides no instances of defeat, perhaps because its resignation rate is unusually high (Table 23). If it is excluded the rate for electoral defeats rises to 16%. Both figures are far higher than the average dismissal rates for all unions (5%), and above all the individual dismissal rates except those of the Agricultural Workers and the Public Employees.

Explanations are still required for differences between unions over dismissals and resignations, and for the rise in both these causes of turnover since before the war.

It is the practice of some unions never to dismiss. It should be observed that only one of the unions which prescribe periodic re-elections (the Electrical Trades Union) is in this group. At the other extreme, dismissal has ended the service of more officers of the Agricultural Workers than have left for any other single cause. Several reasons can be suggested for this. The organizers of the union work on their own without staff and with only infrequent contacts with head office. Each is responsible for a widely-scattered membership. Thus, it is a more onerous and responsible job than those of most other union officers. There is evidence that hours are unusually long and branch cares unusually heavy.[1] On the other hand, the union has unusual difficulties of recruitment, for farm-workers are less well equipped than most other groups of workers to meet the requirements of trade union office. This is shown by the number of occasions the union has gone outside the ranks of lifelong farmworkers. In both wars, for example, it has appointed conscientious objectors directed to work on the land. Finally it may be the case that the union is less given to euphemisms than some others.

The only other unions with markedly high dismissal rates are the Shop, Distributive and Allied Workers, and the Public Employees. The first, like the union's high rate of premature retirements, arises from reorganizations in one of the constituent unions before the war.[2] In the Public Employees the high dismissal rate should probably be associated with its high rate of resignations. Two other unions—the National and Local Government Officers and the Civil Service Clerical Association—also have high resignation rates. They are White Collar unions whose officers have a higher educational standard than that of most other trade union officers and can there-fore more easily move to another professional post without loss of salary or status.[3] The same explanation fits the Public Employees'

[1] See pp. 45–46.   [2] See p. 80.

[3] The experience of the Civil Service Clerical Association is that all the resignations but one have been of officers recruited from outside the civil service. So far, all but one of the officers recruited from the Civil Service who have ceased to serve, have retired at the normal age.

Excluding legal staff, editorial staff and public relations officers, the majority of those who have resigned from full-time office in the National and Local Government Officers' Associa-tion since 1946 (10 out of 12) have entered the service of the local authorities or other public employers as industrial relations officers, establishment officers and so on. It has been sug-gested to us that this was due to a big expansion in interest in personnel management since the war, and similar opportunities are likely to be much less frequent in future.

officers. The union's general secretary, Bryn Roberts, who has held office since 1934, and has built the union up from 10,000 to 200,000 members, has instituted the practice of making some appointments from outside the union, largely from such promising young men as he himself discovers and recommends to his executive committee. Consequently their educational standards, and certainly their versatility, tends to be higher than for other trade union officers, and they can more easily switch to another occupation.[1] In addition to that, all three unions make a practice of appointing at an early age so that their officers are more willing than others to think of other posts, and more likely to be considered for them. Taking together all the unions covered by this part of the inquiry the number of officers leaving within two years of appointment or election was 4% of those appointed. The National and Local Government Officers came far and away ahead with 24·4%. The Agricultural Workers were second with 8·3%. The Civil Service Clerical Association came third with 7·7%. The Public Employees slightly exceeded the average with 4·8%, but came sixth after the Transport and General Workers and the Building Trade Workers.

Nine unions come well below the average for resignations: the Engineers, General and Municipal Workers, Railwaymen, Shop, Distributive and Allied Workers, Woodworkers, Boot and Shoe Operatives, Iron and Steel Trades Confederation, Transport Salaried Staffs and Printing, Bookbinding and Paper Workers. The National Federation of Building Trade Operatives had no resignations. There is no characteristic which clearly distinguishes these unions from the others. They include two General unions, but the largest General union is among the rest. They include five unions which elect their officers, but there are three such unions amongst the remainder. A firmer relationship can be established if we separate out the unions which already existed as stable and powerful unions (or whose constituents had these characteristics) before the First World War. Six of the unions come into this class: the Engineers, Railwaymen, Woodworkers, Boot and Shoe Operatives, Iron and Steel Trades Confederation and Printing, Bookbinding and Paper Workers. Three of the remainder belong to the same class, the Mineworkers, Weavers and Building Trade Workers, but all of them have resignation rates rather below the average.

[1] A high rate of resignation naturally affects the rate of promotion, and all three of these unions have a relatively high ratio of promotions to posts (Table 18B). It is possible that *both* characteristics reflect a 'career' approach to the trade union officer's job.

This relationship is not as far-fetched as might appear at first sight. If it is supposed that the tradition is for trade union officers to regard their posts as offices of trust, honour and service, and resignation as a mark of failure, then unions with strong traditions would expect few resignations. In more recent unions, however, the post of officer might be regarded as one amongst a number of possible careers. An officer who found the post uncongenial, or was offered an attractive post elsewhere, might see no reason to stay, and might be allowed to leave with no hard feelings on either side.

The general increase in dismissals since the war might thus represent a change in the traditions of the movement, but there is also a special reason. Everyone whom we have consulted on the point agrees that there was a decline in the standard of newly-elected or newly-appointed officers during the war. The number of posts rose with increasing membership, and many, perhaps most, of the likely candidates were absent on some form of war service. At the same time the conditions of wartime (frequent wage claims, rapid changes in workshop practices, and frequent alterations in regulations) added to the difficulties of the job. In other words, two of the conditions which explain the high dismissal rate of the Agricultural Workers, a shortage of suitable candidates and unusually onerous conditions, became fairly general. Dismissals inevitably rose, and rose all the more immediately after the war when it became easier to find replacements for the least satisfactory wartime appointments.

Since then the rate has remained higher than before the war. Two reasons can be suggested. Firstly, by 1951 the old traditions had been modified. Secondly, alternative employment was more readily available than before the war, so that union executive committees had less cause to worry about the personal difficulties which would face a dismissed officer.

The same consideration could also explain the increase in resignations. If we are right in suggesting that the three unions with the highest resignation rate have officers unusually well equipped to find other jobs of equivalent salary and status, then it is reasonable to account for a general increase in the rate of resignations by improved job-opportunities. Full employment increases job-opportunities all round. Trade union officers are better qualified for jobs as personnel officers than for most other professional occupations, and the number of personnel posts in industry has increased out of all comparison since 1938. In addition, experience of trade union office is one of a

G

number of alternative statutory qualifications for membership of the board of a nationalized industry and several of the nationalized industries have made a point of employing trade union officers in their labour or staff departments.

Before this line of argument is pursued too far, however, it is worth looking more closely into the reasons for resignations, which are given in Table 24.

The high proportion of 'unknowns' (chiefly due to the Transport and General Workers' Union) does not completely vitiate the table, for trade union records are selective in stating reasons for leaving. Few, if any, posts in nationalized industry go unremarked, for they are regarded as an honour, and in several instances the union is consulted before the appointment is made. The same reasoning applies to election to Parliament, and probably also to government posts. On the other hand, the figures in the table for posts in private industry, returning to the 'shop floor' and posts in other organizations, are probably all serious under-estimates.

It is important, however, to note that there is a fairly wide spread of occupations, none of which completely dominates the picture. Post-war nationalization has not denuded the unions of officers. More than half the appointments to nationalized industries came from two unions, the Transport and General Workers (16) and the Mineworkers (10). The Mineworkers, therefore, suffered the highest rate of loss, which works out at almost exactly 1 per cent per annum of their total strength of officers over the years since nationalization (although most of the appointments were bunched in the first year or two).[1] In relation to all the unions covered, the point can be put in this way: since the war the unions have, on the average, lost about one in twenty of their officers each year. Only just over one in five of these, however (or one in a hundred of total strength), has resigned. And only about a quarter of these *post-war* resignations (the proportion in Table 25 is of *all* resignations) have been to take

[1] A number of full-time officers of the old Miners' Federation took up posts with the Ministry of Fuel and Power during the war, and many of these were transferred to the Coal Board when it was established. Most of the appointments of full-time officers of the National Union of Mineworkers to the Board occurred in the first years of nationalization. In addition a considerable number of lay officers of the union have taken up appointments with the Board. We have failed to obtain satisfactory information on the numbers concerned, but it is clear that the numbers have also dropped off in recent years. Of sixteen full-time and lay officers from the South Wales Area who took up posts with the Board up to 1958, six had worked in the Labour Department of the Ministry prior to nationalization, four took up posts with the Board in 1947, and six during the following two years. (Information supplied by the National Coal Board Labour Staff Association.)

TABLE 24

FULL-TIME OFFICERS: SUBSEQUENT POSTS OF RESIGNED
OFFICERS[1]

Subsequent Posts	Numbers	Percentage
Post in Nationalized Industry ..	48	18
Government Post (including colonial and commonwealth governments)	25	10
Managerial posts in private industry	14	5
Post in another union	11	4
Back to 'shop-floor'	13	5
Own shop or business	7	3
Labour Party post	4	1·5
Elected Member of Parliament ..	4	1·5
Posts with other Organizations ..	9	3
Other	9	3
Unknown	122	46
TOTAL	266	100

up a post in nationalized industry. So that the annual loss of officers
to the nationalized industries is between two and three in a thousand.

It is impossible to make satisfactory comparisons between these
rates and those of other organizations. There are no other occupations which lend themselves easily to comparison with the job of
trade union officer, and it is not easy to obtain information about
such other occupations as appear to be remotely comparable. All
that we can say is this: the rate of resignations in these unions is
rather higher than the rate for the administrative class of the Civil
Service, but lower than that of several large firms who have supplied
us with information.

[1] This table covers resignations in all the unions covered, starting from the date at which
each union's records become available.

Assessments

We have found no methods of measuring changes in the quality of trade union officers from period to period, and can make only one or two points on the subject. There is, as we have remarked,[1] a consensus of opinion that the standard of entrants fell off badly during the war, and that at least some of the lost ground has since been recovered. Secondly, many full-time officers in the past were very heavy drinkers and, to judge by memories of both sides of industry, some of them allowed drink to interfere with their work. If this is true we can confidently say there has been a change for the better, without implying that all officers are teetotallers; far from it. The problem of embezzlement has been with the unions from the start. At the least, it is no worse now than in earlier periods.

Our questionnaire[2] for personnel officers, however, was intended to elicit information which would allow comparisons between the officers of different unions at the present time. The questionnaire was answered by 72 personnel officers drawn from a number of large, private multi-plant firms from all parts of the country. All the firms and all but a few of the personnel officers deal with more than one union and some with as many as ten.

Respondents were asked to list the trade unions with whom they have regular contact according to their assessment of the all-round competence of those officers at their jobs. Since the same unions did not recur in each answer, and since the number of unions listed varied from two to ten,[3] we were in some difficulty in finding a suitable method of analysis. In the end we decided that we must neglect the unions which were rarely mentioned and analyse the remaining unions situation by situation. Only four unions were mentioned often enough to be included in the analysis—the Engineers, the Transport and General Workers, the General and Municipal Workers and the Electricians. We analysed separately each situation in which two or more of these four unions were compared.

The only certain conclusion from the analysis was that the Electricians fared very much worse than the other three unions, with four out of 41 possible first places (10%) and 22 out of 41 possible last places (54%). It was very difficult to choose between

---

[1] See p. 83.   [2] Appendix 1.

[3] Several replies mentioned only one union and these were therefore of no use for purposes of comparison.

the other three unions. With 55 mentions the Engineers scored 40% of their possible first places and 31% of their possible last places. The Transport and General Workers had 41 mentions and scored 46% of possible firsts and 27% of possible lasts. The General and Municipal Workers were mentioned 24 times and scored 54% of possible firsts and only 21% of possible lasts.

This would seem to give the General and Municipal Workers a slight edge on the Transport and General Workers, and the latter a slight lead on the Engineers. Even this conclusion, however, must be accepted with caution. If the analysis is confined to direct comparisons of pairs of unions there is almost nothing to choose between them. The Electricians still come last by a wide margin, but the rest of the comparisons are shown in Table 25.

TABLE 25

FULL-TIME OFFICERS: ASSESSMENT BY PAIRS OF UNIONS

Unions	Number of instances of Situation	First Place	Second Place	Ties
T. & G.W.U.	41	18	21	2
A.E.U.		21	18	
T. & G.W.U.	11	7	4	–
N.U.G.M.W. ..		4	7	
A.E.U. ..	22	7	15	–
N.U.G.M.W.		15	7	

From this it would appear that the Engineers have a slight edge on the Transport and General Workers, but fall far behind the General and Municipal Workers, but that the General and Municipal Workers in their turn fall behind the Transport and General Workers. Consequently the only safe conclusion is that the three unions run very close in the estimation of British personnel officers.

There is no doubt about one reason for the poor score of the Electricians, for several respondents added comments to their

questionnaires to explain that the union would have stood higher
had it not been for its political affiliations and their industrial consequences. One quotation will illustrate the point.

The fifth choice, namely the Electrical Trades' Union, would on competence
alone be head and shoulders above any. [The local officer] is a most able man in
every respect, but like his colleagues in this Union is a Communist and a trouble
maker. His ability and intelligence, however, are far more than average.

It is also relevant that officers of many unions, not only of the
Electricians, took the view that personnel officers would be biased
in their attitudes to union officers, and their opinions could therefore not be taken as an objective evaluation.

We attempted to discover the criteria which the respondents used
by asking them to pick out in order of priority the four qualities
which seemed most important to them in making their assessments.
In order of priority, honesty came far and away the first; concern
to uphold procedure agreements and undertakings with management was second; ability to control his or her members and intelligence were third equal; and, fifth, came readiness to talk matters
over with management. Little of what we hoped comes out of the
answers, except that these are sensible criteria to apply to trade
union officers.

All this may appear to be a meagre result for a considerable effort.
By the nature of the inquiry no assessment could be made of unions
mainly confined to one industry such as the Mineworkers and the
Railwaymen. The material was insufficient to permit firm judgments about most other unions. Our conclusions, therefore, relate
only to the three largest and one other large union, and show that
there is nothing to choose between the quality of officers in the first
three.

Even negative results, however, have their uses. We have discovered that many interested people do form strong views about
the relative quality of union officers, including the three largest
unions, on the basis of limited experience, and the answers to the
questionnaire bore this out. Some personnel officers are certain that
one union is far better, or worse, than others. It is worth knowing
that their opinion is not generally shared.

Many observers think appointment gives better officers than
election, and that periodic re-election makes trade union officers the
slaves of their members. Our evidence is that election and even
re-election does no harm to the Engineers in comparison with the

general unions (although the Engineers might do even better without it). Personnel officers might be expected to mistrust Communists. It seems that they do mistrust the Communist officers of the Electricians, but the considerable number of Communists among the officers of the Engineers does not apparently pull the Engineers below the General unions in their estimation. Without doubt the philosophy of the two General unions (certainly that of the General and Municipal Workers) is less hostile to management and to managerial ideas than the traditions and often restrictive approach of the craftsmen. If this affects the judgment of personnel officers, however, then they are able to find compensating characteristics, at least, so far as the officers of the Engineers are concerned.

This chapter has answered some questions about full-time officers, left others unanswered, and raised a new crop of questions. More evidence on some of these unsettled points, however, will be provided by some sections of the chapters on other classes of union officer. Further consideration of them will therefore be left over to the last part of the book.

SUMMARY

1. There are about 2,500 'full-time' trade union officers in Britain. Since 1939 there has been one officer to about 4,000 members.

2. Member to officer ratios vary greatly from union to union. Since the differences between unions have remained fairly constant over the years, the explanation for them must be sought in different methods of administration and negotiation.

3. There are differences between union groups in the amount of time spent on different duties. Negotiations generally take first place, and are particularly important in unions with higher member to officer ratios. In other unions more importance is attached to office work, to branch meetings, to recruitment and to helping members with individual problems.

4. The age of entry into full-time office is over 40 years in unions which elect and under 40 in most unions which appoint. Most officers attended elementary schools and left school at 14, but the number of those who left later and attended grammar or technical schools is far higher amongst younger officers than in the whole sample. Surprising numbers of general union officers attended grammar schools, and held clerical, supervisory and administrative

posts before appointment. Most potential full-time officers held their first voluntary trade union office earlier than those who remain voluntary officers.

5. The selection schemes of the Railwaymen and the Shop, Distributive and Allied Workers suggest that, in the opinion of those responsible for them, the numbers of properly qualified candidates for full-time office considerably exceed the posts available.

6. Since 1938 officers' salaries have risen less than average earnings and wage rates, and some have fallen behind the increase in prices. But they have probably kept pace with other salaries, and there is still a margin between starting rates and average earnings in the industries which each union organizes.

7. In most unions full-time officers have formal or informal means of representing their grievances to the governing bodies. In one or two instances they have formed their own trade unions.

8. Average hours worked are about 57. Most officers spend not more than three evenings a week and not more than one week-end a month on union business, but there are wide variations, even within individual unions.

9. Nearly all officers are superannuable, and a variety of perquisites and allowances adds something (but in most instances not very much) to their incomes.

10. Opportunities for promotion vary widely, according to the number of grades and the proportion in the lowest grade. About 30% of officers appear to hope for promotion, ranging from 49% in the Transport and General Workers to 12% in the Skilled unions.

11. More than half of our sample would like their sons to be trade union officers.

12. Although most full-time officers rate themselves amongst the holders of middle-class posts (and rate their general secretaries close to the top of a scale of social standing), many of them are reluctant to claim middle-class status. Officers who desire promotion tend to rate their own post lower and their general secretary's post higher than those who do not.

13. Our evidence does not show that the time spent at work causes a major domestic problem for trade union officers. There is no relationship between family reactions and the number of evenings and week-ends spent at work.

14. Turnover amongst union officers is now about 4% a year, and has fallen considerably since 1950. Almost half the cases of leaving office are normal retirements, and about one-fifth are deaths.

15. Resignations have risen sharply since before the war. An unusually high rate of resignations seems to be associated with a low age of entry, high educational standards and rapid promotion. An unusually low rate is found in unions with long and stable traditions. Since 1945, appointments to nationalized industries have accounted for two or three resignations amongst a thousand officers in a year.

16. A questionnaire for personnel officers suggests that, in general, they rate the officers of the three largest unions at very much the same level. Officers of the Electricians come well below them.

CHAPTER 6

FULL-TIME BRANCH SECRETARIES

WE shall confine our observations on full-time branch secretaries (not ranked as full-time officers by their unions) to attempts to answer two questions: how many are there? and, how far do their characteristics differ from those full-time officers (narrowly defined)? The small number of respondents to the relevant questionnaire and the small number of unions who employ this type of officer makes any attempt to compare the characteristics of full-time branch secretaries from different unions and union groups not only impossible, but also pointless.

NUMBERS

We have full information from the Printing, Bookbinding and Paper Workers. At the end of December 1958 their branches employed 42 full-time officers, classified into 30 branch secretaries, 3 finance secretaries, and 9 assistant secretaries.

At the same date 47 full-time branch secretaries were included in the superannuation scheme of the General and Municipal Workers, but we know that the total number was larger than this.[1] There is, however, no reason to suppose that an estimate of 'over eighty', which was made in 1953 (and accepted by the union) is not still valid.[2] The total membership of the union has fallen by about 5% since that time, so that a few large branches may have fallen below the numbers needed to support a full-time secretary. We should not go far wrong in putting the number at 80.

A far more difficult problem is presented by the National Union of Mineworkers. They have no superannuation scheme for full-time branch secretaries, and their head office maintains no records of any kind concerning them. Consequently we sought information from most of the Areas of the union. The complexity of the problem, and the large number of different types of full-time secretaries have already been mentioned.[3] In the circumstances we defined as a full-time secretary any branch secretary who spent all his working

---

[1] See pp. 21–22.   [2] See H. A. Clegg, *op. cit.*, p. 37.   [3] See pp. 22–23.

time on union business, whether the business was branch administration or negotiating and consulting with management, and whatever the source of his income. In doing so we have inevitably included a number of secretaries who in other industries would be regarded as full-time convenors and part-time secretaries, but this was unavoidable. Table 26 sets out the results.

TABLE 26

NATIONAL UNION OF MINEWORKERS: FULL-TIME
BRANCH SECRETARIES

Area	Membership (approx.)	Full-Time Secretaries
Derbyshire	35,000	20 ?
Durham	90,000	3–6
Lancashire	40,000	12
Northumberland ..	35,000	7–9
Nottingham ..	45,000	0
South Wales ..	95,000	30 ?
Yorkshire	125,000	55 ?
TOTAL	465,000	127–132 ?
Other Areas ..	235,000	?
Whole Union ..	700,000	About 190 ?

Each of the figures in the last column needs explanation. Most of them are the figures supplied by Area Secretaries. The Durham, Lancashire and Northumberland figures were supplied in the form given in the table. In 1957 South Wales attempted to devise a superannuation scheme for its full-time branch secretaries and called a meeting for the purpose. At the meeting eighteen secretaries asked to be included in the scheme, but there were other secretaries present who for one reason or another did not want to be included, and still others who did not come because their branches had already covered them, because they were too old, or for some other reason. The Derbyshire figure is a guess founded on the even less accurate information that in the Area's forty-nine branches, 'there are no full-time secretaries as such, but in fact many of the secretaries are engaged full-time or almost full-time on union business', either as a check measurer, or by arrangement with the local management. In Yorkshire 'the exact number is not known, but it is estimated at about 50% of the total number of branch secretaries, including at least ten out of the twelve pits in the Doncaster Area'. There are 109 branches in Yorkshire.

Our total of 127–132(?) for the seven Areas should probably be put as 100–150 to give fairly reliable outside limits. It would follow that these Areas have one full-time secretary for each 3,000–4,500 members. The assumption that something like the same ratio applies in other areas is at least partially justified by the knowledge that, although the Scottish Area supplied no figure, a considerable number of its branches support full-time officers. Consequently the limits for the union become 150–230, and it appears that the union has about twice as many full-time branch secretaries as 'full-time officers'.

This gives a total of 280–360 for the three unions. How can we move from here to an estimate for all British unions? We know that no other union whose records we have studied includes any large number of full-time branch secretaries unless they are graded as 'full-time officers' as in the Transport and General Workers and the Boot and Shoe Operatives. We are also confident that no other union maintains full-time branch secretaries in the same proportion to membership as the Mineworkers, since their arrangements are determined by the structure and history of their industry. The unions covered in the survey include about two-thirds of the total membership of British unions. Consequently we take the lower limit of 280, to allow for the exceptional character of the Mineworkers' figure and increase it to 420 to allow for the unions not covered in the survey. Because 420 has a spurious accuracy, we then conclude that British unions maintain about 400 full-time branch secretaries in addition to those graded as 'full-time' officers. If this is correct, our questionnaire sample of thirty full-time secretaries (at one in thirteen) bears almost exactly the right relationship to our sample of 190 full-time officers (which according to our contention is just over one in thirteen). This correspondence is, however, a little tarnished by the knowledge that one or two Mineworkers' branch secretaries whom our investigators thought were probably full-timers preferred to fill in the questionnaire for other branch secretaries.

CHARACTERISTICS

The average age of full-time branch secretaries who replied to our questionnaire was 51·1 years; for those included in the superannuation schemes of the General and Municipal and the Printing, Bookbinding and Paper Workers the figure was 52·0 in December 1958; and the average of the eighteen secretaries of the South Wales Miners who asked to be included in the suggested superannuation scheme in 1957 was 52·0. From this it appears that full-time branch secretaries are slightly older than full-time officers, amongst whom the average age of questionnaire respondents was 50·6, and of officers covered by the survey of records, 50·5.

Using the same method of calculating the relative importance of main duties,[1] Table 27 compares full-time secretaries and full-time officers.

TABLE 27

FULL-TIME BRANCH SECRETARIES: MAIN DUTIES

Duty	Full-Time Branch Secretaries	Full-Time Officers
Helping members with individual problems	26	17
Financial Work	17	3
Negotiating	16	24
Correspondence and other Office Work	14	23
Benefit Claims and Payments ..	13	—
Meetings	9	21
Recruiting new Members and Collecting Individual Contributions	5	12
TOTAL	100	100

[1] See pp. 42–43.

Full-time secretaries spend less time negotiating than do full-time officers, although perhaps not so much less than would be expected given that the secretary is confined to one branch. The reason for this may be that the full-time secretaries have to deal with almost as many members as a full-time officer. On our calculation there is in Britain about one full-time officer to each 4,000 trade union members.[1] The average size of branches covered by our questionnaire for full-time secretaries was 2,878. There are, of course, some issues which a full-time secretary must hand over to a senior officer, but it is probably the large number of smaller issues which takes the time.

The full-time secretary spends more time on helping members than on anything else, because he is much more accessible to the members than a full-time officer. Most full-time secretaries of a miner's lodge spend much of their day at the pit, and their homes or offices (like the offices of the full-time secretaries of the General and Municipal Workers) are usually thronged each evening with members (and their wives) coming for advice on every kind of problem 'from ingrowing toenails to divorce' (the quotation comes from South Wales).

The full-time branch secretary spends more time on office work than the full-time officer, but most of this is financial work which rarely comes the way of the full-time officer. The branch secretary has to deal with all his members' claims for benefit and all the branch returns to and transactions with the district, area or national office, where financial matters are normally in the hands of the staff. The branch secretary has less correspondence to handle than the full-time officer.

At first sight it might appear strange that the secretary not only spends less time at meetings, but less at *branch* meetings (for which the full-time officers' score is 13%), but the explanation is that the branch secretary has only his own branch meeting to attend, whereas the full-time officer may attend several branches.

Finally, the full-time branch secretary spends much less time on recruitment and collecting individual contributions than the full-time officer spends on recruitment alone. This can only be explained by the preponderance of secretaries from the Mineworkers and the General and Municipal Workers. The Mineworkers have virtually 100% membership and their contributions are deducted by the

[1] See p. 37.

Coal Board. Collection in the General and Municipal Workers is the duty of the collecting stewards.

All but one of our full-time branch secretaries left school at thirteen or fourteen, although two had attended a grammar school and one a technical school. One had previously held a white collar job, and two had been unskilled workers. Ten (a third) had held semi-skilled jobs and thirteen (about a half) had been skilled workers. These proportions are similar to those for full-time officers, except that the latter include rather more white collar workers. None of the full-time secretaries, however, came from White Collar unions.

Our information on selection is limited to the Mineworkers, General and Municipal Workers and the Printing, Bookbinding and Paper Workers.

The national rules of the Mineworkers make no mention of the method of selecting branch secretaries.[1] Most of the Area rules prescribe annual election or re-election (South Wales: Rule 28; Derbyshire: Rule 29A; Nottingham: Rule 12B; Scotland: Rule 32; Durham: Rule 149) although one or two Areas merely prescribe election (Lancashire: Rule 7). So far as we can discover, no Area rules make any provision covering full-time branch secretaries so that they must be elected according to the rules for branch secretaries. In some instances (particularly those in which the branch pays a fixed salary and possibly makes provision for superannuation) the secretary is given to understand that re-election will be allowed to stand over so long as he gives satisfaction, but where the rules prescribe re-election this arrangement cannot be binding, and he could be turned out at the appointed time of year.

The Printing, Bookbinding and Paper Workers leave the method of choosing branch secretaries to the branches in a rule laying down that: 'The Secretary of each Branch shall be elected or shall hold office according to the regulations laid down by the Branch in its local rules, or when local rules do not provide for election, shall be elected yearly at a properly summoned General Meeting of the Branch' (Rule 44). Presumably the branches can prescribe re-election or not, as they see fit, and there is no established custom on the point. In fact, however, no full-time secretary has been defeated, and their inclusion in the superannuation scheme appears to assume continuity.

[1] The Model Rules for the Areas, drawn up in 1944 and 1945, give the Area Executive Committees responsibility for the details of administration within their Areas, and for the establishment and maintenance of branches.

The rules of the General and Municipal Workers say that district committees may 'appoint' a full-time secretary for 'a large Branch or number of Branches amalgamated for that purpose'. Such a secretary 'shall not be subject to periodical election by the members of the Branch' (Rule 45). In some instances appointments have been made direct by the district committee, but usually on the creation of a new post the existing elected secretary is appointed, and another election is held to choose his successor. 'The district reserves the right to reject an unsuitable candidate, and would only confirm the successful candidate and recommend him for superannuation after a trial period of a year or two.'[1] Where a branch secretary has chosen to live on his commission without the approval of the union, he is formally subject to the rule requiring re-election every second year (Rule 37).

In the Printing, Bookbinding and Paper Workers the salary of the full-time branch secretary is determined by his branch, usually at a rate somewhat higher than the skilled craftsman's rate and rising or falling with that rate. All full-time branch secretaries (apart from those over age) must be included in the union's superannuation scheme, as employees of the union. In every other respect, however, they work for the branch and any grievances they have must be settled with the branch.

All branch secretaries in the General and Municipal Workers are entitled to a commission of $12\frac{1}{2}\%$ on contributions. In December 1958 this was worth about £650 for a branch of 2,000 fully paid up adult male members, and almost £1,000 in a branch of 3,000 members. If the commission from all sources (including the district sick and accident fund, which is additional to the union contribution) does not amount to a prescribed minimum figure then the district must make up the difference so long as the appointment has been confirmed by the union. Where the district wishes a full-time secretary to have secretarial assistance and the commission does not run to it, it may supplement up to a maximum figure; and it may supply premises, or rent premises for him. In the largest branch the income from commissions probably exceeds the general secretary's salary by a comfortable margin and allows for the appointment of a typist and an assistant secretary besides a salary well above the minimum for the branch secretary. So far as the minimum rate is concerned it is fixed by the Salaries Sub-Committee of the union's

[1] H. A. Clegg, op. cit., pp. 43–44.

General Council, as are the salaries of full-time officers; and full-time secretaries can, if they wish, make informal approaches through their districts.

In other respects the full-time branch secretary in the General and Municipal Workers has two masters. The rules lay down that he 'shall be at all times under the control and work under the direction of the District Secretary'. This, however, is a determination of where ultimate power lies rather than a description of the way in which ordinary business is done. That has to be arranged with the branch and the branch committee. Any typist or assistant secretary who may be employed by the secretary out of his commission (together with, if necessary, a subsidy from the district) is employed by him and not by the union.

Most full-time secretaries in the Mineworkers are employees of the Coal Board. This is the case both in those Areas, such as Derbyshire, in which they hold a sinecure from the Board in order to devote themselves to the industrial relations of the colliery, and in those Areas, such as Yorkshire, where they support themselves out of their daily 'loss of work allowance', their payment under rule as branch secretary, and such payments as the branch may choose to make out of its allocation from the members' contributions or its general purpose funds raised by additional contributions.[1] Such a secretary is still nominally in the employment of the Board, as it were on leave of absence *sine die*. Both types of secretary receive allowances of coal and other perquisites of a miner and qualify for a miner's pension. So long as he fulfils the duties required of all branch secretaries by the Area and the national union, the full-time branch secretary has only his branch to please.

In other Areas, however, for example in South Wales, the full-time branch secretary is the employee of the branch and *not* of the Coal Board. Until 1959 they were excluded from the Mineworkers' Pension Scheme.[2] Salaries for these secretaries are fixed by the branches, and include any payments the secretary may be entitled to from the union. The balance is made up out of the branch allocation and any additional funds it may choose to raise. In 1957 the average salary of the eighteen secretaries who asked to be included in the proposed superannuation scheme was £11 19s. 2d., with a range from £8 13s. 6d. to £14. Increases in most instances followed increases in the national minimum rate for the industry,

[1] At least 70% of the Yorkshire branches have these funds.   [2] See p. 22.

H

so that by December 1958 the average must have been nearer £13. Even so, the salaries are not over-generous for such a high-paid industry.

One consequence of this arrangement is that the full-time secretaries in South Wales are regarded as 'full-time officials' of the union, and as such come under the provision of Rule 12 in the Area's constitution: 'Full-time officials of the Union, whether locally or at the Central Office, shall not be eligible for election to the Area Executive Committee. . . .' This places the South Wales' full-time secretary at a disadvantage compared with his colleagues in other Areas, and is in marked contrast to the arrangements of the General and Municipal Workers. Indeed, since the practice of appointing full-time secretaries is spreading rapidly with the decline in checkweighing, the ultimate consequence may be to debar the majority of the branch secretaries from the Area Executive Committee.

Full-time branch secretaries worked slightly less hours than full-time officers (55·4 a week as against 57·2), slightly less evenings (2·7 a week compared with 3·0), but slightly more week-ends (1·6 a month compared with 1·4). These differences are hardly significant.

Only one of the full-time secretaries had received union assistance in buying a car, although 40% had cars (compared with 69% of the full-time officers). In most instances the full-time secretary covers a much smaller area than the full-time officer, and has therefore less need for a car.

Half the full-time secretaries (compared with 74% of the officers) were supplied with a typewriter, a duplicator, a telephone and a filing cabinet. Two of them were supplied with none of these things. Since full-time secretaries do more office work than full-time officers this suggests false economy on the part of their branches. However, 40% of the full-time secretaries (compared with 78% of full-time officers) had secretarial assistance provided either by the branch or by the union. (Presumably this included secretarial assistance paid for out of the commission of secretaries in the General and Municipal Workers.)

Promotion prospects for full-time secretaries are reasonably favourable in the General and Municipal Workers. Of 97 full-time secretaries who have been included in the union's superannuation scheme, 21 have subsequently been appointed full-time officers. In the Printing, Bookbinding and Paper Workers the corresponding figure is 3 out of 49. We have no information for the Mineworkers.

Since all indications are that the average age of full-time secretaries is slightly higher than for full-time officers, promotion prospects are poor or negligible for most secretaries at any period of time. Newly-appointed full-time secretaries must receive promotion quickly or not at all. Of the seven secretaries of the General and Municipal Workers who left their branch post within two years of appointment, four became full-time officers of the union.

Amongst full-time secretaries 55% would be pleased if their sons became full-time union officers compared with 53% amongst full-time officers. Family attitudes are almost the same as those of full-time officers, and so are the ratings of the social standing of their own posts and the posts of their general secretaries.

We have information concerning turnover only for those full-time secretaries who are included in the superannuation schemes of the General and Municipal Workers and the Printing, Bookbinding and Paper Workers. In the former union the annual rate since 1927 is 6·8% as against 4·3% for full-time officers. In the latter it is 6·5% (since 1939) as against 5·2%. The difference can be almost entirely explained by promotion from full-time secretary to full-time officer, which is more common in the General and Municipal Workers. Reasons for leaving their posts are compared in Table 28.

The differences between the proportion of deaths in the two unions is probably to be explained by the different periods covered. The differences between full-time branch secretaries and full-time officers seem to be that some full-time secretaries become full-time officers, that they suffer less from ill-health, and that there are fewer resignations among full-time secretaries. This last difference, however, can be entirely explained by the low resignation rate of both groups in the General and Municipal Workers. The relatively high rate of resignations amongst full-time secretaries in the Printing, Bookbinding and Paper Workers, is only partially explained by the difference in periods covered. It might possibly reflect disappointment at the low rate of promotions to full-time offices, or adverse comparisons between salaries and the earnings of skilled workers in the trade.

The eighteen full-time secretaries who were to have been included in the proposed South Wales Miners' superannuation scheme had an average length of service of 7·5 years, compared with 14·3 years for the full-time secretaries included in the superannuation schemes of the General and Municipal Workers and the Printing, Bookbinding and Paper Workers. Probably the difference

TABLE 28

FULL-TIME BRANCH SECRETARIES: REASONS FOR LEAVING[1]

Reason	Full-Time Branch Secretaries			Full-Time Officer		
	N.U.G. M.W.	N.U.P. B.P.W.	Both Unions	N.U.G. M.W.	N.U.P. B.P.W.	All Unions
Normal Retirement	49	49	49	53	79	45
Premature Retirement	—	4	1	—	—	6
Death ..	17	4	12	18	7	16
Ill-Health ..	—	2	1	14	—	7
Resigned ..	8	29	15	10	7	18
Defeated ..	—	—	—	—	—	3
Dismissed ..	4	6	5	5	7	5
Appointed Full-Time Officer ..	22	6	17	—	—	—
TOTAL ..	100	100	100	100	100	100

is a consequence of the rapid expansion in the numbers of full-time secretaries in the South Wales Area of the Mineworkers, as check-weighing has been replaced by payment by the yard.

SUMMARY

There are probably about 400 full-time branch secretaries in Britain who are not graded as full-time officers. Full-time branch secretaries share the characteristics of full-time union officers except in a few respects which are to be explained by the different nature of the two jobs (such as a somewhat different allocation of time between duties), or by the concentration of full-time branch secretaries in a few unions.

[1] The information for the General and Municipal Workers covers the years 1927–1958, and for the Printing, Bookbinding and Paper Workers the period is 1939–1958.

CHAPTER 7

TRADE UNION STAFFS

NUMBERS

WE have obtained information about numbers of staff[1] from fifteen unions, and from the National Federation of Building Trade Operatives. The details are set out in Table 29. Excluding the Building Federation the total is 2,394. If other unions employ staff in the same ratio to membership as these fourteen unions (which include about 60% of the total membership of British unions), then the total staff of all British unions is about 4,000. If allowance is made for the staff of the Trades Union Congress, the various federations, and clerical staff employed by branches the total would be between 4,200 and 4,300, and if allowance is to be made for possible errors in calculation the limits should probably be put at 4,000–4,500.

Unions with the highest ratios of members to full-time officers tend to have high ratios of staff to officers. Thus all seven unions with more than 5,000 members per officer had ratios of staff to officers which were above average, except the National Union of Mineworkers, which equalled the average. At the other end of the scale, all six unions with less than 2,500 members per officer had staff to officer ratio below average, except the Shop, Distributive and Allied Workers. Thus sizes of staffs go some way towards redressing the extremes in the ratio of members to officers. The variation in this figure is from one in 1,100 to one in 16,200. When membership is compared with officers and staff together the variation is from one in 600 to one in 3,100. However, this is not to say that there is an inverse correlation between numbers of full-time officers and staff. Four of the six unions with less than 2,500 members per officer have 2,000 members or less per staff employee.

Costs of administration thus vary very considerably from union to union. Every 600 members of the Building Trade Workers have to find the salary of one full-time employee. At the other extreme the figure of one officer or staff member for 3,100 union members in the Mineworkers is somewhat misleading because of its full-time

[1] The definition of staff is discussed on pp. 19–20.

TABLE 29

TRADE UNION STAFFS: NUMBERS

Union	Total Staff excluding Full-Time Officers (to the nearest 10)	Percentage working at Head Office	No. of Staff per Full-Time Officer	No. of Members per Staff Employee	No. of Members per Full-Time Officer	No. of Members per Staff AND Officers
T. & G.W.U.	670	13	1·2	1,800	2,200	1,000
A.E.U. ..	320	59	2·3	2,700	6,300	1,900
N.U.G.M.W.	250¹	16	1·7	3,100	5,200	1,900
N.U.M. ..	150²	13	1·6	4,400	7,200	2,700
N.U.R. ..	100	100	4·2	3,800	16,200	3,100
U.S.D.A.W. ...	280	50	1·9	1,200	2,400	800
N.A.L.G.O. ..	220	82	3·3	1,100	3,700	900
A.S.W. ..	40	50	0·4	5,100	2,100	1,500
A.W.A. ..	15	33	0·4	4,400	1,700	1,200
N.U.B.S.O. ..	40	25	0·8	2,000	1,700	900
I.S.T.C. ..	60	83	2·9	2,000	5,800	1,500
N.F.B.T.O. ..	30	33	1·8	—	—	—
N.U.P.E. ..	50	60	1·1	3,500	4,000	1,900
A.U.B.T.W.	70	86	1·0	1,200	1,100	600
T.S.S.A. ..	50	80	4·0	1,700	6,700	1,300
N.U.P.B.P.W.	80³	25	5·3	2,000	10,100	1,700⁴
All Unions ..	2,420	41	1·6	2,300	3,800	1,400

¹ The head office of the General and Municipal Workers has no record of district staffs except when they are included in the union's superannuation scheme. Many of the clerical staff, particularly women, are not so included. On the basis of investigation in three districts, in which the ratio of superannuated staff varied from 6 out of 27 to 13 out of 15, we made an estimate of 200–210 district staff. This estimate excludes clerical staff employed by full-time branch secretaries, just as the figure for full-time officers excludes full-time branch secretaries.

² The Mineworkers has a staffing complement for head office and for each area office. There is nothing to stop individual Areas from employing additional staff out of their own funds. In fact, only a few Areas do so, and we would estimate the total at less than ten. We have not included them in our total for the union.

³ This figure includes clerical staff employed in the branches.

⁴ If the union's branch officers were included, the figure would be 1,200.

branch secretaries (although many of them are not paid by the Mineworkers). But it can be said that the salary of one full-time trade union employee is spread over 3,100 members in the Railwaymen without the same need for qualification.

There is no clear explanation for the differences. They do not have a close relationship to union groupings. The Ex-Craft unions provide the Building Workers at one extreme and the Engineers at the other. Two general unions are well below average and the other is well above (or probably slightly above if full-time branch secretaries and other branch employees are included).[1] The Single-Industry unions range from the Boot and Shoe Operatives to the Mineworkers. Only one Skilled union is included in the list; and of the two White Collar unions one has the next to lowest ratio and the other is about average.

The number of staff employed at head office serves as some measure of the centralization of union administration. This does not help to solve our problem, for two of the most centralized unions (by this measure) are the Railwaymen and the Building Trade Workers, who are at opposite extremes of the scale of ratios of members to union employees. The nine unions with more than average centralization include five with members to employees ratios above average and four below.

We are driven towards the conclusion that the staffing of trade unions is to some extent governed by Parkinson's Law: 'Work expands to fill the time available to perform it.' At one time or another a union has adopted a certain staffing ratio and its administrative arrangements have been adapted accordingly. Since then these arrangements have determined the staffing ratios. The Shop, Distributive and Allied Workers, for example, have one of the lowest ratios of members to officers. It has already appeared that these officers give more time to office work than do most other union officers.[2] Nevertheless, the union has almost the lowest ratio of members to office staff. Is it the volume of office work which determines the numbers, or the numbers which determine the volume of office work?

[1] Making allowance for both these groups, the General and Municipal Workers' ratio would be about one in 1,500.
[2] See p. 98.

The 'Administrative' Grades

In most unions a number of members of the staff perform jobs which seem to carry as much responsibility as that of the junior grade of full-time officer (in several instances considerably more). Some of these posts carry salaries equal to or higher than the salaries of junior full-time officers. It is not easy to make exact assessments on these points, for office jobs are not easily compared with work in the field, and there may be other reasons for differences in salary besides differences in responsibility, but we have fairly full information for four unions and estimate that about thirty of the 320 members of the Engineers' staff, thirty of the 250 members of the General and Municipal Workers' staff, fifteen of the 150 Mineworkers' staff, and twenty of the 100 Railwaymen's staff come within this 'administrative' grade. For the four unions this gives 95 out of 820 or about 12%. On this basis the total for all unions might be as much as 500. This, however, is probably an overestimate, for several reasons. A number of small unions have no one in this class; the 12% ratio would give roughly 80 in the 'administrative' grade in the Transport and General Workers, which is certainly far too high a figure; and in some White Collar unions such as the National and Local Government Officers' Association the distinction between 'officers' and 'staff' which we have adopted is one of salary-scale, so that all senior staff are necessarily 'officers'. Accordingly 300–400 would be a more realistic estimate.

Most of the members of this 'administrative' grade perform duties which do not normally come within the responsibility of full-time officers. They include, for example, office managers, chief clerks and chief cashiers (finance officers, finance clerks, etc.) at head office and at regional offices. Such officers are never (or very rarely) graded as full-time officers in unions which elect full-time officers, and only in some instances in other unions. There are other posts, however, which are normally filled by officers but in some instances (even in the same union) are held by members of the staff.

Both education officers and research officers come into this class. The head of the education, research and political department of the Transport and General Workers is a member of the staff. So is the Engineers' research officer; responsibility for education is shared between several people at the Engineers' head office. Until recently the education officer of the General and Municipal Workers was an elected officer, but he has been succeeded by a member of the staff who was previously head of the research department. The Miners' research officer is also a member of the staff. The Miners have no national education officer. The Railwaymen have no separate posts for education or research officers. The Shop, Distributive and Allied Workers have both education and research departments and grade their heads as officers.

The major Areas of the National Union of Mineworkers have Compensation Secretaries who are elected Area Officers, except for Durham, Scotland and South Wales, where the responsibility lies with the head of the compensation department,[1] who is a member of the staff. The South Wales Area also employs a graduate education officer, and an electrical and mechanical engineer.[2]

The education scheme of the General and Municipal Workers is largely administered by the districts and in the majority of the districts it is a part-time responsibility of one or more of the district officers. In the Scottish district, however, it is the full-time responsibility of an elected officer who is a university graduate. In one or two other districts education is the responsibility of a member of the staff. In some districts a full-time officer has responsibility for dealing with appeals under the Industrial Injuries Act and common law claims; in others they are handled by a member of the staff.

Each member of the Executive Council of the Amalgamated Engineering Union (and its general secretary) has a personal assistant. Most of them have been branch or part-time district secretaries in the union, and are therefore (like the Research Officer and several other senior members of the staff) members of the union, and not of the Clerical and Administrative Workers' Union which organizes the rest of the staff. Naturally enough, a good deal of the work they do is work which would otherwise fall on their overburdened council men

In some unions the collection of contributions is thought to require special attention. In the Agricultural Workers this is because the membership is so scattered. In the Shop, Distributive and Allied Workers many members in privately-owned shops are shy of making contact with the union on their own initiative. And in the Lancashire cotton industry house-to-house collection is the

[1] South Wales has three compensation secretaries, each responsible for a zone, who are staff members.

[2] When the old South Wales Miners' Federation absorbed the mechanics' unions in the area they took over two 'mechanical agents'. It was found that election did not produce the right type of man for the work, so that two elective offices were abolished and replaced by this new post. Appointments are made by the Area Executive. The present officer is a miner who had acquired national certificates in Electrical and Mechanical Engineering. His work is mainly concerned with safety matters connected with mining equipment.

custom. In the smaller local associations of the cotton unions the task is done by the full-time secretary, but the major associations, as, for example, the Oldham or Bolton Card Room Association, employ several full-time collectors. The Shop, Distributive and Allied Workers recently revived a practice of one of their constituents and appointed full-time 'collector-canvassers', of which there are now thirteen. They form a grade half-way between the staff and the full-time officers, and several have been promoted to full-time office. The Agricultural Workers are currently experimenting with full-time collectors who will also do all the office work for a number of branches, so that the branch secretary can be replaced by a 'branch convenor' to call branch meetings. The full-time collectors of the Weavers and the Shop, Distributive and Allied Workers have been graded as staff.

By our calculation the total number of staff doing work which usually comes within the scope of full-time officers is about forty in the Engineers, General and Municipal Workers, Miners,[1] Railwaymen and Shop, Distributive and Allied Workers, and thus perhaps 100 for all British trade unions. Because, for the reasons already mentioned, the Transport and General Workers, the White Collar unions, and many small unions have few staff members in this position the number is more likely to be below 100 than above.

STAFF SALARIES AND THEIR SETTLEMENT

In the past the salaries and negotiating rights of trade union staffs have caused some trouble. The Clerical and Administrative Workers' Union and other clerical unions have tried to get the Trades Union Congress to intervene.[2]

[1] A marginal case are workmen's inspectors in the coalmining industry. These are appointed either under Section 123 of the Mines and Quarries Act, 1954, or under Joint Boards. In some areas the work is done by part-time inspectors, but South Wales has eight inspectors (four under Section 123 and four under a Joint Board) and Yorkshire has four (under a Joint Board). Section 123 inspectors are paid by the Area and Joint Board inspectors from a fund, half of which comes from the Coal Board and half from a special levy on the men. These inspectors, who are concerned with safety matters, work under the direction of the Area Executive Committee. We have *not* included them in any of our estimates.

[2] In 1921 the Trades Union Congress established a Joint Board for Trade Union Staffs to hear disputes between employing unions and their employees. It did not have much success in resolving them. In 1924–25, for example, there were five cases (*Trades Union Congress Report*, 1925, pp. 261–264). The Board decided it was not competent to deal with one; in another the Transport and General Workers' Union disputed the right of the National Union of Clerks (as it then was) to represent its staff; in a third the Award of the Board was not observed; and in a fourth it was rejected. During the same year the Board tried to get the parties to agree upon a scale of wages for all offices in the London area. No agreement was reached, and the Board reported (*Trades Union Congress Report*, 1926): 'that they were not able to take further initiative in the matter, as they had done as much as they felt they could usefully do. . . .' Next year the Board did not meet.

The trouble is not that trade union salaries are generally low, or that conditions of work are generally bad. Most of the salary scales which we have seen do not compare unfavourably with those of other clerical staffs, for example, in national and local government, nationalized industries and some large private firms. Hours are reasonable and the pressure of work in most trade union offices is by no means unbearable. Most of the large unions have well-built modern head offices in London (several of them built since the war). A number of district and regional offices still occupy inadequately-converted private houses, but many of these have been rebuilt or reconstructed in recent years.

The grounds for complaint is that trade unions should be above suspicion when they act as employers. Some unions have paid low rates and offered poor conditions in the past, and more have been slow to grant their staffs the same right to trade union representation to protect their interests which unions claim for all other workers. The evidence of low rates is contained in the complaints of the Clerical and Administrative Workers to the Trades Union Congress, and in the award of a considerable increase to clerical employees in the London office of the National Society of Painters by the Industrial Court in 1953.[1] One national union was disturbed some years ago to learn the rates being paid to clerical staffs in some of its regional offices and instituted a minimum rate to encourage the laggards.

One of the reasons for these lapses is a tendency to paternalism in trade union employment practices. In the early days, much more than now, the word applied literally, and a number of full-time officers staffed their offices with their relatives. Even where this was not so, many tended to regard their offices as personal fiefs. Consequently, as often happens with paternalistic employers, they thought they were treating their employees with considerable generosity when, in fact, they were being mean. They failed to look at the other side of the picture or to allow their employees freedom to present their case, with proper outside assistance.

Part of the difficulty has been that many unions expect, or demand, that their employees shall belong to the union, and it is therefore impossible for their employees to secure completely independent spokesmen for their case. We have collected details of the methods of settling salaries and grievances in fourteen major unions. The Clerical and Administrative Workers' Union organizes all or most of the staff in half of these, including the Engineers, the

[1] Award No. 2461.

Miners and the larger building unions. In the other half, including the three General unions and the Railwaymen, all or most of the employees are members of the union for which they work.

In the seven unions in which the Clerical and Administrative Workers organize the staff, it has negotiating rights of some kind. In the Engineers, for example, it submits claims to the Wages Sub-Committee of the Executive Council. Minor grievances are handled by the general secretary. In the Mineworkers there is a similar procedure. In some other unions claims are submitted in the first instance to the general secretary, and in the Building Trade Workers the representatives of the staff negotiate with the national officers of the union. In several unions (including the Building Trade Workers, where the Clerical and Administrative Workers share their authority with a 'staff fraternity') it is the custom that the whole negotiations are handled by the chosen representatives of the staff without bringing in the full-time officers of the Clerical and Administrative Workers, although the course of negotiations may be affected by the knowledge that they could be brought in if the staff representatives insisted.

The staff of several other unions belong both to the unions which employ them and to their own independent staff association. The Shop, Distributive and Allied Workers have both an officers' association and a staff association, each of them having the right to negotiate on behalf of their members with the National Executive Committee of the union. On one occasion the staff association could not agree with the Executive on the proper settlement of the complaint of a member of the staff who was aggrieved by a decision on his grading, and the dispute was submitted to outside arbitration by the consent of both parties. The officers and staff of the National and Local Government Officers' Association also belong to a staff association, and it meets the union in a properly constituted 'Whitley Council'.

In other unions the staff have set up committees to represent them without formally constituting an association. This is the arrangement in both the Transport and General Workers' Union and the head office of the General and Municipal Workers (where the committee is only informally recognized). The committees consist of elected representatives of the various grades of staff, and negotiate with the general secretary. Grievances are first put to the head of departments, thence to the officer in charge of administration and finally to the general secretary.

The staff of the National Union of Railwaymen have a Staff Board which was first established in 1919. The president, the general secretary and an ordinary member of the Executive Committee meet two members of the staff, elected at a general meeting of the staff, who belong to various London branches of the union according to their place of residence. These staff representatives raise grievances first with the Office Manager, then with the general secretary, and finally submit them to the Board. The Board has no authority to determine salaries, but the staff representatives can make representations through the Board to the Executive, and understandings reached by the Board are normally ratified.

In those unions whose staff are also members, the staff have the rights of other members to appeal against decisions of the union, and an aggrieved member of the staff could take his case to the annual conference, or to the executive or to whatever body is responsible for the final decision of an appeal.

The arrangements of the Agricultural Workers deserve separate mention. The organizers have a trade union of their own in addition to their membership of the Agricultural Workers.[1] All the members of the head office staff belong to the Clerical and Administrative Workers' Union as well as the Agricultural Workers. This includes the heads of departments, who are the equivalents of national officers in other unions. (They are generally recruited from field organizers, and provide the candidates for the general secretary's post, and have been treated as full-time officers for our purposes.) Consequently all the head office staff except the general secretary make representation on salaries or on other matters through him to the Executive Committee. Since it is sometimes said that to be a staff representative is not the way to promotion in a trade union it is worth noting that the present general secretary of this union was previously, as head of a department, the elected representative of the head office staff.

One limitation which some unions (for instance, the General and Municipal Workers) place upon their staff, is to debar them from election to the governing bodies of the union—annual conferences, executive councils and area, district or regional committees. The reasons for the limitation are understandable, but the Shop, Distributive and Allied Workers have a member of the staff and three full-time officers serving on the Executive Council of the union

[1] See p. 62.

(which has sixteen members). If the number increased so that the Council was dominated by its employees, the union might wish to put a limit to their rights, just as other unions limit the number of representatives allowed to any one section in the union. As it is, these four have been elected as members of the union, in the same way as other executive councillors.

As outsiders we would repudiate the view that trade unions are bad employers. Certainly most of the larger unions are at least tolerably good employers. We cannot, however, escape the conclusion that many unions have been unduly conservative in dealing with the problem of staff representation.

SUMMARY

1. The total staffs of British trade unions are probably between 4,000 and 4,500. Unions with a low ratio of members to officers tend also to have large staffs, but the variation in the sizes of staffs is not so great as in numbers of full-time officers, so that the variation in ratios of members to full-time employees is less than the variation in ratio of members to officers.

2. Probably 300–400 members of trade union staffs are in the 'administrative' grade, and perhaps 100 perform duties which in other unions (or occasionally in other areas of the same union) are carried out by 'full-time officers'.

3. In the past trade unions have not had the best of reputations for dealings with their staffs, and even now some of the arrangements for settling salaries and grievances are not above criticism.

CHAPTER 8

BRANCH SECRETARIES

NUMBERS

BRANCH sizes for a number of major unions are set out in Table 30A. It can be seen that the average size of the branches covered by our questionnaire is double that of the unions for which we have extracted information from the Chief Registrar's figures.

TABLE 30A

BRANCH SIZE: COMPARISON BETWEEN UNIONS

Union	No. of Branches	Average Branch Size	Average Size of Branches covered by Questionnaire
T. & G.W.U.	5,167	237	516
A.E.U. ..	2,536	350	468
N.U.G.M.W.	2,308	336	794
N.U.M.[1] ..	925	730	1,113
N.U.R. ..	1,419	250	410
U.S.D.A.W. ..	1,721	205	437
N.A.L.G.O. ..	1,352	182	
A.S.W. ..	1,409	137	*Union Groups*
E.T.U. ..	700	329	
N.U.A.W. ..	3,748	40	Skilled .. 243
N.U.B.S.O. ..	55	1,404	Ex-Craft .. 418
I.S.T.C. ..	706	181	Single-
N.U.P.E. ..	1,335	138	Industry .. 541
A.U.B.T.W. ..	923	89	General .. 610
T.S.S.A. ..	423	206	White
N.U.P.B.P.W.	229	662	Collar .. 242
C.S.C.A. ..	1,376	100	
All Unions Covered ..	26,332	226	464
All Unions (estimated) ..	42,500	—	—

[1] The National Union of Mineworkers returns only the number of its constituent Areas, but not of their branches, to the Registrar. The Head Office estimate is that the number of branches is between 900 and 950.

This exaggeration, however, is common to the main unions covered by the questionnaire, and has already been explained as due to the greater ease with which our investigators made contact with the secretaries of larger branches. The size of General and Municipal Workers' branches is the most overweighted, and those of the Engineers and Mineworkers are the least exaggerated. The share of each of the major unions in the sample of branch secretaries is compared with their proportion of total branch secretaries in Table 30B. All major unions except the Transport and General Workers are over-represented here also, and the explanation follows the same lines. Our investigators made contact most easily with the secretaries of the major unions. Confirmation of both these explanations is provided by the position of the Mineworkers in the sample. They are the most overweighted in Table 30B, and they have the largest branches of all the major unions (unless the Boot and Shoe Operatives are included in that category).

TABLE 30B

BRANCH SIZES: PROPORTIONS IN SAMPLE COMPARED WITH ALL
UNIONS

Union	Proportion of Branches to Total Trade Union Branches	Proportion of Branches in Sample
T. & G.W.U.	12	10
A.E.U.	6	11
N.U.G.M.W.	5	7
N.U.M.	2	6
N.U.R.	3	7
U.S.D.A.W.	4	7
Building Unions	⎫ 68	9
Other	⎭	43
TOTAL	100	100

These differences between the sample and the total population, both in size of branch and in the number of branches covered, are certainly not so great as to invalidate the conclusions which we propose to draw.

Of the five unions with the largest average size of branch, four (the General and Municipal Workers, the Miners, the Boot and Shoe Operatives and the Printing, Bookbinding and Paper Workers) employ a considerable number of full-time branch secretaries. No branch which has a full-time secretary (or none whose secretary would admit to the title) is included in this sample. They were covered by another questionnaire, described in Chapter 6. Their omission, however, affects the comparison between the Registrar's figures and our samples in Tables 30A and B. If we accept the figure of 80 full-time secretaries in the General and Municipal Workers and assume that the average size of branch employing such a secretary is 2,500,[1] the average size of the remaining branches becomes 258, still leaving the union with branch sizes above average. It is not so easy to make any allowance for the Mineworkers, since most of their branches are large and the practice of employing full-time secretaries is not confined to the larger branches. We know of full-time secretaries in branches with as few as 500 members. Consequently the exclusion of branches employing full-time secretaries would not necessarily make a marked alteration to their figures in the two tables.

Apart from this, most of the differences in size can be explained by the common-sense consideration that branch size will vary with the concentration of the workers organized by each union, and, other things being equal, the larger the union the larger the concentrations of membership. This principle explains why the Transport and General Workers, the Engineers and Railwaymen have branches over average size. The first two are the two largest unions, and the Railwaymen are large and have the advantage of some concentration. The Agricultural Workers have the most scattered membership, and the Building unions probably come next to them in that respect. Union policy or tradition must also have some effect, for size and concentration cannot explain the difference between the Electricians and the Iron and Steel Trades Confederation. The former is the larger union, but the latter is the most concentrated.

[1] This is about the figure at which the branch secretary's commission yields the minimum salary.

I

The explanation is that the Iron and Steel Trades Confederation normally has a branch for each department in a steel works.

Throughout these calculations we have assumed that the number of branch secretaries is the same as the number of branches, although we know that a number of full-time officers act as branch secretaries, some of them for several branches. We can make no worthwhile estimate of the number of branches concerned, but, if our figure of 41,800 branches can be accepted, this and the existence of about 400 full-time branch secretaries probably reduce the total number of voluntary branch secretaries well below 40,000.

Another consideration is that some unions provide in their rules for more than one branch secretary. The rules of the Shop, Distributive and Allied Workers, for instance, allow for both a financial secretary and a correspondence secretary; and the Transport and Salaried Staffs' provide not only for these two officers, but also for an organizing secretary. Even in these unions, however, it is common for the posts to be held in plurality. Only 259 of the Shop, Distributive and Allied Workers 1,721 branches (15%) have both a financial secretary and a correspondence secretary. Unfortunately we have no information on the proportions in the other unions concerned.

TABLE 31

BRANCH MEMBERSHIP: PROPORTION OF WOMEN

Proportion of Women	Branches with Full-Time Secretaries	Other Branches
Less than 10%	57	56
Between 10% and 30%	13	13
Between 30% and 60%	13	15
Over 60%	10	15
No Answer	7	1
TOTAL	100	100

Taking all these considerations together, we propose to work on the assumption that the total number of voluntary branch secretaries is about 40,000.

The sex distribution of the branches, both of the 211 branch secretaries in our sample and of the 30 full-time branch secretaries, is shown in Table 31. Since approximately 17% of British trade union members are women, our samples are not markedly unrepresentative in this respect.

THE NATURE OF THE JOB

Our Oxford survey impressed us with the wide range of duties of branch secretaries. Few if any of them can restrict themselves to the conduct of correspondence and the keeping of records. In most unions the branch secretary is also the branch treasurer. He is expected to be able to deal with his members' queries on the law and to deal with the union's legal department. He is often guide, counsellor and friend to all the members. In some unions he operates a little employment agency. He may have to sit on joint committees or joint councils. In a number of unions he has to supervise the work of collectors. In a minority of instances the lead in matters of policy is taken by another officer of the branch, perhaps the chairman. But in the great majority of branches it is the secretary who is the leader. This is true of all types of union—White Collar, Skilled, Ex-Craft, Single-Industry and General. At the same time, however, most secretaries are very 'rule-conscious' and anxious to carry out their job within the spirit, if not always the letter, of the rules.

We tried to make a more exact analysis of their work by much the same methods as we used for full-time officers and full-time secretaries. Table 32A sets out the duties of branch secretaries by detail for union groups. Table 32B sets out only the total scores of all kinds of office work for the major unions. The numbers of secretaries involved are too small for minute divisions of duties to have much significance, but major differences between totals of this kind are worthy of some attention.

TABLE 32A

BRANCH SECRETARIES: MAIN DUTIES BY UNION GROUP

Main Duties	All Unions	Skilled	Ex-Craft	Single-Industry	General	White Collar[1]
Financial Work ..	20	25	19	20	27	7
General Correspondence	16	15	17	18	12	22
Meetings	16	17	15	14	12	23
Helping Members with individual problems ..	13	9	10	19	12	13
Benefit Claims and Payments	12	17	19	6	14	2
Negotiating	8	1	2	14	9	8
Arrears and Meeting Notices	6	9	9	2	4	9
Branch Minutes ..	5	4	2	5	3	14
Membership Transfers and Branch Register	4	3	7	2	7	2
TOTAL	100	100	100	100	100	100

TABLE 32B

BRANCH SECRETARIES: SECRETARIAL WORK BY UNIONS

Union	Rating of Office Work[2]
T. & G.W.U.	65%
A.E.U.	75%
N.U.G.M.W.	54%
N.U.M.	35%
N.U.R.	68%
U.S.D.A.W.	78%
Building Unions	78%
All Unions	63%

[1] The distribution of branch secretaries (see p. 33) shows that, in contrast to the samples of full-time officers and shop stewards, the proportion from White Collar unions was large enough to allow inferences to be drawn about the structure and behaviour of the group and they are therefore included in all union group comparisons in this chapter.

[2] This is made up of financial work, correspondence, benefit claims and payments, arrears and meeting notices, minutes, membership transfers and branch registers.

To assist in the interpretation of these tables, we next set out the time spent by branch secretaries on union business, and also the relationship between time spent and size of branch, which is measured in minutes per member per week.

The primary explanation for the differences in time spent on branch business per member shown in Table 33 is variations in branch size. Time spent on union business increases with the size of branch (although not proportionately) so that minutes per member are lowest in the Mineworkers, with the largest branch size of unions included in the table, and highest in the Skilled unions (and the Building unions) which have the smallest branches. The General and Municipal Workers has larger branches than the two other general unions, and its figure of minutes per member is by far the lowest of the three. Not all the differences, however, can be explained in these terms, for example the high rate of minutes per member spent by branch secretaries in the National Union of Railwaymen.

Turning to Table 32A, we note that branch secretaries in general spent something like a third of their time on financial work (including the payment of benefits), almost another third on office work and the remainder in meetings, giving individual help to members,[1] and negotiating, in that order. The branch secretary is primarily a part-time office worker.

Amongst union groups the most outstanding departure from this norm is to be found in the White Collar group. Branch secretaries of White Collar unions do very little financial work of any kind. The explanation is that it is the custom in White Collar unions to appoint branch treasurers who handle financial business. Most other unions expressly entrust all financial business to the branch secretary, or, if a treasurer is appointed, grant him only formal powers and leave the branch secretary to fill in the books. In White Collar unions the time thus saved is spent neither in helping individual members, nor in negotiating. Some of it goes on branch meetings, and even more on correspondence, branch minutes and other work. This seems to be another variant on Parkinson's law. Branch secretaries of White Collar unions should be more competent in office work than branch secretaries in other unions, since they are

[1] Branch secretaries with whom we have discussed the point suggest that this system of measurement underestimates the time spent on members' individual problems, since the payment of benefits is to some extent giving individual help, and a proportion of correspondence deals with individual members' affairs. We accept the point, without being able to make an exact correction.

TABLE 33

BRANCH SECRETARIES: TIME SPENT ON UNION BUSINESS

Union or Union Group	Hours on Union business at work per week	Hours on Union business in own time per week	Minutes of[1] own time per member per week
All Unions	4·1[2]	11·2	1·4
Skilled	1·4	9·7	2·4
Ex-Craft	1·2	11·8	1·7
Single-Industry	7·0	12·4	1·4
General	5·8	13·5	1·3
White Collar	3·0	5·6	1·4
T. & G.W.U.	5·6	14·3	1·7
A.E.U.	1·4	12·3	1·6
N.U.G.M.W.	8·8	13·2	1·0
N.U.M.	11·8	15·8	0·9
N.U.R.	3·0	15·9	2·3
U.S.D.A.W.	2·0	12·5	1·7
Building Unions	0·8	10·8	3·4

[1] It was not clear from the answers to our questionnaire whether branch secretaries had properly distinguished between time at work spent on *branch* business and time at work spent on other union business, for instance (if they hold a second office) in their capacity as shop stewards. Consequently, after some hesitation we decided that the best comparison was between the hours of their own time spent by branch secretaries from different unions and groups. The amount of time spent on union business at work is related to the volume of negotiating done by branch secretaries, and in some instances also to the method of collecting contributions. It may also be that some failed to make an adequate distinction between time spent on union business and time spent on other spare time activities not directly connected with their unions. Our first questionnaire for local officers (see p. 29) showed that 17% of the sample covered were holding or had held 'local government office, been a magistrate or served on any local official committee (e.g. youth employment . . . etc.)'. Although the questionnaire did not adequately distinguish between different types of local officers, at least a quarter of those holding public offices were branch secretaries. Of this sample 74% belong to some 'organization unconnected with trade unions', 39% were active in them and 28% held office. The main organizations mentioned were: Social Clubs (26% membership); Co-operative Societies (21%); Sports Clubs or Teams (21%); British Legion (14%); Other Ex-Service Organizations (13%); Workers' Educational Association (13%); Church or Chapel (10%).

[2] This average includes 68 secretaries who stated that they spent no working time on union business, but not 51 secretaries who failed to answer this part of the question. Since many of the latter may, in fact, also have spent no working time on union business, the average is probably too high and this gives further support to our decision to disregard working time spent on union business in comparisons between unions.

trained for it. Consequently they might be expected to despatch it more rapidly than other secretaries. Presumably, however, their training and capacity reflects their interest, for they spend a considerably larger share of time in office work than the secretaries in any other group.

Both Skilled and Ex-Craft branch secretaries spend more than average time on benefit payment (because they have the most benefits). Negotiating hardly concerns them. Presumably they leave local negotiations to the stewards. Secretaries in the Skilled unions have a heavy load of other financial business, as have General union secretaries, who give rather less time to correspondence and meetings than the rest. Single-Industry branch secretaries stand out for the amount of time they give to negotiating and to helping their members with individual problems.

Table 32B allows us to take the story further. Office work is less important for secretaries in the General and Municipal Workers than for most other branch secretaries. Part of the reason may be that economies of scale apply here, particularly to financial business, and time spent on financial work falls faster with increasing branch size than does total time spent per member.

The same reasoning might apply to the Mineworkers (whose score for all kinds of financial business is 9% compared with an average of 32%), but it is more likely that their exceptionally low score for office-work is due to the 'check-off' system, whereby union contributions are deducted by the employer and transferred in bulk. It is often said that the consequence of the 'check-off' is to rob union members of personal contact with union officers. This appears to be incorrect, since the Mineworkers' secretaries are thus enabled to give more time to the problems of their individual members than the secretaries of any other union. (This item received the highest score from the Mineworkers' branch secretaries. Negotiating also scored considerably more amongst Mineworkers than amongst other branch secretaries. It should be remembered that negotiating is part of the normal duties of a Mineworkers' branch secretary.)

At the other extreme come the branch secretaries of the Shop, Distributive and Allied Workers, with exceptionally heavy loads of office work. The Engineers have almost as high a score, and the Railwaymen are above average.

In order to examine the weight of financial work more closely, let us suppose that time spent on financial business is determined by the number of members, the system of book-keeping and the number of benefit payments to which members are entitled. This assumption will be given further examination later,[1] but for the moment it can be allowed some credence, for there is no obvious reason why secretaries should linger over their financial business. Three groups and four unions come well above the average for both kinds of financial business taken together: Skilled unions (42%),[2] Ex-Craft unions (38%), General unions (41%), the Transport and General Workers (38%), the Engineers (39%), the Railwaymen (38%), and the Shop, Distributive and Allied Workers (52%). Skilled and Ex-Craft unions provide a much wider range of benefit than other unions and this explains the Ex-Craft group and the Engineers, and provides half the explanation in the Skilled and Building groups. Consequently it would appear that the accounting methods of the Skilled unions and the Building unions, the Transport and General Workers, the Railwaymen, and above all the Shop, Distributive and Allied Workers, are unusually complex.

The provision of a branch treasurer who actually handles the branch finances effects a considerable economy in the time of branch secretaries, as Table 34 reveals. It shows minutes per member separately for unions in which we know that the practice is to appoint such a treasurer and for unions where we know that it is not.

Despite the irregular behaviour of the figures in the last column of the table, the advantage of a responsible treasurer seems to be clearly established.

The irregularity of the last column supports the view that economies of scale in branch work occur mainly in financial business. Where financial business is handled by a treasurer, time spent per member no longer varies closely with size of branch.

We thought it would be interesting to make a comparison between full-time and other secretaries in relation to time spent on branch business per union member. An over-all comparison might be misleading, however, because only a few unions employ many full-time secretaries, and differences might be due to this bias. Consequently we have made comparisons only for the Mineworkers and the General and Municipal Workers. In the Mineworkers full-time branch secretaries spend 2·1 minutes per member on branch business each week as compared with 0·9 minutes spent by part-time secretaries. In the General and Municipal Workers full-time secretaries give 1·2 minutes per member, and part-time

---

[1] See Appendix 5.   [2] For the Building unions the figure is 45%.

TABLE 34

BRANCH SECRETARIES: COMPARISON OF TIME SPENT PER
MEMBER IN BRANCHES WITH AND WITHOUT TREASURERS

Branch Membership	Minutes per Member in Unions without Treasurers	Minutes per Member in Unions with Treasurers
Under 100 ..	3·9	3·4
100–200 ..	3·7	3·8
201–300 ..	2·8	0·9
301–400 ..	2·1	1·6
401–600 ..	1·9	0·8
601–1,000 ..	1·4	0·9
Over 1,000 ..	0·7	0·6
All Branches ..	1·8	1·0

secretaries 1·0 minutes. This confirms our view[1] that, in the Mine-workers, branches with full-time secretaries are not so much larger than other branches. Consequently a full-time secretary can provide members with a better service. In the General and Municipal Workers, however, the branches with full-time secretaries are so large that a full-time secretary is necessary if the members are to have any kind of reasonable service. Presumably, however, these branches benefit not only from the slight increase in time per member, but also from the quality of service that the greater experience of a full-time secretary enables him to give. It must also be noted that if the time of assistant secretaries and typists was added in the rate of minutes per member would be much higher in these branches than in the others.

Frequency of contact between branch secretaries and full-time officers affects the nature of the branch secretary's job. We included

[1] See p. 115.

a question on the point, and the answers of those who gave information (96%) are summarized in Table 35.

TABLE 35

BRANCH SECRETARIES: CONTACT WITH FULL-TIME OFFICERS[1]

Union or Union Group	Secretary meets a Full-Time Officer on Union business				Total
	Once a week or more often	Between once a week and once a month	Between once a month and once a year	Less than once a year	
All Unions ..	12	42	37	9	100
Skilled ..	11	38	40	11	100
Ex-Craft ..	8	45	30	17	100
Single-Industry	4	45	39	12	100
General ..	30	48	20	2	100
White Collar	—	24	72	4	100
T. & G.W.U.	36	46	18	—	100
A.E.U. ..	4	35	35	26	100
N.U.G.M.W.	22	64	14	—	100
N.U.M. ..	20	60	20	—	100
N.U.R. ..	—	42	42	16	100
U.S.D.A.W.	29	35	29	7	100
Building ..	11	52	21	16	100

Taking all unions together it seems that almost as many branch secretaries see a full-time officer on business less than once a month as see one more frequently. Amongst union groups the general unions stand out for good contacts and the White Collar unions for

[1] The analysis of replies of individual unions should be treated with reserve because of the small numbers involved. This applies also to subsequent analyses by unions in this chapter.

poor contacts. All three general unions enjoy good contacts, as does the National Union of Mineworkers, and the Engineers and the Railwaymen have poor contacts. The infrequent direct contacts in White Collar unions and in the Railwaymen perhaps explain the importance of office work for their branch secretaries. (See Tables 32A and B.) Correspondence may have served as a substitute.

In interpreting the figures, it must be remembered that the ratio of officers to members is less important than the ratio of officers to branch secretaries. Some of these ratios are set out in Table 36.

TABLE 36

MAJOR UNIONS: RATIOS OF FULL-TIME
OFFICERS TO BRANCH SECRETARIES

Unions	Ratios
T. & G.W.U. ..	1 : 9
A.E.U. ..	1 : 18
N.U.G.M.W. ..	1 : 16
N.U.M. ..	1 : 10
N.U.R. ..	1 : 65
U.S.D.A.W. ..	1 : 12
All Unions ..	1 : 17

The table shows that it is surprising that the contacts in the National Union of Railwaymen are not a good deal worse than they are, and explains why the General and Municipal Workers and Mineworkers are able to maintain good contacts, despite their high member to officer ratios. The relatively poor contacts in the Engineers also reflect a slightly worse than average ratio of officers to branches. The poor contacts of the White Collar unions are to be explained partly in terms of the high member to officer ratios (for example, in the Civil Service unions) but also in terms of the small size of their branches.

ORIGINS

No less than 23% of our sample left school at fifteen and over, and just over half of these at sixteen or seventeen; 14% went to grammar schools and 5% to technical schools. This shows a noticeably higher educational standard than full-time secretaries and full-time officers. A large part of the explanation, however, is the heavier representation of White Collar unions in this sample. They provided 33% of those who left school at fifteen or later and 30% of those who had attended grammar schools. As with full-time officers, the proportion of those educated at grammar and technical schools was considerably higher under 40 (27%) than over 40 (16%), although the small group of under 30's was only 15%. Much of the difference is explained, however, by the relative youth and the high educational standards of branch secretaries in White Collar unions. Excluding them, the proportion with grammar or technical school education becomes 17% under 40 and 14% over 40.

The distribution of occupations; 4% unskilled, 27% semi-skilled, 40% skilled, 13% clerical, 9% supervisory (and 7% other or no answer) also reflects the larger share of the White Collar unions in this sample.

The average age of our respondents was 46·6. Their membership of the unions to which they then belonged averaged about twenty years and their average tenure of office had been 8½ years. Consequently it seems that branch secretaries have, on the average, eleven or twelve years of service in the union when first elected, and that the average age at election is about forty. There are, however, considerable variations. Six per cent of them were under thirty, and 7% had held the office of branch secretary for less than a year. Eleven per cent were over sixty, and 7% had served for over fifteen years.

SELECTION

Union rules invariably prescribe election as the method of choosing branch secretaries; most of them add a clause enjoining periodic re-election (usually at intervals of one or two years). In fact, as our local survey showed, original elections often do no more than confirm the only candidate for the post, and re-elections are even more frequently treated as formalities, or forgotten.

Preliminary inquiries had suggested that the most urgent problem was to find capable candidates for vacant posts (and this was confirmed by the number of branch secretaries' posts filled *pro tem.* by full-time officers). Consequently we concentrated our questions on this aspect of selection, and asked: 'If you were to resign as Branch Secretary do you think there would be anyone willing to take over?' Table 37 tabulates the answers. If a wish to be thought indispensable coloured some of the answers, there is no reason to suppose that it affected one union or union group more than others.

TABLE 37

BRANCH SECRETARIES: AVAILABILITY OF REPLACEMENTS[1]

Union or Union Group	Replacement available	No replacement available	Unsure	Total
All Unions ..	55	26	19	100
Skilled	43	35	22	100
Ex-Craft ..	57	24	19	100
Single-Industry ..	63	24	13	100
General	52	22	26	100
White Collar ..	56	28	16	100
T. & G.W.U. ..	48	28	24	100
A.E.U.	59	23	18	100
N.U.G.M.W. ..	53	20	27	100
N.U.M.	83	—	17	100
N.U.R.	64	22	14	100
U.S.D.A.W. ..	57	14	29	100
Building Unions	30	50	20	100

Another question covered partly the same ground: 'In your experience, is the ability of your Branch to get a full complement of officers getting harder, remaining about the same, or getting easier?' Table 38 summarizes the replies.

The two tables together show that the Single-Industry group has a high morale in this respect, due to the exceptionally good scores

[1] This question was not answered by 1% of the total sample.

TABLE 38

RECRUITMENT OF BRANCH OFFICERS

Union or Union Group	Recruitment harder	No Change or no Answer[1]	Recruitment easier	Total
All Unions ..	35	59	6	100
Skilled	49	49	2	100
Ex-Craft ..	35	58	7	100
Single-Industry	31	64	5	100
General ..	43	57	—	100
White Collar ..	12	68	20	100
T. & G.W.U.	50	50	—	100
A.E.U.	48	39	13	100
N.U.G.M.W. ...	47	53	—	100
N.U.M. ..	8	84	8	100
N.U.R. ..	57	43	—	100
U.S.D.A.W. ..	29	71	—	100
Building Unions	50	50	—	100

of the Mineworkers on both tables, and to the relatively high availability of branch secretary replacements in the Railwaymen. The General unions come rather below average on both tables, and this result is compounded of a slightly better than average performance by the Shop, Distributive and Allied Workers, a slightly worse than average performance by the General and Municipal Workers and a poor result from the Transport and General Workers. The Engineers find growing difficulty in filling branch offices in general, but are not worse off than other unions for candidates to take on the branch secretary's job. The Skilled group have a poor score in both tables, largely because the Building unions have a

[1] Again 1% of the total sample failed to answer.

worse one. The White Collar group appears to have improved its capacity to fill branch offices in general, although the reserves of branch secretaries are no better than those of other unions.

Variations in the availability of replacements in the sample as a whole can be partly explained by two factors. It varies inversely with the amount of his own time which a secretary spends on branch business. Replacements were available for 68% of the secretaries who gave less than four hours of their own time to union business, 57% of those who gave between four and eight hours, 51% who gave between eight and fifteen hours, and only 42% who gave more than fifteen hours. Secondly, the availability of replacements also varies inversely with the importance of office work in the branch secretary's job. The score of all kinds of office work amongst secretaries who thought someone would be willing to take their place was 60%. Amongst those who thought there was no one to take over it was 71%. And amongst the doubtful it was 66%.

Another consideration is the method of branch organization. Some unions base their branches on residence, and others on the place of work. Some make use of both practices. The difference is usually regarded as a matter of considerable importance in studies of trade union structure, which look upon the residential branch as generally outmoded by the conditions of modern industry. We therefore included a question which divided the branches into those which drew their members from only one place of work, such as a colliery (23%); those which covered two or more places of work, but only one employer, such as a Railwaymen's branch organizing in several stations or depots (24%); and those which included members working for two or more employers (53%). In most respects we could find little connection between this division and the other characteristics of the branch secretaries, but it did appear to have some bearing on this point. In the first group 54% could rely on a replacement, in the second group 67%, and in the third only 48%. On the other hand, this can be largely explained by the relatively high score of the Single-Industry group, most of whose branches fall into the first two categories, and the low score of the Skilled group, most of whose branches are residential. And it could therefore be a consequence of other differences between these two groups.

The proportion of women in a branch appeared to be relevant. Only a quarter of the branch secretaries with more than 60% of women members felt sure of finding a successor. If this is a causal factor, it could explain some differences between unions and groups, for the proportion of women members varies considerably. In the Shop, Distributive and Allied Workers, for instance, women constitute 47% of the members, 20% in the General and Municipal Workers, and 13% in the Transport and General Workers, compared with 17% in all unions, 8% in the Engineers, 3% in the Railmen, and none in the Mineworkers. We were unable, however, to make much of this possibility. Certainly it cannot serve to explain the relatively low score of the Building unions.

It is possible, however, to suggest that a relationship between the proportion of women members and the recruitment of branch secretaries may be part of a more general relationship, between the recruitment of branch secretaries and the difficulty of recruiting and retaining union members. Women are notoriously less trade union-minded than men. The turnover of women workers in industry is generally higher than that of men, and this adds to union problems both of recruitment and retention.

So far the explanation is plausible, and it is also understandable that insecure membership should affect the availability of candidates for branch secretary's job. The need to struggle to retain his membership probably adds to the time a branch secretary spends on his union work, and it also adds to his worries. To have to beg and cajole money out of unwilling subscribers (or to find others to undertake the task) is an obligation few would find congenial. Add to this his fear that cajolery may fail, his membership dwindle, and he himself be regarded as a failure, and there are sufficient grounds to lend credibility to a connection between membership security and the recruitment of branch secretaries.

Membership security varies widely between unions. The Mineworkers, for example, have no problem in this respect. In some areas they enjoy closed shop agreements which date back to the days before nationalization. All areas, except Durham (which prefers to rely on the old method of collection of union dues by branch officers), are covered by an agreement for the deduction of union dues by the Coal Board. Recruits to the industry have to sign a form before their contributions can be deducted, but the arrangement allows the union to maintain almost universal membership amongst manual workers. The Mineworkers' branches and their officers have, therefore, no need to look for members. So long as the collieries employ miners, the union will have members.

The Building unions boast a trade union tradition as long and proud as that of the miners, but for a number of years past they have been struggling for members. Over the past ten years their membership has fallen about 10%, more than twice as fast as the slow decline in total trade union membership. Moreover, this figure does not reveal the alarm of the union leaders as the creeping decline has continued. The effect on the branches in the Midlands and the South of England has been considerable, and our local survey revealed several branches in imminent danger of collapse. Part of the problem is the casual character of much building work. No sooner is a site properly organized than the job finishes and workers move to a different site where loyal members may find themselves once more in a minority among non-unionists and lapsed members.

In between these two extremes, other unions have a mixed experience. It might be expected, for instance, that the Shop, Distributive and Allied Workers, would have as troublesome a problem as the Building workers. Almost half their members are women, and the distributive industry is not generally responsive to trade unionism. The majority of the union's membership, however, is in Co-operative employment, and trade union membership is a condition of employment for most Co-operative employees. In this section of the trade, therefore, the union is protected from the adverse conditions which its officers experience in trying to find and keep members in private retailing undertakings.

The two other General unions also experience these two extremes of complete protection and extremely unstable membership, but with large sections of their members in a variety of intermediate positions. In this they probably reflect the general experience of British unions. Many skilled Engineers are protected by closed shop agreements, or by informal understandings with employers, but since their union went into competition with the General unions for the general run of semi-skilled engineering workers, including women, its membership must have become less stable.

Over the last ten years the Railwaymen's membership has fallen twice as fast as that of the Building unions—by more than 20%— but the cause has been a decline in employment, not an increasing difficulty in persuading railway workers to join the union. For more than forty years the union has maintained a high degree of membership among the grades which it organizes, with 100% membership in many railway establishments. Consequently their

K

branch secretaries do not have to spend much time looking for members.

Our figures for branch secretaries of individual unions cover only small numbers. This does not destroy the value of our hypotheses in matters in which the behaviour of branches is likely, because it is governed by the rules or by the structure of the unions, to be fairly uniform throughout each union. In frequency of contact with full-time officers, in the weight of financial business, and in branch stipends, the experience of ten or twenty branches spread over the country is likely to represent the experience of other branches, although considerably larger numbers would be needed for certainty. Especially where there is corroborative evidence, we have thought it worth while to make use of branch secretaries' answers on these points. In a matter of opinion such as the avail-ability of replacements, however, much larger numbers would be needed to constitute reasonable evidence. We have therefore quoted the figures of individual unions only to show they are con-sistent with our argument that the willingness of members to under-take the job of branch secretary is related to stability of membership. The basis of this suggestion is our local survey and general experience of trade union affairs.

We therefore suggest that the availability of recruits for the post of branch secretary is probably inversely related to the weight of the work (and the proportion of secretarial work in the job), and positively related to the stability of membership.

The White Collar unions were the only group to think that the recruitment of branch officers was not becoming more difficult. If this is not a chance result of a small sample, it can be explained by the continued expansion of White Collar unions at a more rapid rate than other unions over the last forty years. Among many White Collar workers trade unionism is still acquiring respectability.

REMUNERATION

One obvious influence on recruitment has so far been left out of account—the stipends of branch secretaries. From the answers to our questionnaire it seems that the average annual payment to branch secretaries is £51 12s. However, this figure must be hedged about with a number of qualifications. First of all, many union rules vary the secretary's stipend with the size of the branch. The average size of branch in the sample is double the actual average for British unions, but in many unions payments do not fall *pari passu* with membership, so that a figure of £30–£35 might seem to be a likely national average. On the other hand, it is quite clear that the answers to our questionnaire understated the payments to the 211 secretaries in the sample, for two reasons. The unions which pay higher stipends tended to be the most reticent. Out of the whole sample 14% did not answer the question, but for the Transport and General Workers the proportion was 38%. Secondly, many of the stipends returned by secretaries were very considerably below the amounts prescribed by their union rules for branches of that size. It is likely that they made such deductions as are allowed by the Inland Revenue for expenses before filling in the questionnaire, but in some instances this does not seem to explain the whole of the gap.

The range of payment is from nothing to over £300 a year. Since most unions relate payment to the size of branch, and since the demands made on a branch secretary vary from union to union, it might be thought that the range could be explained in these terms. If it could, payment per hour of work should be fairly constant. A branch secretary with few members and few duties would receive a small stipend, and a busy secretary with a large branch and many duties would receive a larger stipend to recompense him for the long hours he must spend on union business. In fact, the range in shillings per hour is less than the range in pounds a year,

TABLE 39

BRANCH SECRETARIES: PAYMENTS

	Annual Payments							Total
nil	–£8	£9–£20	£20–£40	£40–£80	£80–£160	£160–£320	£320–	
8	7	14	22	33	10	4	2	100[1]

	Hourly Payments							Total
nil	–6d.	7d.–11d.	1s.–2s. 5d.	2s. 6d.–3s. 11d.	4s.–6s. 5d.	6s. 6d.–9s. 11d.	10s.–	
9	8	17	42	17	2	4	1[2]	100[1]

[1] 14% of the sample did not state what stipend they received, and 16% did not give sufficient information to permit a calculation of hourly payments.

[2] One of the two branch secretaries receiving over 10s. an hour for union work was actually being paid at a rate of more than 15s. an hour.

but it is still considerable, as Table 39 reveals. We have assumed that hourly payment should be measured in terms of hours spent on union business in the secretary's own time, since it is presumably for this that he requires compensation.[1]

If we assume that remuneration for a post held by an adult at less than 1s. an hour is merely a token payment, and any payment below 4s. an hour cannot be regarded as adequate remuneration for a paid adult post, then Table 39 seems to indicate that most branch secretaries receive a considerable honorarium in compensation for their

TABLE 40

BRANCH SECRETARIES: PAYMENTS BY UNIONS AND UNION GROUPS

Union or Union Group	Annual Payment	Hourly Payment (own time)
All Unions ..	£51 12s. 0d.	1s. 10d.[2]
Skilled	£33 19s. 0d.	1s. 6d.
Ex-Craft[3]	£35 13s. 0d.	1s. 2d.
Single-Industry[4] ..	£56 0s. 0d.	1s. 9d.
General	£104 6s. 0d.	2s. 9d.
White Collar[5] ..	£7 16s. 0d.	6d.
T. & G.W.U. ..	£80 0s. 0d.	1s. 11d.
A.E.U.[3]	£29 3s. 0d.	11d.
N.U.G.M.W. ..	£186 11s. 0d.	5s. 4d.
N.U.M.	£55 2s. 0d.	1s. 3d.
N.U.R.	£105 0s. 0d.	2s. 8d.
U.S.D.A.W. ..	£34 9s. 0d.	1s. 1d.
Building Unions ..	£34 2s. 0d.	1s. 2d.

[1] Although 22% of union secretaries appear to suffer loss of earnings by union work. See p. 138.

[2] A further reason for supposing that the questionnaire answers are underestimates is that the average hourly rate of payment for all Oxford branches worked out at 3s. 3d.

[3] A.E.U. figures are all inclusive of 75% personal allowance.

[4] Including 3 secretaries who receive no remuneration.

[5] Including 10 secretaries who receive no remuneration.

services. For most of them this does not amount to anything like the 'rate for the job', if it was a full-time occupation, but a small minority find in it a remunerative spare time occupation.

Comparisons between unions and union groups are given in Table 40.

The information in Table 40 can be supplemented by union rules on standard payments to branch secretaries which are given in Table 41. In order to facilitate comparison the table shows payments for a branch of 500 adult male members, none of them in arrears.

TABLE 41

BRANCH SECRETARIES: PRESCRIBED PAYMENTS
1938 AND 1958

Union	Annual Payment		
	1938	1958	Increase
T. & G.W.U. ..	£48 15s. 0d.	£97 10s. 0d.	100%
A.E.U.	£33 13s. 4d.	£58 18s. 4d.	75%
N.U.G.M.W. ..	£81 5s. 0d.	£162 10s. 0d.	100%
N.U.R.	£54 3s. 4d.	£142 3s. 9d.	163%

NOTE: The Shop, Distributive and Allied Workers leave the payment of all branch officers to the decision of the branch. The national rules of the Mineworkers make no mention of branch secretaries' stipends except that they, and the salaries of other branch officers and the expenses of branch committee members, are to 'be borne out of the percentage allowed to the Branch in question by these Rules from contributions payable by its members to the Union'. One or two Areas prescribe the stipend (for example, in 1958 a branch secretary in Nottingham would have received £26 11s. 2d. for 500 adult male members), but most Areas leave the rate to be decided by the branch. All that can be said is that the practice varies considerably from place to place.

Table 40 seems to show that hourly payments average between 1s. and 2s. an hour except in the White Collar unions (some of which make no payment at all), in the General unions (whose high average is due to the apparently very high payments of the General and Municipal Workers) and in the National Union of Railwaymen.

The table must, however, be interpreted together with the figures in Table 41 and information concerning the methods of payment.

Table 41 reveals that the payments in the General and Municipal Workers are not so exceptional—at least, for the size of branch in our example—as would appear from Table 40. The Railwaymen's annual stipend is only slightly smaller. Part of the explanation for the high hourly rate in the General and Municipal Workers is the large size of their branches in the sample, for payment on a *per capita* basis must provide a higher hourly payment as the size of branch increases if (as is the case in all unions) the amount of time spent on each member falls with increasing numbers. At least part of the explanation for the large difference between hourly payments in the Transport and General Workers and those in the General and Municipal Workers is that very few of the secretaries of large Transport and General branches answered the question.

This, however, is only part of the story. The Mineworkers have even larger branches than the General and Municipal Workers, but hourly payment is much less. This is because the Mineworkers, along with many other unions, do not pay secretaries a standard proportion of branch income. The latter method is used by the Transport and General Workers, the General and Municipal Workers, the Railwaymen[1] and the Electricians, but there are two other popular methods—a diminishing percentage as members increase, and a fixed honorarium. The first method is used by the Engineers, who pay only 2*d*. per member per quarter beyond 300 members. Those Areas of the Mineworkers which prescribe the rate of payment also lay down a diminishing rate as numbers rise, as well as a percentage well below that of either of the two larger General unions, even at the lowest level. Consequently, in these two unions hourly payments do not rise as the size of branch increases, or at least not so fast as in the two larger General unions.

The custom in the White Collar unions is to make no payment at all, or to allow the branch to pay an honorarium. Consequently, the relation between size and income may not exist, and is at best not automatic, and the average payment in the group is very low. In fact, 10 of the 23 White Collar branch secretaries who completed this part of the questionnaire stated that they received no payment at all.

Comparison between Tables 37 and 40 shows that there is no relationship between payment and the availability of replacements. If there were a close and positive relation the General unions should have the best reserves of new secretaries, and the General and Municipal Workers should be outstanding; both have average

---

[1] Although the Railwaymen also have an additional allowance for branches with less than 120 members.

scores. Of the three General unions the Shop, Distributive and Allied Workers have slightly the best reserves, and almost the lowest remuneration. The Mineworkers have far better reserves than other unions, and the remuneration is below average. White Collar union secretaries are hardly paid at all, but their score on availability of candidates is a little above average.

Table 41 gives information for only four unions, but between them they cover about 35% of British trade unionists. They show a very marked fall in remuneration since 1938 compared with retail prices (up by 175%), wage rates (up by 205%) and average earnings (up by 280%). Not even the largest increase, that of the Railwaymen, has managed to keep pace with the retail price index. To some extent this decline has been masked by an increase in branch size since 1938, for the growth in union membership since then has increased branch sizes rather than numbers of branches, but even if the total number of union branches had not increased since 1938 the fall in payments would still be considerable. Part of the difficulty is that many unions fix branch secretaries' stipends in terms of union contributions and these have not increased in proportion to wages or prices. On the average they rose by about 60% between 1938 and 1958, and in the two General unions contributions were exactly doubled. In other unions salaries have been *reduced* in relation to income. The Engineers have left their rates of payment unchanged since 1938, but have added a 75% personal allowance. The Electricians have reduced their branch secretaries' percentage of branch income from $7\frac{1}{2}$% to 6%.

If we can assume, on the evidence of Table 41, that branch secretaries' stipends have nearly doubled since 1938, then they have risen only half as fast as the wage-rates of adult male workers. It would be unwise, however, to deduce from this that all the difficulties of unions in relation to their branch secretaries are to be explained by a severe decline in payments, for it is not easy to relate the performance of branch secretaries to their payments. The evidence would more readily support the suggestion that unions which pay more than others for their branch secretaries' services are wasting their money, for other unions do as well for less; and, indeed (unless the behaviour of White Collar unions has no relevance to other unions), it is not clear that unions derive any advantage at all from paying their secretaries.

Much more evidence would be needed to establish this point, and there is some evidence to the contrary. Certainly some branch secretaries attach considerable importance to their stipends. The secretary of a branch of one of the highest-paying unions wrote in:

The duties of a branch secretary are many, and I can honestly state that we are not paid sufficient for the work we perform. The union as a whole could not function successfully if the branches were not properly organized, and that is the responsibility of the branch secretary.

Branch secretaries attend to branch accounts, banking, making out balance sheets every quarter, a half-yearly and an annual balance sheet.

Appearing at Medical Tribunal Boards on behalf of members. Advising members on domestic problems, at the same time having sufficient domestic problems of his own.

It has become my experience that home life can be interrupted, and broken up, because your home is nothing more than another Public House without the sale of drink, everyone visits you and requires you to perform miracles for them. If you don't appear co-operative you are subjected to the vilest abuse.

Perhaps the only safe conclusion is that payment cannot be the dominant incentive for branch secretaries. It is also a fair guess that its importance has declined since 1938 as incomes from work have risen, so that the heavy decline in stipends since then has had less effect than it otherwise might have done.

Another consideration is that branch secretaries may lose money because of their trade union activities. In answer to the question: 'Do you suffer any loss of pay as a result of union activity?' 22% of the sample claimed that they did. Over half of these estimated their loss at less than £1 a week (over one-third put it at less than 10s.). Most of the remainder put it between £1 and £2, leaving three out of the 211 respondents with average losses of over £2 a week. Unfortunately the wording of the question does not make clear whether these losses were caused by their activities as branch secretaries, or through other union work.[1]

PROMOTION

For branch secretaries promotion within the union can mean two things: election to the higher committees and councils of the union; or selection for a full-time office.[2]

Almost 40% of our sample were members of district committees or held some other district office; 9% held regional offices in unions

[1] 23% of the sample were shop stewards, 3% branch delegates, and almost 40% held district offices or served on district committees.

[2] In some unions there are other possibilities. At least three members of the clerical staff of the Transport and Salaried Staffs' Association were previously branch secretaries, and others held other branch offices. Several of the personal assistants to national officers or Executive Council members in the Engineers were formerly branch secretaries or part-time district secretaries. But both these instances seem to be exceptional.

which have both districts and regions (or their equivalents); and 4% were members of their national executive committee or held some other national office. Although our sample over-represents the secretaries of larger branches, who might expect to get more than their share of such posts, this suggests that there is considerable opportunity to take part in the higher counsels of the union if they wish to do so.

We attempted to measure the desire of branch secretaries for this type of work by asking those who did not already serve on district, regional and national committees whether they would be willing to do so if the opportunity arose. Of those to whom the question applied 73% replied that they would. In other words it seems that most unions need not lack candidates for such posts.

The opportunity for full-time office is much more restricted. There are some 2,500 full-time officers. With a turnover of between 4% and 5% per annum there are 100–125 posts to fill each year. From our sample of full-time officers[1] it seems that 38% (or between 38 and 48) of these posts can be expected to go to union members who are currently branch secretaries. Since there are about 40,000 branch secretaries this means that in each year the chances of each branch secretary achieving full-time office are little better than one in a thousand. Since the secretaries in our sample had held their posts as secretaries for an average of $8\frac{1}{2}$ years we may assume, as a first approximation, that branch secretaries, on the average, hold office for about seventeen years. On this assumption the chance of a branch secretary now in office being promoted to a full-time post before he ceases to hold the post are about one in a hundred. For newly-elected branch secretaries the chances are about one in fifty. In any union the opportunities are affected by the number of officers and branches in the union, amongst other things. Table 36 (which gives the ratios of officers to branches) suggests that in the Transport and General Workers, with its large number of officers, and in the Mineworkers, with its small number of branches, the chances may be twice as good as average. By a similar calculation the likelihood of a branch secretary attaining a full-time post in the Railwaymen is far below average.

These figures are rough and ready, but they demonstrate that, even in the most favourable circumstances, few secretaries can expect full-time office, or that, if many do, most of them will suffer frustration.

[1] See p. 51.

On the other hand, it suggests a plentiful supply of candidates for full-time office, so long as it can be shown that an appreciable proportion of branch secretaries desire promotion. It seems that many of them do want it, for 30% of our sample said that they thought they would like to become a paid union official.[1] It may be that secretaries of larger branches are more eager than secretaries of small branches, but assuming the proportion is constant, this suggests that 12,000 branch secretaries would like to have the 120 full-time posts which are filled each year (or the 40-odd that are likely to go to branch secretaries). Assuming that all the posts which go to branch secretaries go to those who want them, the chances of a secretary now in office, and who would like a full-time post, actually achieving it are about one in thirty.

These figures may surprise trade union leaders and executive members who have difficulty in finding good candidates for vacant offices. And they exaggerate the availability in candidates in other ways besides the over-weighting of large branches. Many branch secretaries who would like full-time office are quite unsuitable. For instance, 20% of secretaries over fifty years of age (and 21% over sixty!) said that they would. (The 41–50 age group was the most eager with 41%. The under 30 group scored 38%, and the 31–40 group only 33%.) Moreover, there is an important difference between a secretary saying he would like full-time office and actually applying or standing for election. But at least the figures suggest that more candidates would be available if the unions sought them out.

We asked for reasons for answers to this question. A fifth of the respondents who did not want full-time office gave no reason. Of the remainder, 31% gave age or health as their reason and 10% said they lacked the ability or the qualifications. The domestic problems created by full-time office deterred 6%, the hours worked by full-time officers were mentioned by 10%, and the attitude of members to them by 1%. Another 4% honestly confessed that they lacked sufficient interest in the union, and 1% preferred to remain in the rank and file. Only three secretaries mentioned the low salaries of union officers.

Reasons for wanting full-time posts were even more varied and difficult to classify. In this group 24% did not give a reason, and of the remainder 28% gave idealistic explanations in terms of service to their fellows, and 24% stated that they thought the work was interesting and satisfying.

[1] 65% said 'no', 2% were unsure, and 3% failed to reply.

On this score there were few significant differences between unions and union groups. The Mineworkers (50%) and the Railwaymen (43%) are well above the average, and the White Collar group (24%) noticeably below. Otherwise the variations between union groups was between 27% (Skilled) and 33% (Single-Industry) and the variation between unions no greater. The score of the White Collar group can perhaps be explained in terms of a connection between occupational status and a desire for full-time office (Table 42). We shall have more to say about this relationship in

TABLE 42

BRANCH SECRETARIES: JOBS AND DESIRE FOR FULL-TIME POSTS

Grading of Branch Secretary's Employment	Number in Grade[1]	Proportion who think they would like a Full-Time Post
Unskilled	9	44%
Semi-Skilled ..	56	38%
Skilled	84	27%
Clerical	27	22%
Supervisory and Administrative	18	39%

the next section. Once more the numbers of branch secretaries of the Mineworkers and the Railwaymen are too small to support any generalization about their unions. We would, however, be prepared to believe that these two unions experience more competition for full-time posts from their branch secretaries than do most other unions. Despite complaints about apathy from miners' leaders, miners still seem to show an exceptional interest in their union and an exceptional identification with it. Alternative opportunities for advancement are still unusually restricted in mining communities, in which trade union work has a high status. It is also possible that some branch secretaries in the Mineworkers are keen to say good-bye to the pits, especially at an age when high-paid face-work is becoming increasingly onerous. In the Railwaymen, financial rewards might provide a stronger incentive than in

[1] The remainder (17 respondents) either gave no answer or no information by which their ob could be graded.

most other unions. The officers of their union are better paid than
the officers of most other manual workers' unions, whereas railwaymen have received less than the average for adult males for many
years, and the National Union of Railwaymen has a smaller proportion of its membership in the higher-paid railway grades than the
two other railway unions.

ATTITUDES

One factor in desire for full-time office may be the attitude of
branch secretaries to the relative social standing of their own posts
and full-time union posts. The sample provided an indication that
desire for full-time office falls as the status of the branch secretaries'
occupations rise.

Since the significance of the proportions diminish with the numbers in the grade, the clearest finding is that semi-skilled workers
are noticeably more interested in full-time union posts than skilled
workers, and not much importance can be attached to the apparent
keenness of unskilled workers for full-time posts, although it
supports the hypothesis. Supervisory and administrative workers
are well out of line with what might be expected of their social
standing, but an explanation can be offered for this. Supervisory
and administrative workers are comparatively rare in trade unions,
and are likely to possess more ambition and more of the skills
required for full-time office. The fact that they are union members,
and even more that they are branch secretaries (at least, in other
than White Collar unions), indicates an unusual interest in trade
union affairs. This is especially so where they hold office in manual
workers' unions, as did several of our respondents.[1] Consequently
it might be expected that the desire for full-time posts would be
high amongst clerical and administrative workers *who are already
trade union branch secretaries*.

Branch secretaries were asked the same question about social
standing as we put to full-time officers, except that they were asked
to rate their own job and that of 'the average local full-time union
official'. Table 43 shows the results and makes comparisons with
the ratings which full-time officers gave to their own positions.

It seems that branch secretaries hold much the same view about
the accepted social standing of full-time union posts as do union
officers themselves, except that a few branch secretaries are willing

[1] This explains why the score of administrative and supervisory workers is markedly
higher than secretaries of branches of White Collar workers.

TABLE 43

BRANCH SECRETARIES: SOCIAL STATUS

Job Rated	Rating by	Range in Status Scale					Total
		Medical Officer of Health —Civil Servant (Executive Grade)	Nonconformist Minister— Elementary School Teacher	Jobbing Master Builder— Policeman	Routine Clerk— Carpenter	Shop Assistant and below	
Jobs held by branch secretaries	Branch Secretaries[1]	←——20——→		35	31	14	100
Full-Time Officers	Branch Secretaries[2]	23	60	13	←——4——→		100
	Full-Time Officers	10	69	←——21——→			100
Full-Time Branch Secretaries	Full-Time Branch Secretaries	4	75	←——21——→			100

to go a little further up the scale than the full-time officers are. Almost all of them rate their own jobs lower (6% put their own jobs above that of the local full-time officer, and 3% put it on the same level). For all that, they seem to exaggerate their own accepted social standing if its rating is to be based on their full-time occupation. Of the 93% of respondents whose jobs can be identified and rated, 24% held administrative, low-grade clerical and supervisory posts, but 55% rated themselves above a routine clerk, and 76% held skilled, semi-skilled or unskilled jobs although only 33% thought their accepted status was equivalent to a fitter's or a carpenter's, or below that.

This might be explained in terms of the widespread 'status-optimism' of western societies, discovered by many social surveys which include questions on social standing, which persuades the majority of their populations that their neighbours see them as 'middle-class'. In this survey, however, we were dealing with active trade union officers whose developed class-consciousness might be expected to place them above this kind of self-deception; and, from some of the comments which were written in, it is clear

[1] 21% of the sample gave no answer to this question.
[2] 11% of the sample gave no answer to this question.

that another factor was at work. They, or some of them, felt that their position as union officers elevated their social standing. One respondent wrote:

> This is indeed a very difficult question to answer because you cannot divorce your status as a General Labourer from the fact that you are a Public Figure by being an active Trade Unionist.

The relationship between occupation and desire for full-time office was paralleled by a slight relationship between attitude to status and full-time office. As a group, those who desired full-time office rated the difference between the standing of their own job and that of a full-time union post to be greater than those who did not, but the difference was relatively small.

We asked two more related questions, whether the respondents thought their social standing would go up and whether they thought their earnings would go up if they were to become local full-time officials. Table 44 gives the answers, and shows that the proportions tally fairly well with their separate ratings of their own social status and that of full-time officers.

TABLE 44

BRANCH SECRETARIES: ASSESSMENT OF STATUS AND
EARNINGS OF FULL-TIME OFFICERS

Expected change on becoming a Full-Time Officer	Social Standing	Earnings
Go up a great deal	6	13
Go up considerably ..	18	22
Go up a little	41	32
Remain about the same ..	27	14
Go down a little	2	7
Go down considerably ..	1	4
Go down a great deal ..	—	—
Don't know or no answer	5	8
TOTAL	100	100

About two-thirds of branch secretaries expected that their status and earnings would rise if they became full-time officers, and they were a little more confident about earnings than status. It is therefore unlikely that many branch secretaries who would consider seeking full-time office are deterred because they think that the change would harm their social and economic position.

Branch secretaries gave an account of the attitude of their families to the time spent on union work similar to that of full-time officers. A rather larger proportion (59% instead of 49%) reported that their wives or families were 'quite happy' about the amount of time they spent on union work. It should be noted that branch secretaries probably spend as much time at work (including both union work and their full-time job) as do full-time officers. If we accept the replies of both groups as a correct report of hours worked, then full-time officers average 57·2 a week, and branch secretaries 11·2 hours of their own time spent on union business. In most industries the agreed working week has been 44 or 45 hours for manual workers, and with overtime the average hours actually worked by adult males has fluctuated about 48 for some years past.

Family displeasure gradually increased with hours worked, except for a sharp improvement in relationships above thirty hours a week on union business. (There were only eight officers in this group.) The connection is, however, not marked enough to support a stronger conclusion than that the hours actually worked have some small effect at home.

TURNOVER

Our questionnaire for branch secretaries included nothing on turnover, except that we asked how long our respondents had been branch secretaries. The average tenure was 8½, and this would suggest an average tenure of office of something like seventeen years.[1]

The Oxford survey suggested that turnover and the availability of replacements are closely connected. So long as he gives reasonable satisfaction a branch secretary can, within wide limits, determine the date of his own retirement. Several secretaries told us that they were only awaiting a suitable successor to enable them to retire. The other side of the story is that most branches have only one secretaryship. If a large number of members were keen to hold the

---

[1] Two secretaries had held office for forty-one years!

post, most of them would be disappointed. In the early years of a secretary's tenure he is usually not looking for a successor, and would probably resist the challenge that an ambitious competitor would offer. In the course of a seventeen-year term of office a number of likely candidates may play an active part in the branch and then leave, or turn to other interests, or be promoted to a supervisory post in industry. The incumbent has no right to expect them to wait patiently until he chooses to retire, and no right, therefore, to expect one of them to be ready as soon as he wishes to lay down his responsibilities. He may have to wait, to pick his man and to nurse him along for a time.

This consideration affects what has already been said about the availability of successors. It may be sensible to attribute a higher morale to a branch whose secretary thinks he can find a successor than to one whose secretary does not, but it does not follow that the second branch is in dire straits. The administration of the branch will suffer only if the situation persists until the incumbent decides to retire.

For similar reasons it is difficult to know how to interpret turn-over amongst voluntary officers. Amongst full-time officers a high turnover would provide *prima facie* evidence of low morale. A very low turnover amongst branch secretaries might cause poor morale. It may be that no replacements have been forthcoming in those branches whose secretaries have been in office for over twenty years, but it may also be that their long term of office has thwarted the ambition of keen young trade unionists for many years, and reduced the morale of the branch. A very rapid turnover would, of course, also suggest that something was wrong with the branch. In view of these considerations there is no reason at all to suppose that any other average period of office would be an improvement on seventeen years.

The first questionnaire for local officers (see p. 29) included the question: 'Have you ever had to refuse, or resign from, a union job because of other commitments? If so, what sort of things got in the way? Was there anything in the union work itself which played a part in your decision?' Only 12% of those who replied gave an affirmative answer to the first part of the question. Almost half of them mentioned domestic reasons, a quarter referred to other commitments, and 10% quoted problems of shift working. Little can be based on this. Other questions, however, revealed that promotion in industry may take its toll of branch officers. The

answers are summarized in the next chapter[1] because they seem to
have more relevance to shop stewards.

SUMMARY

1. Allowing for branches with full-time branch secretaries or
with full-time officers acting as secretaries, there are probably about
40,000 voluntary branch secretaries in British unions. The average
size of branch is 226, but in our sample it was 464.

2. The secretaries in our sample averaged just over 11 hours a
week of their own time on union business. More time was spent
in unions with large branches than in unions with small branches,
but the difference is far less than the difference in size of branch, so
that time spent per member falls considerably as size of branch rises.

3. Branch secretaries spend most of their time on office work,
particularly on financial business. The two most successful ways of
reducing the load seem to be the 'check-off' and the provision of a
treasurer who handles branch finances. Where financial work is
kept down, the amount of time spent on members' problems rises
(except in the White Collar group). Contacts between branch
secretaries and full-time officers seem to be related to the ratio of
branches to full-time officers.

4. The average age of the sample was less than 47 years. Their
average age of entry into office has been about 40 (after 14 years'
membership in the union), and the average term of office was
probably about 17 years.

5. Little over half were confident that replacements would be
available if they left their posts. Availability of replacements varied
inversely with the amount of their own time secretaries gave to
union business, and also with the weight of office work. Variations
between unions and union groups appeared to be related to the
security of union membership.

6. Some unions pay branch secretaries nothing, or only small
honoraria. The average payment is almost £1 a week (1s. 10d. an
hour). Differences between unions depend on the method of payment (whether or not *per capita* payments decline as numbers
increase) and average size of branch. These go some way to explain
the apparently high payments in the General and Municipal
Workers. The payments received by the great majority of branch

[1] See pp. 175–176.

L

secretaries are small in relation to the time which they give to their work, but a few make it a profitable spare-time occupation.

7. About 30% of the sample would like to be promoted to full-time office. Ambition seemed to be inversely related to the social standing of the secretaries, except that supervisory and administrative workers who serve as branch secretaries in the General unions are relatively eager for promotion.

About half the sample served on higher committees in their unions, and most of the remainder professed themselves willing to do so.

8. Their estimate of the social standing of full-time officers was much the same as that of the full-time officers themselves. They reckoned their own standing noticeably lower, but still well above that which their occupations seemed to warrant. Apparently their union office enhanced their standing.

9. Only 3% thought their social standing would fall if they became full-time officers, and 65% thought it would rise. Only 11% thought that their earnings would fall if they became full-time officers, and 67% that they would rise.

10. As with full-time officers, only a minority said that their families were displeased at the amount of time they spent on union business. Displeasure seemed to have some small relation to the amount of time actually spent on union work.

11. We have no conclusive evidence about turnover amongst branch secretaries.

CHAPTER 9

SHOP STEWARDS

NUMBERS

THE shop stewards' questionnaire was answered by 226 respondents. Three-quarters of the total were shop stewards proper or convenors of stewards (62% stewards and 12% convenors). Of the remainder 8% were branch negotiators, and the rest were made up of Chapel Fathers from the printing industry, 'corresponding members'[1] in the Association of Engineering and Shipbuilding Draughtsmen, secretaries and members of the Staff Sides of Local Whitley Committees in the Civil Service and of Local Departmental Committees on the railways and so on.

We were able to calculate average constituencies from their answers to the question 'for how many members are you personally responsible?', and these are given in Tables 45 and 46.

The figure for convenors may be more suspect than the others, for two reasons. We made no distinction between 'shop convenors' and 'works convenors'; and secondly, our respondents may have had difficulty with the words 'personally responsible'. Many of them are shop stewards as well as convenors. Some may have returned their constituency which they serve as steward, and others the number of members for whom they have overall responsibility as convenors.[2] The large average constituency of branch negotiators is almost entirely due to the Mineworkers. Even so, the questionnaire was clearly answered by officers of the larger branches for the figure is double the size of the average Mineworkers' branch. It may be that in the smaller Mineworkers' branches the secretary can carry all the negotiations, and the need for an additional negotiator is stronger in large branches, but whether or not negotiations are the secretary's business is more a matter of local custom than of the size of branch.

[1] 'Corresponding members' are the links between the members of the union in each drawing office and the union.

[2] When convenors who stated they were personally responsible for under 100 workers were eliminated (for such figures probably relate to their responsibilities as stewards, not convenors) the average size of constituency was 1,648—probably a more realistic figure than the 978 shown in Table 45.

TABLE 45

Shop Stewards: Size of Constituencies

Type of Steward	Numbers	Size of Constituency
All Respondents	226	327
Shop Stewards	139	69
Convenors	28	978
Chapel Fathers	9	71
'Corresponding Members'	6	55
Staff Side Secretaries,[1] etc.	10	89
Branch Negotiators ..	19	1,172
Local Departmental Committee Members ..	3	182
Others	12	—

TABLE 46

Shop Stewards: Constituencies by Unions and Union Groups

Union or Union Group[2]	Numbers in Sample	Size of Constituency
All Unions	226	327
Skilled	37	46
Ex-Craft	70	133
Single-Industry ..	45	563
General	61	148[3]
T. & G.W.U. ..	33	161[3]
A.E.U.	50	175
N.U.G.M.W. ..	23	148

[1] This figure would be just over 1,000 if we had included one respondent who was responsible for 6,500 members.

[2] The White Collar group produced only 12 'shop stewards' and is therefore excluded from the analysis. The Transport and General Workers, the Engineers and the General and Municipal Workers are the only individual unions with a large enough share in the sample to warrant separate analysis.

[3] The averages for the General unions and the T. & G.W.U. do not include one convenor who stated that he was responsible for 18,000 workers. With this figure included, the average for General unions is 463 and for the T. & G.W.U. is 756.

The very low average size of constituency for Skilled union shop stewards is probably to be explained by the relatively small numbers of workers in any one apprenticed trade employed in most modern factories. Outside the shipyards, their membership does not often justify the election of a convenor of stewards. The large constituency of the single-industry group is to be explained by the presence of the Mineworkers' branch negotiators in the group.

If convenors are excluded, the constituencies of the three largest unions are: 91 in the Transport and General Workers, 78 in the Engineers and 59 in the General and Municipal Workers. Since these three unions organize the production workers in engineering and other manufacturing industries, it is only to be expected that the constituencies of their shop stewards should be larger than those of the Skilled unions, but the difference is not so large as the figures in Table 46 suggest.

We do not think that any significance can be attached to the remaining differences between the three major unions. Table 47 sets out the average size of constituencies in the undertakings covered by our Oxford survey, and these reveal no obvious pattern except that almost all the figures derived from questionnaire answers are exaggerated (apart perhaps from those for the constituencies of Chapel Fathers of the printing unions).[1]

The upshot is that the Engineers and the two larger General unions probably have larger constituencies than the Skilled and smaller Ex-Craft unions, and that branch negotiators have considerably larger constituencies than shop stewards. In actual figures it would probably be unsafe to say more than that the average constituency in the first three unions may be fifty or more, and in the smaller unions almost certainly under fifty; whereas the branch negotiator's charges probably run into three figures.

Several obstacles prevent us progressing from these figures to a serious attempt to estimate the number of shop stewards in Britain.

First of all, our figures are necessarily related to unions or groups of unions. We cannot give a satisfactory analysis in terms of industry, because the engineering industry, with 39%, dominates the sample and most other industries are poorly represented. Even if we could, it would not solve our problem, for the size of constituency seems to be determined by the organization of work and

---

[1] Probably the explanation is the same as for the exaggeration of branch sizes in our sample (see p. 114). Our investigators found it easier to get in touch with stewards who had bigger constituencies.

TABLE 47

SHOP STEWARDS: SIZE OF CONSTITUENCIES IN OXFORD

Union	Establishment	Average Constituency
T. & G.W.U. ..	A	76
	B	24
	C	27
	D	53
A.E.U.	A	47
	B	45
	E	52
N.U.G.M.W.	D	45
	F	100
	G	43
N.U.P.B.P.W. ..	Average for Oxford	86
Typographical Association	,, ,, ,,	44
Association of Engineering and Shipbuilding Draughtsmen ..	,, ,, ,,	18

the distribution of unions in each place of work. Where there are many small shops there will be many stewards and small constituencies. Where departments are large and compact, there will be fewer stewards. The more unions, generally speaking, the more stewards. In some circumstances Skilled and Ex-Craft unions such as the Electricians and the Foundry workers have many members and large constituencies, and in others even the three major unions have only small constituencies.

We have no reason to suppose that large *works* have large constituencies. On the contrary, our local survey suggested that a works tends to rely on one steward (or one steward per union) up to well over a hundred workers. Once the critical figure is passed, the workers are split up amongst a number of stewards. The largest works in Oxford has the highest ratio of stewards to members.

There is also the problem of definition. A man is either a branch secretary or not. A properly-accredited shop steward is equally a

shop steward. But what of a man who habitually speaks on behalf
of his fellow trade unionists because he is a collecting steward,
because he is a branch officer, or just because he is that sort of man?
Are all Local Departmental Committee members on the railways to
be counted as shop stewards, or only the secretaries? Are branch
committee members in the Mineworkers to be counted as stewards
if they form the first line of communication with the colliery
management? If so, how do we know where they perform this job
and where they do not? Where a firm employs only one pattern-
maker, or draughtsman or electrician, does he become his own
shop steward? Our definition of a shop steward is a local union
representative who has definite responsibility for the first stage of
local negotiations, but is neither a full-time officer nor a branch
secretary with recognized negotiating rights in that capacity.
Whether this applies in any particular instance can be determined
only by investigation.

If we accept the figure of 50 as the most reasonable, on our
evidence, for the average size of constituency, and suppose that half
of British trade unionists are represented by shop stewards,[1] this
would produce a figure of about 80,000 shop stewards. If we further
supposed that half the remainder do not have local representatives,
and the rest are represented by branch negotiators with constituencies of 250 (approximately equal to the average size of branch),
this would bring the total up to 90,000; but the figure is no better
than a guess.[2]

[1] The majority of the members of some unions, such as the Engineers or the Electricians,
are represented by shop stewards. In other unions, such as the Miners, the Shop, Distributive
and Allied Workers, and White Collar unions, representation is exceptional. The practice
of the industry is the determining factor, and in the Transport and General Workers and
the General and Municipal Workers some secretaries have stewards and others do not. In
addition, stewards are rare when unions are relatively weak. All in all, it seems reasonable
to suggest that half British trade unionists are represented by stewards.

[2] The President of the Engineers told the 1960 Trades Union Congress that his union had
23,523 shop stewards (Report, p. 357). He has told us that this figure is 'reasonably accurate',
being based on the records of District Committees, which are responsible for the control of
stewards and the payment of nominal fees to them. Consequently the ratio of members to
stewards is about forty to one. B. C. Roberts (Trade Union Government and Administration in
Great Britain, 1956, p. 63) gives a figure of 'over 25,000' stewards in the Transport and
General Workers, yielding a ratio of about fifty to one. Some parts of the unions rely on
branch negotiators, so, if the figure is correct, the average constituency of stewards proper
must be less than fifty. On the other hand the Building Trade Workers, who have recently
completed a central register of stewards, have just under 800, or rather less than one to a
hundred members.

On balance, these figures suggest our total is too small, although we would suggest that
the Trade Union Congress's own estimate of 'at least 200,000' (1960 Report, p. 128) errs in
the other direction.

The Nature of the Job

We attempted to analyse the job of the steward by much the same means as we applied to the branch secretary, except that we tried to introduce a new set of categories—the industries in which our stewards worked.

Engineering, as might be expected, dominates the group with 39% of the sample. The only other industries with sufficient numbers to justify separate analysis are transport (road and rail) and public employment (national and local), with 11% each. Three industries is not enough to make analysis by industry much use for most purposes.

We also asked a question concerning the numbers employed at each steward's place of work. Table 48 gives the answers.

TABLE 48

Shop Stewards: Size of Undertaking

Numbers employed at place of work	Proportion of Sample	Proportions in British Manufacturing Industry[1]
Over 10,000 ..	7 ⎫	21
2,000–10,000 ..	15 ⎭	
500–2,000 ..	30	27
100–500	34	32
Under 100 ..	14	20
Total ..	100	100

The table shows that large, middling and small undertakings were all reasonably well represented. Indeed, the distribution of stewards between undertakings is not very different from that of workers in British manufacturing industry.

Shop stewards of all kinds gave nearly eleven hours a week to their work, over six hours out of their working time, and over four and a half hours of their own time. Convenors spent little more of their own time on union business (just over five hours), but averaged eighteen hours of their working time. For most

[1] The figures for manufacturing industry are taken from the *Ministry of Labour Gazette*, September 1959. They exclude establishments with 10 or less employees.

purposes we have neglected the proportion of their own time spent
on union business. On the face of it, the expenditure by stewards
of much of their own time on union business is surprising. We
discussed the point with a group of stewards, however, and they
insisted that our respondents had not exaggerated. The continuation
of negotiations after working hours, seeing constituents at other
times, preparing for negotiations, and occasional meetings could
add up, they suggested, to an appreciable period each week. But it
is also likely that our respondents included time taken in collecting
contributions and by union work arising from the other union posts
which they held. The variation in time spent is considerable: 8%
spent none of their working time on union business, and 6% more
than thirty hours; over half the sample came between two and
eight hours. The respondents who spent none of their working time
on union business should probably not be included as shop stewards
under a strict interpretation of our definition.[1]

Our Oxford survey had revealed that stewards sometimes cover
a wide range of duties. In practice the steward is often the man
who brings to the attention of the foreman or departmental manager
any grievance of an individual or group in his shop or section.[2] If
he cannot settle the grievance on the spot, he will probably pursue
it further in conjunction with his convenor or a shop stewards'
committee. In order to perform this task he must talk to his constituents, and not only about particular problems and grievances,
but also to find out what they are thinking so as to anticipate
trouble. He may have to try to instil discipline into them, to
persuade them to come out on strike or to censure an individual
for some breach of faith or rules—or, perhaps even more likely, to
dissuade them from walking out while a grievance is still under
discussion, or before a case of disciplinary action has been before
the branch.

The steward is also responsible for the organization of his department. He must try to see that everyone, or everyone who is
eligible, is a member of his union, and many stewards are also
responsible for collecting dues.

Where workers are paid by results the steward is likely to be
involved in rate-fixing, in trying to agree an acceptable rate for

---

[1] Only one steward stated that he spent no time on union business either at home or
at work!

[2] In most dispute procedures (including that of the engineering industry) it is the formal
responsibility of the individual worker to take the first step; in practice this is frequently
ignored.

each job, and this can be very time-consuming in a shop where products constantly change and new rates have therefore to be arranged.

Many undertakings have works' councils or joint consultative committees to discuss safety, wastage, sanitation, and welfare provisions, and perhaps also production problems and management's plans for the future. Where such bodies exist the stewards (particularly works' convenors and shop convenors) are likely to be members of the workers' side.

Despite this wide range of duties, however, and differences of shop-floor organization from industry to industry, the survey seemed to reveal that straightforward negotiating with foremen and managers, and discussions with constituents were the most time-consuming duties. Many stewards mentioned no other aspects of their work. Accordingly our questionnaire was designed to test whether this was generally true, and to discover the relative importance of these central duties. The results are set out in Table 49.

The table reveals a number of minor differences. Most groups and unions give more time to negotiating with management above foreman level than with foremen. The last two columns suggest that differences under this heading may reflect the proportion of convenors in each section of the sample, for convenors clearly concentrate on negotiations above that level. The Engineers appear to have very few 'other meetings' to attend. Rate-fixing is, naturally enough, most important in the engineering industry and therefore to the Engineers.

Where rate-fixing is important it is very important. Most of the duties with low scores are (naturally enough) mentioned in second or third place if they are mentioned at all. Rate-fixing, however, was the main duty for thirteen stewards, the second duty for thirteen more, and the third for only six of them.

However, it is not so much the differences which strike the eye, but the startling similarity in the pattern of a steward's duties wherever he may find himself. The shop steward is a negotiator even more exclusively than the branch secretary is a clerical worker for his union. He spends his time talking either to his members and his colleagues, or to foremen and managers. In every union and group, stewards spend as much time or almost as much time talking to management as to union members, and convenors spend much more time with management. (If joint committees are included as negotiation with management, then *all* groups of stewards spend

TABLE 49

Shop Stewards: Importance of Main Duties

Duty	All Stewards	Skilled	Ex-Craft	Single-Industry	General	T. & G.W.U.	A.E.U.	N.U.G. M.W.	Shop Stewards Proper	Convenors of Stewards
Discussions with members and shop stewards ..	32	26	34	26	36	38	35	33	34	33
Negotiations with management above foreman level	21	23	21	25	18	21	23	13	20	36
Taking up grievances with foremen	16	19	19	16	14	9	20	20	20	7
Works' Committee, Joint Consultative Committee, etc.	11	11	10	13	10	10	7	11	9	10
Other meetings	8	8	5	8	10	9	3	10	6	5
Rate fixing	6	6	8	7	5	4	10	8	7	5
Correspondence	6	7	3	5	7	9	2	5	4	4
TOTAL	100	100	100	100	100	100	100	100	100	100

more time on this function.) For the rest of his union work he
attends meetings unless he is one of the stewards who have important
rate-fixing responsibilities (and this is also a form of negotiation
with management), or is a White Collar worker (for whom correspondence is important).

This consistency in the pattern of the stewards' work has its effect
on a number of the questions included in our questionnaire. Several
of the analyses used for full-time officers and branch secretaries with
some success have been omitted because they yielded no other result
beyond showing that stewards in one set of circumstances behave
very like stewards in another.

The average time spent on union business per constituent was
3·9 minutes a week, counting only working time, and 6·6 minutes
counting all time spent on union business. The distribution was
fairly wide. A quarter of those who answered the question[1] spent
less than one minute of their working time per member, whereas
9% spent more than ten minutes; one third spent between one and
three minutes.

For reasons already given we attach more importance to the
proportion of working time spent on union business. This is closely
related to the size of constituency, as shown in Table 50.

Table 50 shows that except for the stewards with large constituencies of over 200 (most of which are held either by convenors,
staff side secretaries and chairmen, or branch negotiators) the time
per member falls with the size of the constituency, but not so
rapidly. With an increase from less than 20 to over 100 constituents,
time spent per member falls by not much more than a half. This
suggests that the size of the constituency has a considerable effect
upon the volume of business.

There is no need to pursue the analysis of time spent per member
by union group or by union, for this can be read off from Table 46,
which shows average size of constituencies. Stewards of Skilled
unions, for example, devote an unusually high time per member to
union business. The Mineworkers and the White Collar group
have low scores and, consequently, so do branch negotiators.
Convenors, however, do rather better than might be expected with
an average of 2·6 minutes, compared with 4·1 for shop stewards
proper.

[1] Only 75% of the respondents gave answers which enabled us to work out working
time per member, and 78% gave answers which enabled us to work out total time per
member.

TABLE 50

Shop Stewards: Minutes per Member and
Size of Constituency

Size of Constituency	Number of Stewards	Minutes per Member
Under 20 ..	16	7·8
20–49 ..	55	6·3
50–74 ..	23	4·7
75–99 ..	21	4·2
100–199 ..	28	3·3
200–499 ..	21	1·3
Over 500[1] ..	20	0·5
Incomplete Information	42	—
TOTAL ..	226	1·1

We dealt with the collection of union contributions by a separate question. Union rules differ considerably on this point. The two larger General unions, for example, make provision for collecting stewards who are paid the same commission as branch secretaries ($12\frac{1}{2}\%$ in the General and Municipal Workers, and $7\frac{1}{2}\%$ in the Transport and General Workers). Collectors are appointed by the branch by a procedure quite separate from the appointment of shop stewards, but, naturally enough, one man often does both jobs. In other unions there is no provision for the appointment and payment of stewards, and stewards can collect by local arrangement. In still others, such as the Engineers, union rules provide that contributions must be paid at branch meetings,[2] and therefore imply

[1] The average size of constituency in this group was, in fact, 2,474.
[2] Amalgamated Engineering Union, Rule 7, Clause 12.

that collection by stewards is contrary to rules. Table 51 sets out our findings.

TABLE 51

SHOP STEWARDS: PROPORTION COLLECTING
UNION CONTRIBUTIONS

Union Group or Union	Proportion collecting Contributions
All Unions	55%
Skilled	45%
Ex-Craft	60%
Single-Industry ..	35%
General	73%
T. & G.W.U. ..	76%
A.E.U...	68%
N.U.G.M.W... ..	74%

The Single-Industry figures are affected by a 'nil return' from the Mineworkers, where the 'check-off' makes collection by stewards inapplicable, and by a very low score on the railways. The proportion of stewards who collect contributions is, however, not a direct indication of the proportion of members who pay their contributions to stewards. In the General and Municipal Workers, for instance, the claims for collecting stewards' commissions show that almost all contributions are collected by stewards, but, of course, not all shop stewards are collecting stewards. It may be that in other unions also the proportion of contributions collected by stewards exceeds the proportion of shop stewards who collect contributions. But we cannot prove it.

Even so, the small difference between the proportion in the Engineers and the two larger General unions is interesting. It shows that shop stewards do almost as much collecting in a union which makes no provision for it, does not pay for it, and in which the practice appears to be contrary to rule, as in unions whose rules prescribe for the appointment and payment of collecting stewards.

It is a reasonable inference that the organization of production workers in modern manufacturing industry demands collection by stewards, and that shop stewards are willing to add collection to their other duties without payment by the union. How else could the Engineers collect contributions in a large factory in which they organize hundreds or even thousands of members who certainly could not be persuaded to attend branch meetings regularly?

Shop stewards seem to have rather more contact with full-time officers than do branch secretaries. Meetings at least once a week were reported by 20% of the sample (compared with 12% of the branch secretaries); meetings between once a week and once a month by 40% (compared with 42%). Of the remainder, 31% reported meetings between once a month and once a year, and 9% less than once a year. The breakdown between union groups and unions was very similar to that for branch secretaries (see Table 35).

ORIGINS

The educational standard of shop stewards was fractionally below that of branch secretaries. Only 16% had continued to attend school beyond the age of 14 years, compared with 23% of branch secretaries, and 18% went to grammar or technical schools, compared with 19% amongst the branch secretaries. Taking technical schools separately the shop stewards came first[1] with 9% compared with the branch secretaries' 5%. The shop stewards also provided our only three respondents who had attended public schools, and the only respondent who had still been at school at the age of 18.

The difference between the two samples can be more than explained by the smaller representation of the White Collar unions amongst the shop stewards. Deducting those unions from both groups, the shop stewards are left with an insignificant educational advantage.

Educational standards varied with age as amongst full-time officers and branch secretaries. Those with grammar, technical and public school education constituted 20% of those under 40 and 17% of those over 40. This difference owes nothing to the White Collar unions' representatives. Strangely enough, however, the educational standard of those between 30 and 40 is lower than the average (11%). The high performance of the under 40 group as a whole is due to the remarkably high score of the under 30 group (44%).

[1] Almost a quarter of the stewards of the Skilled unions had been to technical schools.

The occupational analysis showed a slightly greater proportion of unskilled and semi-skilled workers than amongst full-time officers and branch secretaries, and (naturally enough) a smaller number of White Collar workers than amongst branch secretaries. The figures are: 8% unskilled, 36% semi-skilled, 37% skilled, 6% clerical and 4% supervisory and administrative; 5% gave no classifiable answer and no less than 4% appeared to be working full-time on union business.

Shop stewards were the youngest group of the three with an average age of 42·4 years (46·6 for branch secretaries and 50·6 for full-time officers). Probably as a consequence they did not average such a long period of service in their current unions (16·5 years compared with 20 for branch secretaries). On the average they had held office as stewards for a slightly shorter period than that of the branch secretaries—just over seven years compared with 8½. Unions which employ stewards have more stewards than branch secretaries. Unions sometimes have to dismiss branch secretaries, but dismissal of shop stewards seems to be very rare. If our sample was representative we could probably infer that the average tenure of office of stewards is about fourteen years; and since there is no particular reason for supposing that it is an unrepresentative group in this respect, we assume that is not very far from the truth. It also seems a reasonable inference that the average age of appointment as shop steward is about thirty-five years.

SELECTION

Some union rules make no mention of shop stewards. Not all those which mention them prescribe the method of appointment, and those which do are far from precise. The Engineers, for example, lay down that 'District Committees shall authorize the appointment of Shop Stewards . . . Shop Stewards elected by members are subject to approval by the District Committee'.[1] In the General and Municipal Workers stewards can be elected by a show of hands or a ballot by 'the members concerned at the place of employment', or by a show of hands at the branch; or, with the consent of the members concerned, appointed by the District Secretary.[2] Neither union mentions re-election. Consequently the selection of stewards is often a matter for regulation by regional or

[1] Rule 13. The preface to the rules, however, includes a table of union officers with a column for 'period of election'. Against 'shop stewards' the column reads 'annually'.
[2] Rule 41.

district committees or by local custom, and we tried to learn something about these customs from our questionnaire.

Regular re-election appears to be the general practice, for 81% of our sample stated that they were subject to it. About half had been opposed at their original election, and almost a quarter had been opposed at least once on coming up for re-election. Details for the unions and union groups are given in Table 52.

TABLE 52

SHOP STEWARDS: RE-ELECTION AND THE INCIDENCE OF OPPOSITION

Union or Union Group	Proportion subject to Regular Re-election	Proportion opposed at First Election	Proportion opposed at Subsequent Election
All Unions ..	81	46	23
Skilled	66	31	3
Ex-Craft	81	50	22
Single-Industry ..	92	57	37
General	76	39	18
T. & G.W.U. ..	73	36	27
A.E.U.	88	54	28
N.U.G.M.W. ..	78	39	4

None of our respondents challenged our assumption that their original appointment was an election. No more need be inferred from this than that there would be an election (or a re-election) if there was more than one candidate. In some instances, no doubt, both the union and members are satisfied if a man can be found willing to undertake the post, and formalities are left aside.

Although it may frequently be a formality, regular re-election appears to be the custom in all these groups and unions. If the Single-Industry figure is neglected because it is strongly affected by the figures for the Mineworkers and the Railwaymen, whose

M

'stewards' are generally branch negotiators with re-election prescribed by rule, or committee members with re-election prescribed
by agreement;[1] the variation is further reduced from 66% in the
Skilled group to 88% in the Engineers. Making the same exception,
the experience of opposition at first election seems to be reasonably
constant, from 31% in the Skilled unions to 54% in the Engineers.
There is more variation in the proportion of opposition at subsequent elections. It occurs about once in four elections in the Engineers and the Transport and General Workers' Union, and only
rarely in the Skilled group and the General and Municipal Workers.

We have a tentative explanation for these differences. The branch
and committee negotiators must be left aside as governed by a
different set of rules. For the rest the degree of opposition should
be related more to conflicts over policy within the union. This
factor might be expected to be particularly influential in re-election.
When a post falls vacant several contestants may well try their luck,
but when 'Joe' has been doing the job for a time it requires more
than mere personal ambition to challenge him. The additional
incentive is a difference over policy or even a factional loyalty.
These, however, are relatively rare in the General and Municipal
Workers' Union, and in some skilled unions. They are more
common in the Transport and General Workers and particularly
widespread in the Engineers. No doubt the greater militancy of
the Engineers and some sections of the Transport and General
Workers' Union has its effect. Perhaps the peculiar difficulties over
membership in the building unions (which have already been mentioned) are of some importance in the Skilled group's score.

Once more, however, differences are less striking than similarities,
and it does appear that, despite union rules or their absence, the
customs of the workshop in manufacturing industry impose a fairly
common pattern for the selection of stewards, regardless of union.

The same uniform response was aroused by our question on
replacement ('If you were to resign as shop steward do you think
there would be anyone else to take your place?'). In the whole
sample 86% answered 'yes'. For the three major unions the proportions were: Transport and General Workers, 88%; Engineers, 82%;
General and Municipal Workers, 83%. A similar consistency was

[1] The Railwaymen's Local Departmental Committee representatives are elected and
re-elected under an agreement between the railway unions and the British Transport Commission. Many branches apparently hold preliminary elections to determine which candidate
has the backing of the branch, and our railway respondents may have had these elections in
mind.

evident in the replies of the union groups and other individual unions.

In this respect also the characteristics of the shop steward seem to be independent of the union to which he belongs. The difference between branch secretaries and shop stewards in almost every union and union group seems to suggest that the recruitment of stewards is much easier than the recruitment of secretaries. The difference may be a consequence of the smaller demands made on the steward, who does all or most of his union work in working hours. Another consideration is that only a regular attender at branch meetings is likely to be elected as branch secretary, but any willing member in the shop can be considered for the steward's job.

The figures also suggest that tales of shops or works which cannot find a steward are not typical, although in some instances it is extremely difficult to persuade anyone to act as shop steward in a factory which has recently been organized, or shop stewards are being established for the first time; and such difficulties may be the common experience in these circumstances.

REMUNERATION

Recruitment might be affected by financial considerations, for although most unions do not make provision for the payment of stewards (unless they are officially collecting stewards), and where provision is made the sum is small, stewards may lose money as a result of union work.

Stewards almost invariably receive some recompense from their employer for time spent away from their work on union business at the firm's request, and usually at the union's request, so long as this is done with permission. By far the most important agreement covering the work of shop stewards is that of the engineering industry, which lays down only that 'shop stewards shall be afforded facilities to deal with questions raised in the shop or portion of the shop in which they are employed'. The employers and their federation interpret this to cover payment. Difficulty arises for a steward who is not paid time rates. How should a worker paid by the piece, or by some other system of payment by results, be paid when he is not producing? Some firms are willing to grant no more than the time rates which serve as a 'fall-back' to the pieceworker. Others are willing to pay a steward's hours on union business at the average piecework or bonus earnings of his hours at work. Several local associations of engineering employers recommend average earnings when time is lost at the firm's request and time rates when the initiative comes from the union. Even average earnings may not adequately compensate a steward or a convenor who spends most of his time away from his work for the odd jobs which he does get finished may provide earnings well below those of his fellow-workers, and in this instance the only adequate compensation is to pay the average earnings of the shop. Consequently stewards may lose income, and where piecework earnings are high they may lose heavily. Only 21% of our sample said that they lost pay through union activities, and most of those lost less than 10s. a week. Less than one in twenty of the whole sample lost more than £1 a week.

Once again the characteristics of shop stewards appear to be fairly constant from union to union. Amongst the three major unions, 76% of the Transport and General Workers' stewards, 71% of the Engineers' stewards, and 83% of the General and Municipal Workers' stewards did not lose pay through union activities. There was little variation in other unions or in the union groups. The slightly lower score of the Engineers might perhaps be due to a higher incidence of piecework amongst their members.

There is nothing in our answers to show whether those stewards who are paid for their union work (as collecting stewards or otherwise) set this off against their loss of earnings at work. It could be that the payment of collecting stewards in the two General unions explains their smaller proportion of loss compared with the Engineers, and the higher rate of payment in the General and Municipal Workers accounts for theirs being the lowest proportion of the three; but this is not clear. It is worth noting that shop stewards may receive payment in other ways. Many shop stewards' committees in large undertakings dispose of considerable funds.[1] It is relatively easy for stewards to use their position as collectors to raise an additional 1d. or 2d. a week above union subscriptions to defray the expenses of their work. Raffles and football pools may be arranged for the same purpose. The unions themselves have no control over these funds, which can be used for such diverse purposes as producing a paper, paying the expenses of delegates to the meetings of unofficial shop stewards' organizations, and employing a secretary to the shop stewards' committee, or even an accountant to check on piecework systems of payment. One obvious expendi-

---

[1] The evidence taken by the Court of Inquiry into the Briggs' Motor Bodies Dispute, 1957, gave a striking instance of this. (Cmnd. 131 of 1957.)

ture is to compensate stewards for a loss of pay because of a difference between their earnings and average piecework earnings. There are instances, probably rare, where the compensation exceeds the losses and the total income of a steward from his employer and from funds collected from his members (neglecting any payment as collecting steward) exceeds the income he would earn if he were not a steward.

PROMOTION

For shop stewards, as for branch secretaries, promotion within the union can mean election to higher committees of the union or to a full-time post (or perhaps, in some instances, election to a branch secretaryship or chairmanship).

There is a conflict in our evidence concerning the proportion of our sample already serving on higher committees, since in answer to the question: 'Do you serve on any higher union committees (e.g. District, Regional or National)?' a quarter of the sample said that they did, whereas in answer to the earlier question: 'What office(s) do you hold in your union?' only 14% mentioned district (10%), regional (3%), and national (1%) committees. Probably the 25% should be accepted on the grounds that the other question did not require the respondents to list *all* their offices in the union and one answer seemed sufficient. Some may not have regarded membership of a committee as an 'office'.

However that may be, two-thirds of those who stated that they did not serve on higher committees said that they would be willing to do so. This comes close to the 75% of branch secretaries not already serving and willing to do so. Perhaps the difference reflects a greater interest on the part of secretaries in internal union work, but the more important conclusion is that we can be even more certain that the supply of candidates for these posts is plentiful.

There are some differences between union groups in these respects, which are shown in Table 53.

The differences in the proportions already serving may be partly explained in terms of the low ratio of 'stewards' to members in unions which rely on branch negotiators (see Table 45). Consequently branch negotiators would be more likely than other stewards to hold higher offices in their unions, and the score of the Single-Industry group would be expected to exceed that of other groups. There is provision in the Engineers' rules for the representation of shop stewards on district committees and for that reason

TABLE 53

SHOP STEWARDS: SERVICE ON HIGHER COMMITTEES

Union Group	Proportion already serving	Proportion of those not serving who would be willing to do so
All Groups	25%	66%
Skilled	10%	58%
Ex-Craft	28%	57%
Single-Industry ..	37%	65%
General	16%	81%

the Ex-Craft score might be expected to be higher than those of the General and Skilled unions.

Differences in proportions already serving should be more easily explicable if taken in conjunction with the analysis of the answers to the question: 'Do you think that you would like to become a paid union official?' There were significant differences between groups and between unions in these answers, and consequently the full analysis is set out in Table 54.

These variations are much wider than those between branch secretaries in answer to the same question.[1] In both instances Skilled unions have the lowest score and Single-Industry unions the highest, but the difference here is 14% to 39%, compared with 27% to 33% amongst branch secretaries. The low score of the Skilled group tends to confirm our suggestion that interest in full-time office varies inversely with occupational status.[2] Only one of the twelve White Collar 'stewards' would have liked a full-time post. The high score of the Single-Industry group reflects even higher scores amongst Mineworkers (58%) and Railwaymen (88%).

The greater variation between unions and groups amongst stewards than amongst branch secretaries cannot be explained in terms of occupation, for although there is a correlation between occupation and desire for full-time office amongst stewards, as amongst branch secretaries, it is, if anything, slightly less marked.

[1] See p. 140.　　　　[2] See p. 141.

The details are given in Table 55, and can be compared with Table 42.

TABLE 54

SHOP STEWARDS: DESIRE FOR FULL-TIME OFFICE

Union Group or Union	Proportion who think they would like full-time posts
All Unions ..	29%
Skilled	14%
Ex-Craft	31%
Single-Industry ..	39%
General	31%
T. & G.W.U. ..	27%
A.E.U.	22%
N.U.G.M.W. ..	35%

TABLE 55

SHOP STEWARDS: JOB AND DESIRE FOR FULL-TIME POST

Grading of Shop Steward's Job	Number in Grade[1]	Proportion who think they would like a full-time post
Unskilled ..	17	12%
Semi-skilled ..	82	34%
Skilled	84	31%
Clerical ..	14	7%
Supervisory and Administrative	8	0

[1] Twenty stewards out of the whole sample were unclassifiable or gave no answer. Of the ten whose stewards' job was their full-time occupation, three would have liked full-time union posts.

This time the unskilled are out of line and the supervisory workers give the answer which their occupation would lead us to expect. Part of the explanation for this second difference (apart from the small numbers in the grade) may be that these supervisory workers were not supervisors who had retained membership of manual workers' unions, as were many of those in the branch secretaries' sample. The low desire of unskilled stewards for full-time posts may be due to their feeling of unfitness (for this is the second most commonly voiced reason for not wanting such a post). This feeling is perhaps less likely to be found amongst unskilled workers who are also branch secretaries, and can therefore handle clerical business.

Apart from this the only explanation we can offer is that the degree of identification with the union and the union hierarchy should perhaps be considered, and that this is by no means the same amongst stewards as amongst branch secretaries. We have accumulated much evidence in this chapter to show that in many respects the characteristics of stewards vary less according to their union than those of secretaries. Stewards are strongly identified with their union in the sense that their power depends on the union membership of their constituents. But except in skilled occupations, it does not much matter which union. The post of steward does not identify a steward with the hierarchy of his union, whereas full-time posts are only available *within* the union, and therefore this question demands of stewards an answer revealing their attitude to their own union. If their tie to the particular union is smaller than that of the secretaries, the variation in their answers due to other factors is likely to be larger than amongst secretaries. Certainly there is a marked contrast between the variations revealed in this table and the consistent scores of different groups of stewards in earlier tables.

Reasons given for not wanting office tally fairly closely with the branch secretaries' answers.[1] A third of those who did not want office gave no reason. Age or health (19%) was the most popular reason and lack of qualifications or ability (18%) came second. The gap between the two reasons is smaller amongst shop stewards perhaps because their average age is lower. Further reasons were: the long hours worked by full-time officers (11%), the domestic problems created by full-time office (7%), the attitude of union members to full-time officers (6%), lack of interest in the union (6%), and preference to remain in the rank and file (5%). Two

[1] See p. 140.

stewards (compared with three secretaries) quoted the low salaries of union officers as a deterrent.

Amongst reasons for desiring full-time office, the opinion that it was interesting and satisfying work (20%) and idealistic statements (19%) were the most popular with stewards as with branch secretaries; 18% failed to give a reason.

From our sample we know that 35% of full-time officers held office as shop stewards immediately prior to their election or appointment to full-time office. There was almost certainly some overlap between them and the 38% who held office as branch secretaries, but no reason to suppose that this overlap differs from that in our samples of stewards and secretaries (23% of our branch secretaries were also stewards and 7% of our stewards were also branch secretaries). This suggests that 35-44 of the 100-125 full-time union posts which fall vacant each year will be filled by stewards. Since 29% of stewards think they would like full-time posts, this suggests that (according to our guess at the total number of stewards) about 29,000 stewards would like to fill these 42 posts. These figures must be read in the light of all the cautions which we set out in relation to similar calculations concerning branch secretaries.[1] Even so, they suggest that the unions ought to be able to find sufficient candidates for full-time posts.

ATTITUDES

Table 56 makes clear that the majority of shop stewards, as of branch secretaries, would expect an improvement in earnings or social status to be the consequence of promotion to full-time office. Like the branch secretaries, shop stewards are slightly more confident that their status would not fall than that they would suffer no loss of earnings.

There is a correlation amongst shop stewards, as amongst branch secretaries, between desire for promotion and their rating of the gap in social standing between full-time officers and themselves. Of the stewards who would like full-time posts 30% thought their standing would go up 'a great deal' or 'considerably' if they became full-time officers. Amongst those who did not want full-time posts only 18% thought this.

The figures in this table agree quite closely with the rating by each steward of his own job and the job of a local full-time officer.

[1] See p. 139.

TABLE 56

SHOP STEWARDS: ASSESSMENT OF STATUS AND EARNINGS OF FULL-TIME POSTS

Expected change on becoming a Full-Time Officer	Social Standing	Earnings
Go up a great deal	7	6
Go up considerably ..	17	20
Go up a little	42	40
Remain about the same ..	27	17
Go down a little	1	11
Go down considerably ..	0	1
Go down a great deal ..	0	1
Don't know and no answer	6	4
TOTAL	100	100

The answers to this question are summarized in Table 57 and compared with full-time officers' rating of their own posts.

The table shows a close agreement between the assessment of the social standing of full-time officers by themselves and by shop stewards, although there are more stewards who are prepared to give a very high standing to full-time posts. Comparison with Table 43 shows that stewards rate themselves a little lower than branch secretaries rate themselves, but part of the explanation for this is the larger number of White Collar workers in the sample of branch secretaries. It is quite clear that the great majority of shop stewards see full-time office as definitely in the middle-class range of jobs, and that well over half of them see their own jobs as definitely working-class. Since the composition of the samples cannot account for all the differences between secretaries and stewards in this latter respect it may be suggested that the post of shop steward has less effect on a man's feeling about his own social position than does the post of branch secretary.

TABLE 57

SHOP STEWARDS: SOCIAL STATUS

Job Rated	Rating by	Range in Status Scale					Total
		Medical Officer of Health —Civil Servant (Executive Grade)	Noncon- formist Minister— Elementary School Teacher	Jobbing Master Builder— Policeman	Routine Clerk— Carpenter	Shop Assistant and below	
Jobs held by Shop Stewards	Shop Stewards[1]	←——12——→		28	46	14	100
Full-Time Officers	Shop Stewards[2]	17	68	←——15——→			100
	Full-Time Officers	10	69	←——21——→			100

ASSESSMENT

An assessment by personnel officers was conducted in the same way as the assessment of full-time officers as part of the same questionnaire, and it has been analysed by the same methods.[3]

Analysis by 'situations' in which the Transport and General Workers, the Engineers, the General and Municipal Workers and the Electricians are all mentioned shows little except that the Electricians fare the worst of the four unions. With 47 appearances they score only 9% of their possible first places, and 51% of their possible last places. The Transport and General Workers, with 46 appearances, scores 43% of its possible firsts, and 33% of its possible last places. Total appearances for the Engineers are 63, and first and last places are 46% and 25% respectively. For the General and Municipal Workers the score is also 46% of first places, but only 19% of last places out of 26 appearances.

Table 58 sets out the assessment by pairs of unions for the three major unions.

[1] 24% of the sample failed to answer this question.
[2] 19% of the sample failed to answer this question.   [3] See p. 86.

TABLE 58

SHOP STEWARDS: ASSESSMENT BY PAIRS OF UNIONS

Unions	Number of instances of Situation	First Place	Second Place	Ties
T. & G.W.U.		19	26	
A.E.U.	46	26	19	I
T. & G.W.U.		6	5	
N.U.G.M.W. ..	12	5	6	I
A.E.U.		11	15	
N.U.G.M.W. ..	26	15	11	–

As with full-time officers, the Transport and General Workers appear to do worse than the Engineers on a direct comparison (for stewards the margin is higher), and better than the General and Municipal Workers, and the General and Municipal Workers seem to do better than the Engineers (in these last two comparisons the margin is smaller amongst stewards). The only possible conclusion is that (by this test) there is very little to choose between them.

THE POSITION OF THE STEWARD IN INDUSTRY

Although our inquiry was not intended to provide a complete study of the role of shop stewards in industry, or in their unions, several of our questions have some bearing on the first of these two topics and the answers are worth recording.

The questionnaire for personnel officers included a query on the preference of personnel officers between dealing with full-time officers and dealing with stewards. According to the terms of the relevant agreement managers have to raise some matters with stewards, at least in the first instance, and others with full-time officers. By prescription or custom, however, there is in most instances a fair range of issues which could be raised with the one

or the other, according to taste. We therefore asked: 'When either
is competent to settle an issue, do you prefer to deal with a full-time
official or with a lay[1] official?'

The results were quite unambiguous. Lay officials were preferred
by 69% of the sample, full-time officers by 17%, and 14% gave no
classifiable answer.

We asked for reasons. By far the most common reason for
choosing lay officers was their 'intimate knowledge of the circumstances of the case', which was expressed by half of those who gave
this answer. Preference for keeping issues within the factory, quick
decisions, the better contact of stewards with their members (or
control over them), and the beneficial results on relationships within
the factory were each mentioned by about one-fifth of those who
chose lay officers. Amongst other reasons one personnel officer gave
the opinion that 'official procedure is detested by the Engineering
unions because it was imposed on them; secondly, bringing in outside officials on both sides from my experience leads to a hardening
of attitudes'.[2]

More than half of those who preferred full-time officers said that
they had a more detached and balanced approach. Other points
were their greater experience and their greater knowledge of
national agreements.

Stewards were asked whether management placed restrictions in
their way which *seriously* hampered them in carrying out their
duties. The result was even more decisive; 94% said 'no'.

A subsequent question asked whether there had been a case of
victimization of shop stewards in their place of work in the last
ten years. To this 81% answered 'no'. Moreover, it is significant
that several of the affirmative answers were hedged about with such
qualifications as 'I think so'.

Victimization may be one of the reasons for turnover amongst
shop stewards, a topic on which our first (abandoned) questionnaire
yields a little information. Some of this has already been given in
the previous chapter,[3] and we can now add a little more. A larger
proportion of this sample (28%) had 'seen or experienced victimization because of union work'. The difference could be due to the

[1] Since in some industries local negotiations are conducted between management and
branch officers, rather than shop stewards, it seemed better to use the general term 'lay
(i.e. not full-time) officer'.
[2] Trade union officers have suggested to us that some personnel officers may prefer to deal
with lay officials because they are less independent than full-time officials, and that they
would not want to give us this reason.
[3] See p. 146.

small number of industries covered by this first questionnaire, but is more likely the result of the omission of the limit 'in the last ten years'. Almost one-third (32%) had at one time or another 'felt that [their] job was in danger, or [their] prospects, because of union work'; but, as one respondent said: 'I have felt that my prospects suffer, but it is so difficult to bring into the open. . . .' Nearly a half (48%), however, had known union work 'lead to promotion by the management'. Several said they had themselves received promotion, and at least one stated that it had been due to union work. Others reported cases of promotion dependent on resigning union office or membership. One or two reported that they themselves had received offers of this kind, but had refused them. Most of these promotions may have been based only on merit, so that union membership was, in fact, incidental, but some respondents had no doubt that 'tough' union members were promoted to render them innocuous, and another reported that the main reason for accepting the post of steward in his firm was to gain promotion from the employer.

Another question asked for 'the main reasons why active trade unionists give up union work'. Of those who replied 43% mentioned promotion, 32% the time entailed by union work, 26% domestic considerations, 23% lack of support or appreciation from the members, and 17% loss of earnings. No other considerations scored more than 5%.

We have no evidence to show that turnover amongst shop stewards is too high. A lower rate might be too discouraging to prospective stewards. But if it is too high, or in those instances in which it is too high, these answers suggest the directions in which remedies might be sought.

The prominence given to promotion at least suggests a more conciliatory approach by employers to shop stewards than is sometimes suggested by accounts of unofficial strikes, of management and stewards locked in battle for supremacy, or conducting a guerilla warfare which from time to time flares up into widespread conflict. Indeed, nearly all the evidence in this section suggests that most firms enjoy good, even intimate, relations with their stewards which may be occasionally disturbed by disputes. They also suggest that one of the most important reasons for the great power and standing of stewards in many British industries is that management likes them to have it and has helped to give it to them.[1]

NUMBERS OF FULL-TIME CONVENORS

Six per cent of our sample of stewards said that they averaged more than thirty hours a week of working time on union business, and 4% were working virtually full-time as union representatives. It is, however, clear that convenors and staff side secretaries are over-weighted in our sample, and we felt that we should attempt some kind of estimate of the numbers of full-time stewards by other means. We therefore attempted to survey the position in two industrial centres, Sheffield and Birmingham.

Before giving the results we must make clear that there are several categories of full-time convenor. Some are recognized as such by the firm and paid a salary or the average earnings of the appropriate shop in order that they may devote themselves to their work. Some employers provide them with an office, office equipment and a telephone, even the services of a typist. Next there is a group who give their whole time to industrial relations work by informal understanding. Officially they are employed and paid to perform a job which they rarely touch, if ever. Finally, there are those who do union work as required, and find that the requirements of this work occupy most of their time. Clearly, a man who spends more than thirty of his working hours on his trade union job is not really employed and paid for his work as a fitter or a driver or whatever else is his official designation on the books of the firm. Where the arrangements are informal there is a strong tendency amongst both managers and full-time union officers to understate the amount of time a convenor spends on union business.

Full-time convenors are to be expected in large rather than small firms. Most of the largest firms in Sheffield are in the steel industry, and the major union, the Iron and Steel Trades' Confederation, organizes its members in departmental branches, whose branch offices deal with departmental matters. Issues concerning the firm as a whole are dealt with by the full-time officers of the union. It should also be noted that industrial relations in Sheffield are typically 'tough' and the Communists have unusual strength, especially in the Amalgamated Engineering Union.

[1] One point which emerged from the Oxford survey was that the time spent by stewards on union business varied considerably with the attitude of the firm towards shop stewards. Unfortunately analysis of the questionnaire revealed no evidence on this.

This background explains why Sheffield appears to have no officially recognized full-time stewards. There have been two in recent years, but both have been dropped, in one instance when the firm tried to dismiss the holder of the post.

Despite this there are convenors who give most of their time to their union work. In one firm the convenor is also joint secretary of the Joint Production Consultative and Advisory Committee. His occasional machine work is carried on for form's sake only, and to safeguard the management lest he should be succeeded by a Communist. The estimates of local employers' representatives and trade union officers suggest that there are about half a dozen convenors in Sheffield who give most of their time to their work as convenor.

There is some confusion over the payment of stewards in Sheffield. The local association of engineering employers recommends average earnings when management calls in the steward and time rates when the steward acts on his own initiative. Union officers suggest that convenors are often paid for loss of earnings from unofficial funds raised by lotteries and levies. It is difficult to avoid the conclusion that there may be instances of dual payment.

The climate of industrial relations is more relaxed in Birmingham and the city's major factories in the engineering, rubber, chocolate and other industries provide about a dozen more or less officially recognized full-time convenors, or workers' secretaries of joint committees, some of whom have offices, secretaries and other facilities provided by the firm. At one works a trade union representative, specially trained in work study methods, is permanently employed in checking the time studies of the firm's rate-fixers. The Local Departmental Committee Secretary at the main railway goods depot gives his whole time to that work.

Besides this there is a far larger number of convenors who give most of their time to union work. Where an engineering factory has one full-time convenor he is more often than not a skilled member of the Amalgamated Engineering Union, for it is easier for a member of a large union to speak for a small union than *vice versa*, and it is rare for skilled men to allow an unskilled man to negotiate on their behalf. On the other hand, the secretaryship of a joint committee is likely to go to the largest union in the plant, which is in many instances one of the two major General unions. In Birmingham it is the policy of the Transport and General Workers'

Union to insist on the business of their own members being handled by their own senior steward, whether he is convenor or not, so that in some of the largest firms there are two stewards giving most of their time to union business.

Local employers and trade union officers seem prepared to agree that about fifty convenors (or other representatives) spend more than half their time on union business in Birmingham, and that most but by no means all of them are in the engineering industry. There are about the same number of full-time union officers in the city.

The Amalgamated Engineering Union informed us as a result of inquiries from their districts that 19 members of the union are officially recognized as full-time convenors in the United Kingdom. It might appear that this evidence contradicts what we have so far said; but the union readily admits that this list may be incomplete and that other convenors are 'virtually full-time'. We believe that the number of these is much larger than the number in the first category, and offer this as further evidence that employers (and unions) are much more ready to accept full-time convenors *de facto* than to recognize them *de jure*.

The position on the railways can be explained a little further. Between the Local Departmental Committees of the railways and the industry's national negotiating procedure there are five Sectional Councils in each of the country's six regions. Each of these has a staff side secretary. The Councils covering salaried staff have as their secretaries full-time officers of the Transport Salaried Staffs Association. The secretaries of the other Councils are lay members of the National Union of Railwaymen, or of the Associated Society of Locomotive Engineers and Firemen. They receive a fairly liberal allowance of leave to attend Council meetings, sub-committee meetings, staff side meetings, and to prepare business. The unions are prepared to pay additional allowances to cover further unpaid leave. Where the secretaryship is held by one of the two smaller unions, the National Union of Railwaymen designates one of its representatives to have overall responsibility for its members. All these officers spend considerable time on the Councils' work, and, in the Councils which cover the major groups of staff, all or almost all their time. Thus the Railwaymen have thirty secretaries or members giving most of their time to this work—some of them all their time. In addition to this there are a few Local Departmental Committee Secretaries in the union who give all or almost all their time to local negotiation and consultation.

N

Obviously this information is insufficient to allow any serious estimate of the number of full-time convenors or their equivalents, and a guess is all that we can offer. We would be surprised if the total number of full-time, or virtually full-time convenors, staff side secretaries, branch chairmen in the Mineworkers, Local Departmental Committee Secretaries on the railways and similar local negotiators added up to less than 500; and the number giving half their time or more to work of this kind might be as high as two thousand.

SUMMARY

1. Our definition of a shop steward is a local union representative who has definite responsibility for the first stage of local negotiations, but is neither a full-time officer nor a branch secretary with recognized negotiating rights in that capacity. This includes officers with a variety of titles such as 'chapel father' or 'corresponding member' and also what we call 'branch negotiators'. The total number cannot be accurately assessed. Our evidence suggests that the average constituency of all kinds of stewards except branch negotiators may be about 50. Assuming that branch negotiators' constituencies average 250, the total for Britain would be about 90,000.

Size of constituency is probably determined by the structure of the firm and the process of production. To some extent these can explain differences between the unions in our sample. Unions which generally organize production workers have larger constituencies than Skilled unions.

2. Stewards average about eleven hours a week on union business, six of them in working hours. In our sample 6% spent over 30 hours of working time each week on union business, and 4% virtually all.

3. The most time-consuming duty of stewards is negotiating with foremen and managers. Next come discussions with constituents or other stewards, followed by various formal meetings. The consistency of the pattern is more remarkable than the minor variations from union to union.

4. The main determinant of the time spent per member is the size of constituency, but time spent declines much less rapidly than numbers increase up to 200 constituents.

5. Most stewards seem to collect union contributions whether or not the union rules prescribe this method of collection and whether or not a payment is made.

6. Frequency of contact between stewards and full-time officers follows a pattern similar to that between branch secretaries and full-time officers.

7. The educational background of stewards is fairly close to that of branch secretaries. The average age of the sample was 42, and the average length of service as steward was 7 years.

8. Four-fifths of stewards are subject to regular re-election. Nearly half were opposed at their first re-election, and a quarter at subsequent elections.

9. The proportion with replacements available is much higher than amongst branch secretaries, and varies little from union to union.

10. Four-fifths of the sample lost no earnings because of union work. One in twenty lost more than £1 a week.

11. Most stewards served or expressed willingness to serve on higher union committees. Nearly a third said they would like to have a full-time post, but the proportion varied considerably from union to union in inverse relationship to the social standing of their jobs.

12. Two-thirds of stewards think their social standing would rise and their earnings would increase if they became full-time officers. Only 1% would expect a decline in status in these circumstances, but 13% would expect a fall in earnings.

13. Stewards rate the social standing of full-time officers slightly higher than do full-time officers themselves and rate their own standing slightly below that which branch secretaries accord themselves. These tendencies are a little stronger amongst stewards who would like to be full-time officers than amongst other stewards.

14. Personnel officers, taking one with another, rate the stewards of the three major unions on roughly the same level of competence.

15. Personnel officers show a marked preference for dealing with stewards rather than full-time officers. This and other evidence leads us to suppose that the power of shop stewards in British industry has been fostered by management.

16. Various pieces of evidence about the numbers of full-time convenors (under whatever title) and convenors giving half or more of their time to union business leads us to suppose that there are far more of them than is often realized.

PART III

PROBLEMS

CHAPTER 10

TOP LEADERSHIP

THIS study has not been specially concerned with trade union leadership as it is popularly understood—with the character and problems of the few dozen men who are the principal officers of the larger unions, many of whom serve on the General Council of the Trades Union Congress.

One reason for this omission is that it was necessary to preserve the objectivity of the study. So far as we know none of the respondents to our questionnaires are personally known to us, and in any event their answers were punched on to Hollerith cards, processed by a computer, and appear in the tables included in this book in a completely impersonal form. The statistics collected from union head offices were comprehensive and therefore included a considerable number of officers who are personally known to us, or to one of us, but the same routine information was collected about each officer, and the results are just as impersonal as those of the questionnaires. The local surveys were, of course, conducted by one or another of us, and so may be subject to personal bias, but where the results have been used they are presented so that individuals cannot be recognized, and we can therefore have no interest in presenting any person more or less favourably than we saw him.

When we started the survey we had intended to include a questionnaire for senior officers of the trade union movement, but it soon became apparent that this would be difficult to handle, and impossible to present impersonally. Comparisons between the general secretaries of the major unions, for instance, are comparisons between individuals and there is no way of providing anonymity which would not destroy the value of the comparison. We therefore decided that there was enough to be done in the areas subject to more objective treatment, and left this aside.

Perhaps the most common speculation about present top leaders is to compare them with their predecessors. In recent years, so far as we can judge, it has become customary to say that the standard of leadership has fallen. We can offer some comment on this point. One of the common forms of the criticism is to say that there are no Bevins and Citrines in the leadership of British unions to-day.

This is true, but since Bevin and Citrine were the greatest leaders that British unions have ever had, it is also true that there was no one of their quality before they entered office. Taking a rather wider view of trade union leadership, we might define it as the members of the General Council of the Trades Union Congress, at least since the reorganization of the Trades Union Congress in 1921.[1] There have been one or two curious omissions (and one or two surprising inclusions), but on the whole the Council has included the majority of the important national leaders of the movement.

Table 59 sets out the membership of the General Council at the end of the years 1933, 1945 and 1959. The two earlier years are chosen because 1945 must be somewhere about the peak of British trade union power, and 1933 was a year when the unions were at a low ebb.

The critic should cast his eye down the three lists and see how many of the names he knows. Some will be unfamiliar to anyone but the specialist, for they are junior officers of large unions or the general secretaries of small unions, but the critic must ask himself whether he can pick out the names of the general secretaries (or presidents) of the major unions. If he can, is he in a position to make comparisons for each group (or for most groups) for these three years? And when he has made his comparisons, do they add up to a definite shift for the better or for the worse?

In our opinion nothing emerges from the test. Amongst the groups about which we feel confident to make a judgment some are better off in 1959 than ever before. Others, certainly, were most capably represented in 1945 when union power was near its peak. There are one or two other groups that were probably better off in 1933 than they have been since.

It would be generally admitted that the public standing and power of British unions has declined since 1948, just as it would be generally acknowledged that they occupied a higher standing and wielded greater power between 1940 and 1948 than ever before. The decline could be ascribed to the failure of the present generation of trade union leaders; but it could also be attributed to changes in the composition of governments and in government policies; or to a changed economic and social environment. It is clearly outside the scope of this study to determine the weight that should be accorded to each of these possible influences.

[1] Before 1921 the executive body of Congress was known as the Parliamentary Committee.

TABLE 59

MEMBERSHIP OF THE GENERAL COUNCIL OF THE TRADES UNION CONGRESS

Group Represented	1933	1945	1959
Mining and Quarrying	E. Edwards W. Forshaw P. Lee	E. Edwards W. Lawther R. W. Williams	E. Hall W. E. Jones B. Walsh
Railways	J. Bromley J. Marchbank A. G. Walkden	W. P. Allen J. Benstead C. N. Gallie	S. F. Greene A. Hallworth W. J. P. Webber
Transport (other than railways)	J. Beard E. Bevin W. R. Spence	A. Deakin C. Jarman A. F. Papworth	F. Cousins L. Forden T. Yates
Shipbuilding	J. Hill	M. Hodgson	E. J. Hill
Engineering, Founding and Vehicle Building	A. A. H. Findlay J. Rowan A. B. Swales	E. W. Bussey J. Tanner G. W. Thompson	W. B. Beard W. J. Carron W. M. Tallon
Iron and Steel and Minor Metal Trades	W. Kean A. Pugh	A. Callighan L. Evans	H. Douglass J. O'Hagan
Building, Woodworking and Furnishing	G. Hicks F. Wolstencroft	L. Fawcett F. Wolstencroft	E. H. Lowthiar G. F. Smith
Printing and Paper	G. A. Isaacs	E. W. Spackman	R. Willis
Cotton	H. Boothman J. Hindle	A. Naesmith A. Roberts	A. Roberts L. T. Wright
Textiles (other than cotton)	A. Shaw	G. H. Bagnall	L. Sharp
Clothing	A. Conley	A. Conley	J. E. Newton
Leather, Boot and Shoe	W. R. Townley	G. Chester	S. A. Robinson
Glass, Pottery, Chemicals, Food, Drink, Tobacco, Brushmaking and Distribution	J. Hallsworth	J. Hallsworth	J. A. Birch H. Hewitt
Agriculture	W. Holmes	A. C. Dann	H. Collison
Public Employees	G. Gibson	G. Gibson	C. Bartlett
Civil Servants	—	—	D. Houghton R. Smith
Non Manual Workers	H. H. Elvin	T. O'Brien	T. O'Brien
General Workers	J. Davenport A. Hayday W. Thorne	H. Bullock C. Dukes H. N. Harrison	J. Cooper F. Hayday T. Williamson
Women Workers	A. Loughlin J. Varley	F. Hancock A. Loughlin	B. A. Godwin E. McCullough
General Secretary	W. M. Citrine	W. M. Citrine	V. Tewson

CHAPTER II

THE STRUCTURE OF UNION BUREAUCRACIES[1]

TRADE union structure has been a subject of study for many years, and we have no intention to venture far into the field except to suggest that there are a number of measures of structure which are not commonly used, and may prove illuminating, at least for some aspects of trade unionism.

B. C. Roberts has already made use of the concept of the ratio of members to full-time officers, and has made a comparison between a number of major unions.[2] The number of officers can also be compared with other units of union structure, for example, with the number of branches and branch secretaries. Moreover, the number of full-time officers needs to be supplemented by information about numbers of staffs and grades of staffs, numbers of full-time secretaries, full-time convenors and so on. Table 60 brings together a number of the measures of the structure of the 'big six' unions which have been used in this study, together with one or two extensions of them.

There are, of course, a number of other measurements which have been used in the study, and others which might be developed from them, but these seemed to us to be the most important.

One of the most notable features of the table is that each successive column relating members to full-time union workers reduces the disparities between the six unions. The first column shows the extremes as 1 : 7. These are not altered by column four, although the ratios of two intermediate unions are bunched nearer the bottom of the scale. Column six reduces the extremes to 1 : 4, and column seven to about 1 : 2·5. The figures in this last column are far less dependable than in the rest of the table (see footnote 3), but the evidence on which they are based has some foundation, so that the change from column six to column seven is in the right direction even if we have exaggerated it, as we may well have done.

A difference of more than two to one is still an important difference, especially in terms of costs. Indeed, the cost ratio is considerably higher than this, for although the payment of some of the

---

[1] We are using the word 'bureaucracy' in its technical sense, with no pejorative intention.
[2] *Op. cit.*, pp. 288–300.

TABLE 60

SOME MEASURES OF UNION STRUCTURE[1]

Union	(1) Full-Time Officers: Members	(2) Full-Time Officers: Branches	(3) Average Size of Branch	(4) Full-Time Officers and Full-Time Secretaries: Members[2]	(5) Full-Time Officers: Staff	(6) Full-Time Union Employees: Members	(7) Full-Time Workers: Members[4]
All Unions ..	1 : 3,800	1 : 17	226	1 : 3,300	1 : 1·5	1 : 1,400	1 : 1,300?
T. & G.W.U.	1 : 2,200	1 : 9	237	1 : 2,200	1 : 1·2	1 : 1,000	1 : 900?
A.E.U.	1 : 6,300	1 : 18	350	1 : 6,300	1 : 2·3	1 : 1,900	1 : 1,600?
N.U.G.M.W. ...	1 : 5,200	1 : 15	336	1 : 3,400	1 : 1·7[3]	1 : 1,600	1 : 1,500?
N.U.M. ..	1 : 7,200	1 : 10	730	1 : 2,800	1 : 1·6	1 : 1,700	1 : 1,500?
N.U.R. ..	1 : 16,200	1 : 65	250	1 : 16,200	1 : 4·2	1 : 3,100	1 : 2,000?
U.S.D.A.W. ..	1 : 2,400	1 : 12	205	1 : 2,400	1 : 1·9	1 : 800	1 : 800

[1] It should be remembered that these figures relate to the end of 1958.

[2] These figures assume that there are 80 full-time branch secretaries in the General and Municipal Workers, 150 in the Mineworkers, and 400 in all unions. (See pp. 92–94.)

[3] This figure is an estimate and excludes secretarial staff employed by full-time branch secretaries.

[4] The figures in this column are based on the evidence (such as it is) contained in the last section of Chapter 9, together with a great deal of guesswork. We assume that there are about five hundred full-time or almost full-time workers who are not union employees. Most of these are shop stewards (as defined in Chapter 9), but the figure for the Railwaymen includes its Executive Council members, and its Sectional Council secretaries. We have distributed about two-thirds of the total amongst the big six as follows:

T. & G.W.U.	.. 75	N.U.G.M.W.	.. 50
N.U.M. ..	.. 50	U.S.D.A.W...	.. 0
A.E.U.	 100		
N.U.R.	 60		

officers included only in the last column (for example, the Railway-men's Executive Council members) comes out of union funds, most of them are paid by employers. This is also true of some of the full-time branch secretaries included in columns four and six. More-over, the average cost of an officer considerably exceeds the average cost of a member of a union staff.

A very similar point can be made in terms of work done. A full-time branch secretary is not a substitute for a full-time officer. He probably does some work that would otherwise have to be done by a full-time officer, but the rest of his work would otherwise have been carried out by a voluntary branch secretary. A few members of union staffs do the work of a full-time officer because they occupy posts which are graded as full-time officers' posts in other unions,[1] but the great majority of union staffs are employed on other work which saves the time of union officers, but cannot be equated with the work of full-time officers.

It is very debatable how far full-time convenors and other negotiators included in column seven would be considered to be substitutes for full-time officers. Indeed, some trade union officers might claim that the existence of full-time convenors made their work more difficult. On the other hand a considerable volume of negotiations carried on by officers in this group would otherwise demand the attention of full-time officers.

For some purposes, a more accurate measure than any used here might be the expenditure on salaries of full-time union workers, divided into those paid by the union and those paid by the em-ployers; but these figures cannot be extracted.

Despite all these qualifications, our estimated figures in the last column in Table 60 seem to us to be the most important measure to show differences in the structure of union bureaucracies. Similar estimates for other unions covered by our inquiry can be obtained from the last column of Table 29, which gives the ratio of members to full-time officers and staff taken together. Outside the big six (already covered in Table 60) only one union included in Table 29 had any number of full-time branch secretaries or convenors—the National Union of Printing, Bookbinding and Paper Workers. We know the number of full-time branch secretaries in the union, and the ratio of members to full-time union workers is therefore 1,200 : 1. We thus have ratios of members to full-time union

[1] See p. 108.

workers for the fifteen unions included in the last column of Table 29.

Thus, taking the average number of members to full-time union workers as 1,300 : 1, five unions (the Transport and General Workers, the Shop, Distributive and Allied Workers, the National and Local Government Officers, the Boot and Shoe Operatives, and the Building Trade Workers) come well below the average. Five unions come a little above the average (the Engineers, the General and Municipal Workers, the Mineworkers, the Iron and Steel Trades Confederation and the Woodworkers). The Railwaymen and Public Employees come well above the average. The three remaining unions (the Weavers, the Printing, Bookbinding and Paper Workers, and the Transport Salaried Staffs) are at the average or just below it.

Four reasons for differences between member-officer ratios are mentioned by Roberts.[1] 'Where there is a well-developed system of organization at the place of work, and local lay officers and committees have considerable discretionary powers . . . much of the work carried out by full-time officials in other unions is done by these lay officials. . . . Where . . . there is a high turnover of membership, there is an acute need for a large force of full-time officers in the field. Also, in some unions . . . there is a tradition of employing full-time branch officers. . . . Where job conditions are extremely stable . . . the need for officials is smaller.'

Stability of membership is an important factor, and instability (which entails constant labour on recruiting and maintaining members) may explain the relatively low ratio of the building unions (which Roberts instances). The Boot and Shoe Operatives, however, have a firm grip on their industry, the National and Local Government Officers[2] do not suffer from high turnover, and a large proportion of the membership of the Shop, Distributive and Allied Workers is protected by compulsory membership agreements in Co-operative societies;[3] and all these unions have outstandingly low ratios.

Roberts' explanation for the Boot and Shoe Operatives' figure is their 'tradition of employing full-time branch officers'. This, however, is a tradition of some importance in the General and

[1] Op. cit., pp. 288–300.
[2] The National and Local Government Officers' Association, however, has a number of ancillary interests such as house mortgages and various types of insurance.
[3] Turnover of membership, however, is still high because of the rapid labour turnover in retail distribution.

Municipal Workers which has a relatively high ratio even when full allowance is made for its full-time branch secretaries.

The stability of job conditions does not seem to be a very important factor. Roberts gives the railways as an example of stability and the building trade as an example of frequent change, and they suit his exposition. But the engineering industry is subject to at least as rapid changes in job conditions as building, and mining is perhaps the best example of all of an industry with frequent and unpredictable change (for this is one of the staple explanations for the high number of strikes per worker returned by coalminers in almost every country in the world in which coal is mined and for which figures are available). The Engineers' ratio can be reduced if full-time convenors are included, and the Miners' ratio if full-time branch secretaries and negotiators are included, but they still remain relatively high.

Roberts' instances of good organization at the place of work are printing, the Civil Service, the Post Office and the Iron and Steel industry, all of which return high ratios,[1] and therefore fit his explanation. It seems to fit other unions also, and may therefore be accepted, but with a qualification. Importance does not attach so much to the 'well-developed system of organization at the place of work', nor to the local discretionary powers, but to the fact that these powers are granted to 'lay' officers. The difference between the Iron and Steel Trades Confederation and the National Union of Boot and Shoe Operatives is not any difference in the effectiveness of organization on the job, nor in the degree of local discretion, but in the preference of the Boot and Shoe Operatives for full-time secretaries to exercise the discretionary powers.

If Roberts' reasoning cannot be accepted as complete, what is the explanation of this variation between unions? The first thing to be said in answer to this question is that other factors must be mentioned. Some industries, such as the railways and the Civil Service, have comprehensive national agreements. Others, particularly those which rely heavily on piece-rates, have to supplement their national agreements by a great deal of local bargaining. Engineering and mining can serve as examples. Consequently one would expect the

---

[1] The Civil Service and the Post Office are not included in our figures in Table 29, although the officer-member ratio of the Civil Service Clerical Association is included in Table 6. It has been suggested to us that two factors in the explanation of the high ratio of members to officers in this union are: the high educational standard of members which ensures competent lay officers, and the generous facilities granted to these officers to carry out union work in the departments' time. The first factor should also apply in the National and Local Government Officers' Association, which has a low ratio.

Mineworkers and the Engineers to have lower ratios than the Railwaymen. In fact, when allowance is made for full-time negotiators[1] (as it must be in considering the effects of methods of bargaining on the ratios) the differences are in the right direction, but not very large; and all three unions have high ratios by any test. Amongst unions with low ratios the building unions certainly have less local negotiations than the Engineers and the Miners, for they have attempted to elaborate a comprehensive national agreement, and have relatively little payment by results. The Shop, Distributive and Allied Workers have less local negotiating to cover than the Miners and the Engineers.

Although most of the members of the National and Local Government Officers' Association are employed under the national salary agreements covering the local authorities and other public services there are, nevertheless, a very large number of personal grading appeals which must be handled by full-time officers. Perhaps this provides an equivalent to local negotiation in a manual workers' union, although the Transport Salaried Staffs' Association, with a high ratio, also handles a considerable volume of grading appeals.

The capacity of the workers covered by different unions could also constitute part of an explanation. Craftsmen, one would imagine, should be more capable of controlling their own affairs than, say, general workers, and have a long tradition of running unions through voluntary officers. Branches of general workers would therefore be more likely to require the assistance of full-time officers than branches of craftsmen. But, in fact, the Woodworkers have a relatively low ratio, and the Building Trade Workers (whose members are predominantly craftsmen) has the lowest of all. The clerical and administrative members of the National and Local Government Officers' Association should be even more capable of running their own branches than craftsmen, for they have training as well as ability (although they lack the craftsmen's traditions); but their ratio is one of the lowest.

The average size of branch might also yield part of the answer. The work of full-time officers may be affected by the ratio of officers to branches as much as by the ratio of members to officers. The very large branches of the National Union of Mineworkers (see Table 60) give a ratio of officers to branches as low as that of the Transport and General Workers, although the ratio of members

[1] See Table 60.

to officers is four times as high in the Mineworkers. The relatively large branches of the Engineers bring its ratio of officers to branches roughly into line with the average for all unions. Turning to Table 30A for unions not included in Table 60, the building unions and the National and Local Government Officers have small branches and relatively large officer-forces. There are, however, exceptions to this rule as well. Above all the Railwaymen stand out with branches of average size and the highest ratio of members to officers. The Civil Service Clerical Association, with an almost equally high ratio, has small branches. And the Agricultural Workers, with the smallest branches of all, has a ratio close to the average.

Another factor of some importance is the reliance of some unions on 'lay' officers for district or regional administration. The Civil Service unions and the railways come into this category. The position of these officers is analogous to that of convenors or stewards, or the Railwaymen's Sectional Council Secretaries. Many of them spend a good deal of their working time on union business, and some spend all of it. In some instances payment is made by the union, in others the employer bears the cost. This enables their unions to manage with a smaller complement of officers than a union in which all executive posts above the branch are full-time.

In some unions recruitment is almost entirely the responsibility of part-time officers. The $12\frac{1}{2}\%$ commission paid to branch secretaries and to collectors in the General and Municipal Workers' Union may be supposed to cut the cost of full-time officers by paying for more recruitment at branch level. In the Engineers recruitment seems to be almost entirely transferred to shop stewards without direct payment from the union.[1]

Other possible influences can be mentioned more briefly. A union with a scattered membership, in terms of industry (a general union), in terms of geography (the Agricultural Workers) or in terms of place of employment (shop assistants) might be expected to require more officers than a concentrated union. A union which offers a wider range of service (insurance, mortgages, and elaborate legal services in the National and Local Government Officers, for instance) needs more officers than one which does not.

[1] Answers to our full-time officers' questionnaire suggest that recruitment is a less important part of the duties of a full-time officer of the General and Municipal Workers than in most other unions, and is negligible for an officer of the Engineers.

We thus have a long list of factors which may affect the ratio of members to officers. To recapitulate: stability of membership, the nature of working conditions, the type of local organization and whether lay officers deal with local negotiations, the type of collective agreement, the type of membership in the union, the average size of branch, the structure of the union and the methods of district and regional organization, the method of recruitment, industrial and geographical concentration and concentration at the place of work, and the services offered. All of them may have some influence, but none of them can be shown to have a decisive influence. There are a number of reasons for the high ratio in the Railwaymen, and for the low ratios in the building unions, so that we can say that the explanations cover the extremes. In between, however, the explanations seem to cancel out rather than support each other. Have we, therefore, to abandon the search for rational explanations?

We suggest that the answer lies in the force of tradition and habit. Table 8 gives the ranking of member-officer ratios in thirteen unions for the years 1939 and 1959, and shows there is very little change over twenty years, although these were twenty years of upheavals in the circumstances and environment of almost every union. Tradition, of course, cannot explain differences. It can only explain why existing differences are perpetuated. We therefore put forward the suggestion that the long list of influences just set down determined the original differences between unions. As time passed, however, each union came to accept its own ratio as the natural order of things, and put up a strong resistance to change, even when altered circumstances warranted it. To-day, therefore, the ratios no longer bear much relation to the factors which originally established them.

We can quote some evidence. In 1910 the Dock, Wharf, Riverside and General Labourers' Union (which is the main predecessor of the Transport and General Workers' Union) had 15,200 members and 37 full-time officers. In the same year the Gasworkers' and General Labourers' Union, which subsequently became the senior partner in the amalgamation which formed the National Union of General and Municipal Workers, had 32,000 members and only fifteen full-time officers. Over the next ten years rapidly expanding membership made considerable alterations in the two ratios, but left the marked difference between the two unions which has persisted to this day and which is only partially narrowed by the practice of the old Gasworkers and present General and Municipal Workers

o

of allowing a branch secretary's commission sufficient to permit full-time secretaries in the largest branches.

There was a reason for the difference. Due to the casual nature of employment in the docks, dockers were very difficult to organize and blacklegs were plentiful. Consequently organization required the constant attention of full-time officers, even more than in the building unions of to-day. But conditions have changed in the docks. In most ports, union membership is now universal and protected by the arrangements of the Dock Labour Boards. It remains the union's view that their special agreements and negotiating arrangements still demand a low ratio of members to officers in the docks, but, even if this is accepted, it does not explain the difference between the General and Municipal Workers and the other sections of the Transport and General Workers, which by and large cover similar types of members.

This is not, of course, to say that the General and Municipal Workers are right and the Transport and General Workers are wrong. It may be that the former has too few officers. It is, however, to suggest that tradition is the main reason for the difference between them. The point can be put in another form which is probably how it would appear to the governing bodies of the two unions. Because of their higher ratios of members to officers the General and Municipal Workers have grown accustomed to spending their income on other things, for instance, higher branch commissions, and could not imagine where they could find the money to double their officer-force. The Transport and General Workers have given tasks to their larger body of officers which are done by others or not done at all in the General and Municipal Workers, and they could not imagine how the work could possibly be carried out by half the number of full-time officers.

One of these duties is acting as branch secretary. Amongst the full-time officers included in our sample almost half of those from the Transport and General Workers were acting as branch secretary for one or more branches and over two-thirds of the officers of the Shop, Distributive and Allied Workers, whereas none of the officers from the Engineers or the General and Municipal Workers were acting as branch secretaries.[1] One obvious explanation for the difference is that there are too few officers in the Engineers and the

---

[1] Although the General and Municipal Workers has full-time branch secretaries, and some full-time district secretaries in the Engineers may perform work which would otherwise fall on branch secretaries.

General and Municipal Workers to make it possible for many of them to take on responsibilities of this kind. Consequently the number of officers determines the work pattern and thereafter the pattern of work demands that number of officers. The ratio of members to officers and staff combined is lower in the Shop, Distributive and Allied Workers than in both the other General unions, although most of its membership is protected by Co-operative Society employment policies. This could also be explained by the hypothesis that the number of officers determines the volume of work.

Why should tradition be so powerful? It is, perhaps, understandable that tradition should defeat proposals for a reduction in officer-force. The officers themselves will oppose it, as will potential candidates, and the branches will be against a reduction in the services available to them. Only a severe financial crisis could override these combined forces, and this might be expected to arise from a fall in membership. If so, a cut in the establishment would stabilize the ratio.

We can, however, also quote an instance of the defeat of a proposal for expansion. In 1936 the Conference of the General and Municipal Workers approved a proposal of the general secretary, Charles Dukes, to appoint a new class of officers solely for recruitment work.[1] The scheme operated for six years only. Its abolition was due to several factors, amongst them that district secretaries used the new officers to do the traditional work of officers, and recruitment became for them, as for other officers, a residual duty. This development was assisted by the rapid rise in membership over those years which meant that new officers were needed for normal duties, and that the ratio of members to officers actually rose, despite the appointment of 77 officers in 6 years. For this reason the example does not prove that tradition will always win. It does show, however, that one of the strongest arguments for appointing new officers is that they will pay for themselves by recruiting new members (at least in unions which have not achieved a high degree of organization). If an increase in membership is achieved, then the effect of the new appointments on union structure is nullified.

This does not have to be a pessimistic conclusion. It could be most optimistic. It means that most unions have considerable room for manœuvre in their staffing ratios and administrative practices,

[1] H. A. Clegg, *op. cit.*, p. 75.

if they understand what they are about. Where a practice has positively harmful effects and can be shown to have no justification apart from tradition there is more chance of change than where it can be proved to be the inevitable consequence of external factors.

To put the point in its sharpest form, some unions may have too many full-time officers and staff members, although every union complains it has far too few. The executive committees and senior officers of those unions which have low ratios of members to full-time officers and staff could well ask themselves whether other unions with higher ratios do not get equally good results, and whether the only reason for the difference in ratios is not a tradition which it is in their power to alter. Similarly a union which is genuinely convinced that it needs more full-time officers but can see no way of paying for them might find that the barrier was in their habitual administrative practices rather than in their budget. It is true, of course, that many traditions are capable of putting up an extremely tough resistance to change; but they can be changed. The history of every industrialized country in the world over the last hundred years is powerful testimony on that score.

If unions are to embark on inquiries of this kind one of their first needs will be detailed information about the structure of other unions which many of them seem to lack, and which this chapter, and, indeed, this whole study, supplies only in part and inadequately.

CHAPTER 12

SUPPLY AND SELECTION

SOURCES OF SUPPLY

THE information we have been able to collect about the supply of shop stewards and full-time officers yields some comfort. Existing stewards take an optimistic view of the availability of replacements, and this view is consistently hopeful when our sample is broken down by union or by industry or by type of steward.[1] Our main source of information about supply of full-time officers is the proportion of stewards and branch secretaries who would like to be full-time officers. Most full-time officers were branch secretaries or shop stewards (or both) before entering full-time office,[2] and it seems clear that many thousand stewards and branch secretaries think they would like to have full-time posts, although only 100–125 fall vacant in any one year.[3] This evidence must be interpreted cautiously. Many of these stewards and branch secretaries might change their minds if the opportunity was directly presented to them. Many are too old. The desire for office is highest amongst semi-skilled workers who are less likely to possess the ability than the skilled and White Collar workers, who are less keen. Nevertheless, the margin is wide. Desire for office is no proof of ability, but the experience of the Shop, Distributive and Allied Workers and the Railwaymen suggests that the number of suitable candidates exceeds the number of vacancies.[4] The evidence therefore suggests that unions which complain of difficulty in recruiting officers should reconsider their methods of selection.

The outlook for branch secretaries is not so promising.[5] Judged by the same standards as the stewards, their overall score is lower, and there are marked differences between unions which suggest that some unions (particularly the Building unions) have a serious problem. We have, however, no reason to believe that the explanation is to be found in a lack of men and women who could do the job (most branch secretaries are drawn from the same source of supply as shop stewards) and it seems reasonable to suppose that

---

[1] See p. 163.   [2] See p. 51.   [3] See p. 139.
[4] See p. 54.   [5] See p. 128.

they lack the will rather than the ability, and they do so because the branch secretary's job, by and large, is less attractive than other union posts. Consequently our problem of supply is to be explained by the characteristics of the job and must be left aside for the moment.

There are, however, two other aspects of the supply which should be mentioned, which may be termed respectively 'promotion loss' and 'higher education loss'.

One of the reasons for turnover amongst lay officers is promotion within their firms, and it is clear that some union members attach considerable importance to it.[1] It would not be surprising if shop stewards and branch secretaries were more likely to receive offers of promotion than the general run of workers, for it can be assumed that their ability exceeds the average in most instances. We have found firms which adopt a considered policy of promoting stewards. In one firm, for example, anyone who holds the post of chief shop steward for three years is offered promotion to the staff. On the other hand there are firms which deliberately abstain from promoting stewards and branch secretaries on the ground that they are at least as concerned about the standards of trade union representation as of their charge-hands and foremen. And there are, of course, stewards and branch secretaries who refuse offers of promotion.

Promotion loss clearly affects the supply of future full-time officers, and it almost certainly affects the supply of potential stewards and branch secretaries, for many of the young men who are promoted in their twenties or early thirties would otherwise have become excellent local union officers. There is, however, no reason to suppose these losses gravely jeopardize general trade union standards. The pool from which full-time officers are drawn remains very large. If the difficulties which certain unions experience in recruiting branch secretaries are to be explained by promotion losses, then the supply of shop stewards should suffer equally (if not more), and it does not.

Higher education losses are of importance only for the supply of full-time officers. Every year several dozen young trade unionists receive scholarships and grants to attend Ruskin College, Hillcroft College, Fircroft College, Coleg Harlech or Newbattle Abbey to pursue residential courses for one or two years; others receive adult

[1] See p. 176.

scholarships which take them direct to the universities, although most adult awards to the universities now go to students who have already spent some time at one of these five colleges. It might appear that this was an excellent source for future full-time trade union officers, and, indeed, a considerable number (particularly of ex-Ruskin students) subsequently obtain full-time jobs in the Labour Movement, as trade union officers, in the Labour Party, in Co-operative Societies or in the Workers' Educational Association. An even larger proportion ultimately obtain professional posts of one sort or another and some of the considerable number who go back to their old jobs remain there.

Certainly the proportion working in the Labour Movement would be larger if more posts of the right kind were available. Most of those who have become union officers in recent years have gone into research departments, education departments or similar specialist jobs whose number is closely limited. A number of those who would otherwise want full-time union posts do not seek them because their union elects its officers and they do not wish to return to their old jobs with nothing better than the opportunity to compete in an election when a vacancy arises. Vacancies may not be available even in unions which appoint their officers, and the qualified students may not be willing to allow their new abilities to rust until their union can find a use for them. There have been several cases of educational loss which have attracted considerable attention. Men of exceptional ability and considerable experience in their unions have added educational qualifications to their other merits only to find that their unions will not offer them a post, or a post which suits their qualifications.

It is as yet impossible to give a thorough assessment of these problems,[1] but in our opinion they are exaggerated. It is only natural that there should be now, as in the past, a number of young working men and women who both find their environment unsatisfying and have the ability to move into other social classes. Some of them naturally turn to the adult colleges as a means of providing themselves with the intellectual and cultural satisfactions that they lack. Their course may feed their dissatisfaction and open up a number of possibilities of permanently changing their environment, perhaps by taking a post which will place them amongst people who have similar interests to their own, possibly also a post

[1] It forms part of the subject of a thesis which Mr. Jay Blumler, tutor of Ruskin, is at present preparing for the degree of D.Phil. in the University of Oxford.

which can ultimately provide the income to satisfy their newly-developed wants. In other words their feet are firmly set on the social ladder, and rightly, because only in this way can they find what they want in life. Others, with different tastes, may be genuinely keen to spend their lives in the service of the Labour Movement, even in a relatively humble capacity.

At the end of their course, however, most adult students are not in a position to see these things clearly. A number of those with a desire for advancement have nevertheless retained earlier ambitions to become trade union officers. Although the two desires are not easily satisfied by the same job, some of them nevertheless look for both in trade union posts. If they fail to obtain them, it may appear that stupid trade union committees are wilfully neglecting highly-qualified men and women, when, in fact, a group of hard-headed men can perceive the disabilities of a man who, whatever his talents and qualifications, is not cut out to be a trade union officer. In some instances we believe that this has happened, and that their failure to obtain union posts has been in their own best interests.

On the other hand some adult students have gone back to their unions and fought elections, perhaps several elections over a period of years, and have ultimately obtained union posts. It is at least arguable that they have had in them more of the stuff which makes a good trade union officer even than some of their more brilliant contemporaries. There are still other adult students who would have made excellent full-time officers, and have made genuine efforts to obtain union jobs, without success.

As unions want more research officers, education officers and other specialists they will find a number of good candidates among trade union adult students; but it is probable that unless the unions ask the colleges to provide courses specifically designed for men and women selected for their suitability for trade union office, only a minority of their alumni will be good candidates for run-of-the-mill trade union jobs. Some trade union executives may be unduly cautious in their attitude to adult scholars; but some caution is justified.

Selection of Full-Time Officers

Our study has produced little information about the process of selection of shop stewards and branch secretaries except to show that, whatever union rules may say, most shop stewards are subject to regular re-election, and that opposition is common in shop elections. But we can say more about the processes of selecting full-time officers.

If the majority of unions include a large number of voluntary officers who would like to be chosen for full-time jobs, and many of them, nevertheless, complain about the difficulty of finding good officers, then the difficulty is one of communication and selection, and these processes need improvement. The Shop, Distributive and Allied Workers' scheme[1] is the most careful attempt to improve communications, and it has shown a plentiful supply of men and women whom the union rates as up to the standard required for full-time office. Whilst recognizing the scheme's advantages, however, it is possible to suggest that it has shortcomings.

One possible drawback is that the number short-listed each two years far exceeds the number of vacancies likely to occur before the next round of interviews. Each vacancy is covered about seven times. The union justifies this by saying that a number of 'short-listed' candidates, in fact, drop out over the subsequent two years, and that others restrict themselves to applying for posts in their own area of the country, and are therefore ineligible for most of the vacancies that actually occur. On the other hand, it follows that many of the short-listed candidates are encouraged to think that they have a good chance of appointment when their chance is small, and it is possible that this leads to the discouragement not only of the unsuccessful short-listed candidates, but also of subsequent potential applicants. It would seem that the union could cover all likely contingencies with a short-list of between twenty and thirty instead of between 47 and 70.

Another possible shortcoming is that all the available and likely candidates may not apply. How far the union is actually combed for potential talent depends on how far existing officers and executive members give time to seeking out good candidates and encouraging them to apply. But its method is clearly far in advance of most other unions in this respect.

Other unions rely on educational schemes which give their leaders some knowledge about the supply of future officers without the formality of interviews and short lists, and have the advantage that students can be tested over a number of courses instead of in one interview. On the other hand, the supply of officers might be

[1] See pp. 52–53.

unnecessarily restricted if posts were confined to those trade union members who attended courses, and still more if it was confined to the best students, judged by academic standards.

It may be possible to achieve a good deal, except in the largest unions, if one or two senior officers regard 'talent-spotting' as an important part of their duties in the manner of the general secretary of the National Union of Public Employees. But this method relies heavily on the chance acquaintances of the men concerned and the quality of their judgment. Many senior trade union officers might not want to take on this kind of responsibility.

In any event it seems fairly clear that a union which finds itself short of good candidates for full-time posts should in the first instance look to its methods of discovering likely men and women; and that there exist methods of improving their techniques in this respect.

These methods, however, apply directly only to unions which appoint their officers, and many trade union rules prescribe election. How can these unions ensure that the best men in their ranks are chosen for full-time posts?

The disadvantages of election are so obvious and so often stressed even in unions which rely on these methods that there is a fairly general assumption that it does not produce the best men. It may perhaps have advantages in giving the membership more control over union policy and more interest in union affairs which, its supporters can claim, outweigh the loss in calibre of officers. Calibre is bound to suffer because the members often have very little notion of the abilities of the candidates between whom they must choose; many good men will not subject themselves to the process of election; in unions which require periodic re-election the officers must always consider their chances of re-election before they act; and so on. Expectations appear to be verified by experience. Anyone who studies British unions can find some officers of very poor quality, but the worst of all, in our opinion, are to be found in elective unions.

In these circumstances it is surprising to find that personnel officers find almost nothing to choose between the abilities of the appointed officers of the Transport and General Workers, the nominally-elected officers of the General and Municipal Workers and the elected and periodically re-elected officers of the Engineers.[1]

[1] See p. 87.

Admittedly the elected officers of the Electricians come off far worse, but there is at least some element of political bias in their grading.

It is possible to suggest an explanation for this puzzle. One of the complaints against re-election is that an officer becomes the servant of two masters. He is subject to the union executive who can instruct him and dismiss him, and to the union members in his electorate who can make demands of him and refuse to re-elect him. So far as it goes this is true, but it is also true that no full-time officer can avoid these dual pressures. He must be subject to the union's executive, if the executive is to govern the union at all. Equally, however, he must represent the members for whom he is responsible in dealings with management. At branch meetings he is the representative of the district, regional or head office; but in negotiation he is also the representative of the men before management. In terms of the time involved, negotiations are by far the most important duty of most union officers (see Table 9). A good deal of the second most important duty (correspondence) is related to negotiations or to the third duty, helping members with individual problems, in which again the officer is acting as a representative. Attendance at branch meetings comes fourth in importance. Consequently, at least in his most important duties, the full-time officer must be a representative of his members as well as an agent of the union executive. In most instances the two loyalties will not conflict, for the executive also represents the members; but in all unions there is some conflict of loyalties from time to time.

The full-time officer is not likely to be respected by management unless he can perform both parts of his job. Personnel officers prize honesty above all other qualities in trade union officers.[1] Next, with equal scores, come concern to uphold procedure agreements and undertakings with management, and ability to control his or her members. These qualities are, of course, not to be found in an officer who is subservient to his members. But an officer who cares for nothing but complying with the orders of his executive is not likely to have much control over his members, and the desire to uphold agreements is not of much use to management without that. Perhaps this explains the apparent indifference of management between unions which appoint and unions which elect.

Representing his members is thus a most important duty for a trade union officer. It may be that election is not a good method of

[1] See p. 88.

choosing the best technician, the most intelligent man or the most competent administrator; but only the most confirmed opponent of democracy would argue that men and women would be better represented if their representatives were chosen for them rather than by them. This is not to say that election is necessarily the best means of choosing union officers, for they require other qualities which may be best perceived by a committee. But it may serve to explain why election, despite its many disadvantages, seems to produce an average standard equal to that of appointment, although election at its worst may fall below any but the corrupt appointment.

If other electing unions imitated the pre-election tests of the Railwaymen, the worst products of the electoral system might in future be eliminated. It is also possible that election applies pre-selection tests of its own. In an electing union a member ambitious for full-time office cannot expect quick and easy successes. He must first win elections in the branch, and then to voluntary district or national posts. Thereafter he may have to stand for full-time office on several occasions before he can expect success. It might be that these successive tests discover and develop representative qualities just as a process of interview and education develops other talents (although even in appointing unions most full-time officers have previously won a number of elections to voluntary posts). On the other hand it may be that, if appointing unions really took advantage of all their opportunities in selection and training, they would leave electing unions far behind; but the test has not yet been made.

It is sometimes suggested that trade unions should look for full-time officers outside their own ranks, and, indeed, will have to do so when the 1944 Education Act has taken its full effect. Some unions already do so. The methods of recruitment adopted by the National Union of Public Employees have been mentioned in an earlier chapter.[1] The Post Office Engineering Union decided in 1934 that its next general secretary must be a man 'with an education of university standard', with the provisos that he must also 'belong to and be imbued with the aspirations of the working class', and 'be a trade unionist by conviction'. The first holder of the post under these conditions was the late John Edwards, a railwayman's son, and a graduate of Leeds University who held a post in the university at the time of his appointment. He was subsequently elected to Parliament and resigned office on becoming a junior

[1] See p. 82.

Minister. The present general secretary is Charles Smith, an Oxford graduate and a former M.P.

Most of the unions which adopt this method are, however, White Collar unions whose members might be expected to take more easily to an outsider than manual workers could. The Post Office Engineers include as many technicians as manual workers, and the Public Employees have acquired some of the characteristics of a White Collar union.[1] The rules of most other unions (including the big six) prohibit outsiders. It would be particularly difficult to find a means of introducing outsiders into unions which elect.[2]

Our evidence does not bear directly on this aspect of selection. The danger is that the outsider will lack the sympathy and understanding required to win the confidence of his members and to represent them before others. We have just stressed the importance of this capacity to represent. It would be silly to suggest, however, that no outsiders possess these qualities, or could develop them. If unions cannot find capable officers within they will have to look outside. We would stress, however, that they do not appear to have exhausted their internal resources—far from it.

[1] See p. 82.
[2] To show the danger of *any* generalization about British trade unions, however, it is worth noting that in 1960 three graduates were serving either as full-time officers or as members of the staff in one district of the National Union of General and Municipal Workers.

CHAPTER 13

PAY

Voluntary and Part-Time Officers

A LTHOUGH we have come across a considerable number of
individual complaints about the payment of shop stewards and
branch secretaries, we have been unable to relate payment to indices
of morale, and would therefore suggest that its importance can be
exaggerated. The supply of candidates for the post of branch
secretary does not seem to be related to the rate of payment for the
work, which varies considerably from union to union down to
nothing.[1] Loss of earnings at work affects only a minority of shop
stewards, most of whom lose less than 10s. a week.[2] It is clearly a
criticism of the unions concerned that they do not insist that their
stewards should suffer no loss, or make the loss good out of union
funds or shop collections, but it does not appear to be an important
deterrent to potential stewards.

It seems, therefore, that remuneration is not one of the most
important incentives to part-time or voluntary officers. They are
moved more by a liking for the work, a desire to serve or a desire
for power than by monetary considerations. Union work is their
hobby. It may be pleasant to receive some payment for one's
hobby, but it does not determine the choice of hobby nor the
pleasure one takes in it.

We do not wish to suggest that there are no problems in the
payment of branch secretaries. The wide variety of methods of
payment may not add to the problems of recruitment, but it does
not follow that each union has the method which suits it best. Some
methods are more costly than others, for example, and if they
achieve no better results, wherein is their justification? Nearly all
methods of payment now yield considerably smaller real rewards
than in 1939, and we have discovered no evidence that branch
secretaries cost too much before the war.

Nor must it be supposed that there is no level of payment which
could affect the supply of branch secretaries. If, for example, the
average payments for branch secretaries provided, not 2s. an hour,[3]

---

[1] See p. 133.   [2] See p. 166.   [3] See p. 134.

but, say, 7s. 6d. for the first ten hours each week and 10s. an hour for each hour beyond that, it is possible that no unions would have a problem in recruiting competent branch secretaries. On the other hand unions might fear that rates of this order would attract the wrong men to the job; and most of them would deny that they could meet payments of this kind without serious increases in subscriptions.

The only branch secretaries whose remuneration yields hourly rates of this kind are some of those with large branches in unions which vary the payment according to the size of the branch. Since a man's time is limited, payment by the size of branch must yield increasing hourly payments above a certain size of branch. In some instances wife and family are brought in to help with the clerical work of the secretary, but even this has its limits, and at some point the service must suffer.

The remedies are to split up large branches or, if sufficient competent candidates cannot be found for all the new posts, to make the secretary's post a full-time job. In some instances at least there would not be a large additional cost to the branch or to the union of making the secretary's income up to a reasonable rate for a full-time post; and *prima facie* it would seem that the additional services would be bound to justify the change. In those unions which restrict the size of branch (like the Engineers) the problem arises only when they make exceptions to their own rules. In other unions the major problem arises with branches of between 1,000 and 2,500 members. There cannot be many branches with more than 2,500 members and a part-time secretary.

Full-Time Officers

There is a good deal more to be said about the payment of full-time officers.

Despite much of what is said about the subject, the starting-point of the salary structure of most trade unions seems to be a reasonable recruiting rate. Table 15 shows that starting salaries of the unions quoted range between £750 and £1,200. There are unions with somewhat lower starting rates. The Agricultural Workers, for example, pays rather less than this figure, but agricultural workers receive considerably less than most other workers; and the problems of the District Association Secretaries in the smaller districts of the

Weavers' Amalgamation have already been described.[1] The information that we have gathered about other unions, however, suggests that almost all the starting rates in the larger unions were between £700 and £1,200 at the end of 1958. The lowest figure was above the weekly rate in all but the most exceptionally skilled of manual occupations, and above the average earnings of male workers (including overtime, piece-work earnings, bonuses and all the rest). In October 1958 the average earnings of adult male workers stood at £12 16s. 8d. a week or about £670 a year.[2] Those unions with starting rates of £800 or £900 were, of course, further ahead. Most workers, if not all, would prefer a dependable annual salary to an annual income of the same value but dependent on fluctuating weekly earnings.

We also know that the majority of our samples of branch secretaries and shop stewards thought that their earnings would go up if they became full-time officers (67% of secretaries and 66% of stewards) and very few thought that their earnings would go down (11% of secretaries and 13% of stewards).[3] This, of course, does not demonstrate that about two-thirds of lay trade union officers would gain on becoming officers, for many of them are not certain of the rates paid to full-time officers in their own unions; but it does suggest that relatively few potential candidates are deterred by the expectation that they will lose money.

There are, of course, many instances, in motor-car towns, in the steel industry or in the coalfields, of workers who would lose heavily—some of them hundreds of pounds a year—by accepting a full-time post in their own unions; but it is important to remember, as our evidence suggests and figures of average earnings demonstrate, that these are the exceptions. Relatively few potential officers are held back, and most unions do not suffer badly from this cause. Moreover, if unions pitched their starting rate so as to make sure that no member would suffer loss of earnings by accepting a full-time office, most of them would have to pitch them at double their present rates. It is generally accepted that earnings in most occupations approximate to a J-shaped curve, with most of its members bunched closely in a narrow band of earnings and a small number earning 50%, 100% or 150% more than the average. So that to attract the best potential candidate a union might have to offer two

---

[1] See p. 60.　　　　[2] *Ministry of Labour Gazette*, February 1959.
[3] See pp. 144–145 and pp. 171–172.

or three times as much as would appear good money to three-quarters of them.

This is not to say that trade unions can be complacent about their starting rates. Table 15 shows that over the last twenty years the salaries of only two out of sixteen grades of officer have risen as fast as average earnings. Only three have risen faster than the rise in average wage rates in the period, and only five faster than the retail price index. From our other information this is fairly typical of trends in the larger unions. Consequently it can be said that what many think has already happened (although it has not) might easily happen in the future. A continuation of the same trend over the next twenty years would leave almost all starting salaries below average earnings, and, indeed, a number of general secretaries would then be earning less than the average earnings of manual workers in the occupations they represent. Disaster has been avoided, but the signal is at red.

In discussing full-time salaries on pp. 56–57 we suggested that they had probably moved fairly closely in line with other *salaries* (which have increased less than wages since 1938, and less still in comparison with the earnings of wage-earners). It might be that the relative decline in full-time officers' salaries could be justified on these grounds. The answers to our questions concerning the social standing of trade union officers should throw some light on this issue. These showed that two-thirds of trade union officers equated the social standing of their general secretaries to a medical officer of health, a company director, or above, and four-fifths put themselves equal to or above an elementary school teacher. Branch secretaries and shop stewards confirm this view, although both groups place full-time officers slightly further up the scale than do the officers themselves.[1]

At the same time it is clear that these questions about social standing caused disquiet. More than one union protested at their inclusion, and a number of full-time officers also objected.

This suggests that trade union officers, and perhaps also trade union members, are uneasy about the class position of full-time union officers. And it is natural that this should be so. The trade union officer sees himself as a more consequential and socially powerful person than, say, the sales manager of a medium-sized firm. But the type of house the manager lives in, the suburb in which it is situated, his wife's clothes and his children's school

[1] See Tables 43 and 57.

P

differentiate him sharply from most of the members of a manual workers' union. A major part of the job of most trade union officers is to represent these men. Could they if they aped *all* these middle-class habits, if, for example, they sent their children to private schools? On the other hand, if they are doing a more important and responsible job than the sales manager, are they not entitled to all the insignia which accompany his position in society—and more?

The conundrum appears to be insoluble. Union members create full-time posts in their organizations which necessarily confer important and powerful social positions on their occupants. The greater the power and the higher the standing, the more the full-time officer can do for his members, but the further he is removed from them. At some point the distance between them must detract from his ability to represent them.

We must not exaggerate. There is plenty of space between the extremes for most trade union officers to maintain an equilibrium without undue psychological strain. Other countries can teach us lessons beyond the bounds of our own experience. If Australian trade unionists are even more shy of middle-class contamination than their British counterparts, some American unions encourage an expenditure and scale of living that would not be tolerated in Britain. In terms of American incomes the average salaries of American trade union officers are not so high as is sometimes supposed in Britain, but the higher salaries are quite beyond our experience.

There are economic as well as social problems in settling the salaries of full-time officers. So long as most full-time officers are recruited from the ranks of union members it would seem reasonable to insist that salaries should exceed average earnings in the occupations organized to encourage recruitment. Thereafter there are two further problems: to make sure that too many officers are not lost to more remunerative posts that might come their way; and to settle appropriate salaries for the higher posts.

The first line of argument would suggest that salary scales should be the 'going market rate' for the work and responsibility involved. Since the war a number of trade union officers have been appointed to the boards of nationalized industries at salaries of anything from £3,000 to £10,000. In the coalmining industry, whose Industrial Relations Department has been largely staffed by ex-miners, many full-time officers have seen men whom they defeated in ballots for

union office accept Coal Board appointments at salaries higher than
their own, because the Coal Board could not denude the union of
full-time officers. Some officers have left their unions for well-paid
posts in private industry. Others have refused posts in both public
and private undertakings. On this basis union salaries might have
to be increased by very substantial amounts. On the other hand
there is no evidence that the opportunities taken by the minority,
or even the offers made to others, have ever been open to the
majority. Indeed, there are some full-time officers (perhaps only a
few) who would be glad to exchange their present posts for others
if only they could find the posts.

Moreover, the minority is small. Taking one year with another,
and one union with another, turnover is about 5% a year, and this
is all the more striking when it is remembered that the average age
of entry into full-time office is about forty.[1] Normal retirement and
death together account for three-fifths of the termination of full-
time officers' careers. More than half the remainder are retired
prematurely, dismissed or resign on health grounds.[2] Even if all the
remainder left because they were discontented with their salaries it
would not prove that union salaries were far too low; and this is
by no means the case.

In consequence, it is not at all clear what salary scale would follow
from 'the determination of the market'. Because ex-trade union
officers hold appointments in nationalized industries at anything up
to £10,000 a year, it does not follow that trade union salary scales
should run to £10,000.

As for the salaries of senior posts, a glance at Table 15 reveals
considerable variation in differentials, and there is even more
variation in fact. Most of the unions for which we have confidential
information have wider differentials than any in the table. It is
common to pay the general secretary twice as much as the junior
grade; several unions pay three times as much; and one pays four
times as much.

It could be argued that salaries ought to increase in proportion
to increased responsibility. But where can we find a post of equivalent standing and responsibility to the General Secretary of the
Transport and General Workers, or the President of the Engineers?
Are they on a par with Cabinet Ministers, or the Chairmen of
Imperial Chemicals, Unilever or the National Coal Board? And if
so, should their posts carry salaries of £5,000, £10,000 or £50,000?

[1] See p. 47.   [2] See p. 79.

We can see no reason for supposing that the Transport and General Workers or the Engineers would benefit from the change.

If it could be shown that senior officers were generally discontented and that promotion was frequently refused, there would be an argument for reviewing differentials. But the evidence is lacking, even in unions with low differentials.

There is, however, one group of officers which was, so far as we know, entirely excluded from our sample of full-time officers. These are the qualified specialist officers within trade unions, particularly union education and research officers and the officers of the Trades Union Congress. The group is much smaller than the 'administrative class' whose numbers we estimate at 300–400,[1] for most members of that class have considerable experience which qualifies them admirably for the jobs they do within the unions, but lack recognized qualifications. Most of the officers of the Trades Union Congress, however, and a number of research and education officers hold university degrees or similar qualifications.

A few trade union officers can hope to attain high salaries in the nationalized industries. Others may increase their incomes by entering government service or becoming personnel officers in private industry (although it should be remembered that there are also those who try and fail). Most trade union officers, however, will not have these opportunities or will refuse them should they be offered. Whether they accept them or not, those who receive offers do so because of the trade union posts they hold and the opportunity these posts have given them to gain experience and to reveal their talents.

Specialist officers, however, are in a different position. They acquired their qualifications before they became trade union officers. A man with a good degree and a number of years' experience of research comes within a certain range of salaries on the labour market regardless of whether his experience was in a trade union or elsewhere. Since most of the qualified specialist officers are young and many of them have not served many years, the test of turnover cannot yet yield convincing results.

This problem has caused a good deal of worry in recent years, not only to the officers concerned, but also to observers of British trade unions, some of whom have found in them a desperate need for qualified men. In these circumstances it is surprising to see how small the problem is in financial terms. Very few of the officers

[1] See p. 106.

concerned would think of themselves, or be thought by others, as above the standard of a University lecturer. The normal University lecturers' scale now runs from £900 to £1,650.[1] Any union which pays its general secretary £2,000 or more has room within it for a scale of this kind. And most middle-sized or large unions could raise their top salary to this level without great expense. In fact, there might be outspoken opposition in some unions. If so, these opponents are no doubt content to do without specialists, or to lose those they have.

This consideration gives us a criterion for judging differentials in union salary-structures. Those unions which want competent specialist officers should fix their highest salaries at a figure of £2,000–£2,500.[2] There is no reason to suppose that most starting salaries are very far from the proper mark, given that they should be determined in relation to the earnings of the occupations from which the union draws its members, and given that the present margin is at least maintained in the future. Other salaries could be settled in between to suit the union's system of grading.

This should allow these unions to employ competent qualified young men and women in their two or three specialist posts. Some of these men and women might ultimately aspire to higher and more remunerative posts. But if the unions experienced a 10% turnover here compared with 5% for other officers, it would not mean that they had failed, or their specialist work was not well done.

In all unions, salaries are determined by conferences or committees consisting entirely or almost entirely of lay members. These members may see no necessity for paying all, or even any of their full-time officers at a rate much higher than their own salaries or wages; and, indeed, it is often a hard struggle for a general secretary or president to win even a small concession from such bodies, even when he is convinced that an increase is vital to the organization.

[1] At the end of 1958.

For simplicity's sake we have written this chapter in terms of salaries alone, without reference to other emoluments. Almost all trade union officers derive some economic advantage from their positions in addition to their salaries, and, generally speaking, the amount increases with the importance of the position. Many university lecturers, of course, also earn more than their salaries, and they enjoy long holidays. This complicates the comparison, but it does not vitiate it.

[2] White Collar unions, especially those which include higher administrative grades, such as the National and Local Government Officers' Association, pay their senior officers at a higher rate than this. If they did not these officers would receive salaries far below those of a considerable number of the members whom they represent. This is a special case to which the arguments we have used have no direct application.

There is, however, another possibility for unions which prefer an extremely egalitarian salary structure. They can pay their specialist officers more than their general secretaries or presidents. In 1958, for example, the salaries of the senior members of the staff of the Amalgamated Engineering Union (including their Research Officer) were fixed (at the instance of the President) above his own salary.[1] In terms of other emoluments, of course, the President still had the advantage, but this is not the point. Trade unions have long employed the services of lawyers, and they have paid the rate for the job. If they want to employ competent specialists in other fields, and at the same time have an egalitarian salary structure for their full-time officers, there is no natural law to stop them—at least in those unions in which specialist officers are graded as staff.

Finally, the problem of persuading unions to pay adequate salaries to their full-time officers is not solved by the withdrawal of salaries from the publicity of union rule-books, and therefore from open determination by union members. It is not true that those unions which put them in the rules pay the lowest salaries. Differentials, on the whole, are lower in the unions which publish their salaries, but the Railwaymen find no necessary connection between openness and meanness. Since unions withdrew their salaries from the public eye (usually between the wars) most salaries have fallen relative to earnings, wages and prices, and the decline has not been greater in unions which publish their salaries. If anything, it has been the other way round. There are few discussions which benefit from an ignorance of the facts, and the discussion of trade union salaries in recent years would, in our view, have been the better for being informed.

---

[1] He is reported to have said: 'Because I am a poor negotiator for myself, that is no reason why I should be a bad employer to you.'

The Engineers' executive proposed a graduated series of increases to the Rules Revision Committee of 1960 which would have brought the minimum for District Secretaries to £950 and the President's salary to £1,500. One delegate stated that 'the officers of the A.E.U. are the poor relations of the trade union movement'. The left-wing members of the Committee argued for a flat-rate increase all round. As a result of a complicated series of amendments, the upshot was agreement to increase the salaries of the junior officers by £100 or £120, and the rejection of the proposals for the higher grades. Thus the salaries of some of the junior officers were higher than some of the senior officers. Subsequently the Committee was recalled. It once more rejected the Executive's proposals, but this time an amendment in favour of a flat-rate increase of £120 was accepted. Thus the President's salary became £1,300.

It is an interesting curiosity of British trade union structure that the majority of 28 to 26 against the Executive's proposal included the two delegates from the Communist-dominated Australian section of the union (which is for most purposes an independent organization). Had the vote been a tie there is no doubt that the President would have given his casting vote for the scheme.

CHAPTER 14

CONDITIONS OF WORK

PROFESSIONALISM

IN the earlier days of trade unionism officers liked to think of themselves as just an engineer or a miner or a carpenter who had been given the temporary job of speaking for his fellow workers, and, because of the volume of work, was having his wages covered by them for the time being, so that he could get on with the work full-time. That was the way many of their members thought of them, and their conditions were settled accordingly. Naturally enough, they were elected by those whom they were to represent. They were to have the accepted rate of wages together with an allowance to cover the special expenses of the work. They were to return to their jobs when their members failed to re-elect them, and they would then lose nothing from their service as a full-time officer because they had all that had been theirs before taking office.

Even in the nineteenth century this simple notion would not work. If a full-time officer failed to secure re-election he might not be able to find work at his trade even if he had not lost his skill after years away from the bench or the coal-face. On the other hand, he would be able to do his job better if he had not too many economic worries, so perhaps he should have a rather larger wage than an engineer or a miner, and maybe a house; and maybe there should be a pension for him when he came to the age at which he could no longer do the job?

As unions grew bigger, with larger complements of officers arranged in a graded hierarchy with offices, with equipment and staffs, all these considerations were reinforced. The distinctions between the member and the full-time officer were emphasized and with them came further distinctions in conditions of work. Nevertheless, the tradition lives on and it can be seen that many of the principles which once applied to full-time officers are now recalled when convenors of stewards find that their trade union work needs all their time. The convenor is to remain 'one of the boys' and to be treated as such except in so far as his job makes this utterly impossible. And trade union members and sometimes full-time officers themselves still think even of the full-time officers' job in the old terms. We have already quoted[1] the opinion of the officer who thought: 'The view of the members of my union (and I believe of most trade unionists) is that the General Secretary, Organizers and other full-time officials have the social standing of a skilled ... worker.'

At the other extreme the trade union officer may be regarded as a professional worker with a career as in any other profession. When the union wants another officer the appropriate committee finds and appoints the best man available. Thereafter he should be subject to the appropriate incentives and sanctions. He must be encouraged to give the best service possible to the union by conditions of service which enable him to do his job without worry or a sense of unfair treatment. He must have the best drawn out of him because he knows that success will be rewarded by promotion, so the union must have a structure of grades and salaries which make certain that opportunity will await the successful officer. If, on the other hand, incentives fail or the union has made a bad choice, then the officer must be dismissed, after clear warning, due notice and everything else that is needed to make sure that his treatment is fair.

Some unions can offer a closer approximation to professional conditions than others. Civil Service unions, for example, can closely follow the gradings, salaries and conditions of the Service in making provisions for their own officers. Skilled or Ex-Craft unions, however, are the most insistent on regarding the officer as another craftsman who happens to be doing a special job. Possibly the reason for the greater professionalism of the General unions and some Single-Industry unions is that from the beginning the differences between the capabilities required by a full-time post and by an ordinary unskilled or semi-skilled job emphasized the need to make special provisions for full-time officers.

The most successful union in terms of growth is the National Union of Public Employees. Between 1938 and 1958 total British trade union membership rose by about 57%. The Public Employees increased their number five-fold. The union has perhaps the most openly 'career' approach to union office of any in the country. The general secretary looks for bright young recruits wherever he can find them, inside or outside the union. Officers can be promoted on the salary scale regardless of the title of their office so long as they are doing their job well. Turnover cannot safely be compared with

[1] See p. 73.

figures for other unions because of the extremely rapid growth of
the officer-force to keep pace with membership, but of those who
left 15% have been dismissed and 60% have resigned. The record
of resignations is exceeded only by the National and Local Government Officers' Association, and the dismissal record only by the
Agricultural Workers.[1]

From this it might appear that professionalism pays; but there is
also evidence on the other side. Amongst other unions which have
grown rapidly are the Electrical Trades' Union (almost four-fold
their 1938 membership) and the Engineers (an increase of 150%).
Both unions follow the old craft practice of election and re-election,
low differentials between different grades of officers, and few or no
dismissals (1% in the Engineers, none amongst the Electricians).

The General unions come down rather hesitantly on the side of
professionalism and their record, although rather better than the
average (the Transport and General Workers and the General and
Municipal Workers have both approximately doubled since 1938)
is not so good as any mentioned so far. The unions with a really
poor growth record are those in declining industries like the railways or cotton, which shows that other factors than the ability of
union officers have their effect on growth.[2]

Consequently there is little evidence to determine what com-
promise between the two possible systems of conditions of service
is the best. Different compromises may yield good or bad results
according to the circumstances. Professionalism is most applicable
in White Collar unions and least in unions with a strong craft
tradition. Amongst Single-Industry unions what suits the Public
Employees would not suit the Mineworkers.

It does not follow, however, that unions would not do well to
review their own compromises and discover whether they have
made the choice which suits them best. It is possible, for example,
that opportunity for promotion explains the difference between the
officers of the Transport and General Workers, 73% of whom
would like their sons to be full-time union officers, and the other
General unions whose scores were 47% (General and Municipal
Workers) and 43% (Shop, Distributive and Allied Workers).[3] Over
the last five years an officer of the Transport and General Workers

[1] See Table 23. Other unions suggest that the bold approach of the Public Employees to
many problems of staffing and organization can be partly explained by its freedom from the
need to build and maintain large financial reserves against strikes. Its members are employed
in the public service, and are most unlikely to be involved in a major stoppage.
[2] See Appendix 6.   [3] See p. 71.

stood one chance in nine of a promotion, against chances of one in thirty-seven in the General and Municipal Workers and one in seventy-five in the Shop, Distributive and Allied Workers.

The dual nature of the full-time officers' job is also relevant to their organization in formal or informal associations. If an officer is just 'one of the boys' the suggestion of a National Trade Union Officers' Union would be as silly as a proposal for a National Union of Full-Time Convenors. If, on the other hand, his job is a career like any other there is every reason for a trade union of union officers, which would aim to improve the rewards and conditions of the profession.

THE HOURS OF WORK OF FULL-TIME OFFICERS

It is generally accepted that full-time officers are overworked. Officers themselves refer to their long hours, their lost evenings and week-ends, and the consequences on family life. Commentators on union affairs from Sidney and Beatrice Webb to modern newspaper correspondents have accepted the complaint at the valuation which trade union officers place upon it.

The replies to our questionnaires confirm that hours are long. Average hours were 57·2 and the 'typical' full-time officer spends three evenings a week and more than one week-end a month on union business. These figures are, of course, estimates made by officers themselves, and it is extremely unlikely that they would be guilty of an under-estimate, so that these figures can be taken as outside limits and the actual averages may well be less. Some officers may calculate that leaving home at 8 a.m. and returning at 10 p.m. constitutes a fourteen-hour day, even if they spend the morning on the Magistrates' Bench or at a Council meeting and manage to slip home for two or three hours in the afternoon before leaving for an evening meeting. Finally the intensity of work on the job must be considered. As we have already said, the pace of work in a trade union office is necessarily variable, and there are times of the year in most trade union offices when only small demands are made upon the officers and the staff.

Long hours deter some potential recruits. Amongst branch secretaries who would not have liked full-time posts, 10% gave the hours worked as their reason,[1] and amongst stewards the figure was 11%.[2] Hours may also have affected some who gave no reason or put other reasons first. Even so, they do not present a very serious picture. Part of the reason may be that, taking both their full-time occupation and their union activities as work, many branch secretaries and some shop stewards work longer hours than full-time officers. Amongst our samples the average time given to union business out of working hours was over eleven hours for branch secretaries and nearly five hours for shop stewards.[1] These figures also, of course, are estimates, but there is no reason to suppose that they are less accurate than the estimates of full-time officers. Assuming that their working hours at their full-time occupation stood at the average for adult males, which was 47·7 in October 1958,[2] the total working hours of branch secretaries in both capacities were nearly fifty-nine and for shop stewards over fifty-two. Our samples were heavily biased towards the larger branches and the busier stewards. Even so it is clear that many branch secretaries could gain leisure by promotion to a full-time post, and many stewards would not lose more than another evening a week. This must be qualified, however, by the consideration that much of the union work of a branch secretary is done at home with his family (even perhaps with the help of his family), whereas evening and week-end work for the full-time officer normally entails absence from home.

So far as our sample is concerned, long hours do not appear to cause as much trouble in the family as might be supposed. Only 1% of the full-time officers stated that their wife and family were 'very displeased' at the amount of time they spent on union work, and 16% 'moderately displeased'. As many as 50% were 'quite happy'.[3] However these figures should be interpreted they certainly do not suggest a disastrous state of affairs. And, indeed, many husbands who are not trade union officers manage to combine absence from home for three evenings a week and one week-end a month with domestic harmony.

All this suggests that the strain imposed on most trade union officers by long and irregular hours is commonly exaggerated; but our evidence also makes clear that a minority of union officers work exceedingly long hours. In our sample 17% worked more than sixty hours a week, and 6% more than seventy hours a week; 10% worked five or more evenings, and 9% worked three or four week-ends a month.[4]

[1] See pp. 120 and 154.   [2] *Ministry of Labour Gazette*, February 1959.
[3] See p. 74.   [4] See p. 65.

It is usual to say that long hours are unavoidable in trade union work. In order to do his work as a representative of his members and a representative of the executive committee to the members the union officer must meet his members and this entails evening and week-end work, just as does the job of a Member of Parliament or a local councillor. If a man finds the job of representing his fellow men satisfies him, he should be able to accept its inevitable disadvantages.

There is much truth in this, but the answers to our questionnaires suggest that it is by no means the whole truth. There is no reason to accept the long hours of one trade union officer as inevitable when other officers in the same union work no more than fifty hours a week, or even less.[1] In these circumstances a little intelligent co-operation between those responsible ought to do away with most instances of excessive hours (say above sixty a week) without too much trouble.

One of the major causes of excessive hours seems to be the practice of taking over branch secretaryships. There is very little to be said in favour of this arrangement, and a great deal against it, unless it is done as a permanent part of the officer's official duties with due relief from other business. It should be stopped, and in most unions it could be. It is common, for instance, in the Transport and General Workers and the Shop, Distributive and Allied Workers, but unknown or uncommon in the General and Municipal Workers. The only available explanation is that the General and Municipal Workers have not enough officers to make it possible for the branch secretary's job to be done in this way, but it is open to the other two unions, with their low ratios of members to officers, to take the easy way out.

Our local survey suggested that a number of branch secretaries are anxious to resign, but feel it is their duty to remain until a successor can be found. If they know the job can be done by a full-time officer, why hang on?

Admittedly there would be difficulties in weaning branches into independence once more, but the evidence suggests that the Transport and General Workers and the Shop, Distributive and Allied Workers could do it. The Agricultural Workers have a special problem because of their scattered membership and small branches, and they have experimented to find remedies. In 1959 they made one or two appointments of full-time officers who have taken over

[1] See p. 63.

responsibility for collecting contributions and carrying out clerical work for a number of branches, leaving the elected branch officers the task of convening and conducting meetings. So far, at least, the union regards the experiment as a success, and reports that the vitality of the branches concerned does not appear to have suffered.

This is a remedy which might in some instances be copied by other unions. Clearly if the work has to be done by a full-time officer there is much to be said for appointing a specialist who is a competent clerical worker. Another device which might work in some instances is to amalgamate a number of branches and allow them a full-time secretary.

This is not the only connection in which trade unions would do well to remember that their full-time officers are not normally trained clerical workers. The same criticism applies most of all to the Skilled unions, and therefore to the Building unions. White Collar union officers are likely to be competent in work of this kind, and a proportion of General union and even Single-Industry union officers come into office from clerical or supervisory posts; but in the Skilled unions the apprenticeship or other training and the previous experience of full-time officers normally has no connection with clerical work. It follows that these unions are paying high rates for inefficient clerical work, as well as discouraging their officers by requiring them to do work for which they are not suited. Ex-Craft unions, for the same reasons, should be careful about loading clerical work on to full-time officers, but they seem to be almost as ready to do so as the Skilled unions.

It is not easy for a union which relies on small-sized districts manned by one or two full-time officers to make satisfactory arrangements for clerical assistance. Something, however, can be done. The provision of a secretary at a regional office for one day a week might save much time and labour for those officers who have reasonable access to their regional centre. All financial business should be transferred to an office staffed to cope with it. And there are instances in which a union would be better and more cheaply served by one officer and one clerical worker rather than two officers, and other instances in which the cost of supplying a part-time clerical assistant to a harassed district officer would yield results more than sufficient to justify the cost. Finally, those unions which require their full-time officers to do a large volume of clerical business without providing them with the necessary office equipment are living in the wrong century.

The Job of the Branch Secretary

This section is confined to branch secretaries because we have discovered no cause for alarm over the morale or the job of shop stewards. Shop stewards do, of course, present a number of serious problems in the British trade union movement. Their close connection with unofficial strikes has attracted much attention. Whether their activities are provided for in union rules or not, their relationships with their union causes trouble, and few unions can be satisfied that they have adequate control over their stewards. Similarly there is a difficulty in integrating the workshop activities of the stewards with the official national negotiating procedures of the major industries in which shop stewards are to be found. But all these are problems outside the scope of this book.

There is more reason for concern over branch secretaries. The recruitment position is not wholly satisfactory, and it is far worse in some unions than in others.[1] The extent to which full-time officers have to take over the work of branch secretaries in some unions is also disquieting.[2]

We have tried to show a connection between the availability of candidates for the post of branch secretary and two other factors: the difficulty of recruiting and retaining members, and the volume of clerical work that a branch secretary has to do.[3] The assumptions behind the attempt to demonstrate these relationships is that it is disheartening for a man to face a continual struggle to maintain a constant, or worse, a declining membership, and that few men or women wish to spend most of their spare time filling in forms and financial returns and making the books balance. Negotiating with the management and supervisors, attending committee meetings and looking after the individual problems of union members is likely to be a more satisfying task than clerical work, and to give a sense of power and of accomplishment. Branch secretaries do all of these things, but some of them do relatively little, and their average comes far below that of shop stewards or full-time officers.

What are the remedies? The practice of the 'check-off' seems to yield at least two considerable advantages to the branch secretaries of the Mineworkers. Their secretaries are assured of their members and for the most part freed from financial business. Some leaders of the Mineworkers, however, are perturbed about the system. They think that the check-off undermines the union by destroying

[1] See p. 127.   [2] See p. 45.   [3] See p. 132.

the contact between the member and his branch officer. The need to collect the contribution provided an occasion for the secretary to give information to the member, and for the member to raise any queries and complaints with the secretary. Our evidence does not support this conclusion, for the Mineworkers' branch secretary appears to be able to spend far more of his time looking after his members' problems than the branch secretaries of other unions; and the organization of the mining industry makes the secretary far more accessible to his members at work, and often at home, than are the secretaries of other unions. It may still be the case that the Mineworkers' secretaries have poorer contacts with their members than before the check-off was instituted. Our evidence cannot settle the point, which would perhaps be best studied by a comparison between the state of affairs in Durham (which has no check-off) and other Areas.

The check-off might, however, have more undesirable effects in other industries than it has in mining. In the engineering industry, in which branch and workplace organization rarely coincide, the contact of the member with his branch secretary is normally through the shop steward. As we have seen, the majority of stewards collect from their members (whether or not they are collecting stewards) and pass the money on to the branch secretary. The check-off might endanger the system of relationships between the members, the shop stewards and the branch secretary. On the other hand, it is possible that its effect would be, where the union is already strong, as in the mining industry, to allow more time for looking after the individual problems of the members. Where communications within the unions are weak, however, the check-off would almost certainly render them weaker.

In any event this analysis is not much of a guide for action. The debate over the rights or wrongs of the check-off (and of the closed shop, with which it is normally, but not necessarily, associated) is not going to be settled on grounds of the convenience of branch secretaries. Those unions such as the building unions, whose branch secretaries seem to be in most urgent need of assistance, are not likely to be able to obtain a wide extension of the check-off for the asking.

The most obvious remedy is an improvement in accounting methods. Trade unions appear to have devised their branch accounting systems more with a view to keeping their funds than to keeping their branch secretaries. Whatever may have been the case at the time when the more archaic of these systems were devised, trade unions to-day have more to gain by improving the recruitment of branch secretaries than by making a marginal addition to the defences against defalcation. There are few unions which could not make some improvement in methods of collection, branch records and returns from the branch to district, regional and national offices, and some unions could do better in all three respects.[1]

In most White Collar unions the branch secretaries are saved from heavy financial responsibilities by the appointment of branch treasurers who take over this part of the work. Those manual workers' unions whose rules prescribe the election of a branch treasurer, however, provide little relief for the branch secretary, for the post usually carries negligible duties, or is normally held in plurality by the secretary.[2] In the nineteenth century the branch of a manual workers' union might have been lucky to find one man who could manage the correspondence and keep the books, but to-day some at least could find two competent men, and divide the clerical business of the union into two fairly equal parts.[3] If the branch secretary's work was thus divided, however, and the division was to be made effective, it would also be necessary to divide his honorarium or commission between the two officers in some equitable fashion. It is not unreasonable to expect that a man would prefer to give five hours of his spare time each week for 10s. than ten hours for £1. It is also possible that some unions might gain from spending rather more on their branch officers at the cost of reducing their full-time staffs, for union officers cannot achieve much if branch organization falls to pieces. Since, however, remuneration does not seem to be related to morale amongst branch secretaries,[4] this should not be necessary.

Other remedies are the provision of full-time branch secretaries, or the appointment of full-time branch clerical and financial officers such as the Agricultural Workers have recently made.[5] No more need be said about this latter device than that the experiment deserves close attention. There is more to be said about full-time secretaries. In most instances they cost more than part-time secretaries, but not always, and in the larger branches of unions which pay part-time

---

[1] These shortcomings are examined in Appendix 5.   [2] See p. 116.
[3] For all unions the score of financial work (including benefit claims and payments) was 32%, and for all other clerical work (correspondence, notices, minutes, etc.) 31%.
[4] See p. 136.   [5] See p. 108.

secretaries a fixed proportion of branch dues, the additional cost per member per week could be slight. Their appointment could also lead to a reduction in full-time officers, although not in proportion to the number of full-time secretaries. There is considerable room in most major unions for the appointment of full-time secretaries to large branches, and for the amalgamation of small branches to give a unit of the required size.[1] On the other hand, the small unions with a scattered membership must rely on part-time secretaries, and so must larger unions in many parts of the country. Moreover, there have been instances (for example, in the General and Municipal Workers, and in the Agricultural Workers) of the division of large branches into a number of small branches which has led to a big improvement in the vitality of branch life and the participation of members.

It would be foolish to be dogmatic about remedies. None that we have suggested can be guaranteed to yield results, and there may well be others. This much, however, can be said: there is good reason to suggest that most unions would do well to consider how to relieve the burdens on their branch secretaries, and they cannot claim that nothing can be done.

[1] Proposals to amalgamate branches, however, often meet strong opposition from active members.

CHAPTER 15

EDUCATION AND TRAINING

WE have said nothing in this study about the training and education of trade union officers, primarily because two of us have written at length on the subject elsewhere.[1] We did, however, include three questions on education for full-time officers and full-time branch secretaries, covering the type of training or education that they had received, its value, and what they felt their needs were. Answers to the first question showed that nearly all full-time officers have had some further education since leaving school. Only 6% of full-time officers and 3% of full-time secretaries had had none. Table 61 shows the experience of the rest.

The table shows that on the average trade union officers have attended three types of course since leaving school. In fact, 37% of full-time officers and of full-time secretaries had attended more than three types. The spread is wide and much the same for both groups. Full-time branch secretaries appear to have a preference for courses run by the National Council of Labour Colleges as against the Workers' Educational Association, whereas full-time officers choose the latter more frequently. This bias is increased by the greater proportion of full-time secretaries who take correspondence courses, for the large majority of correspondence courses for trade unionists are provided by the National Council of Labour Colleges.

Amongst full-time officers 68% had found the course 'very helpful', another 23% 'moderately helpful', but 65% thought more useful courses could have been devised. Amongst full-time secretaries 83% chose 'very helpful' and 13% 'moderately helpful'; 60% thought better courses could have been devised.

Their choice amongst the subjects they would like to see covered is given in Table 62.

Both groups give industrial law first place, which suggests that they feel a strong need for assistance in dealing with the problems of individual members. Thereafter full-time officers, whose major single duty is negotiation with employers, would like training in techniques of collective bargaining, whereas full-time branch secre-

---

[1] H. A. Clegg and Rex Adams, *Trade Union Education, A Report for the Workers' Educational Association*, 1959.

TABLE 61

FULL-TIME OFFICERS AND FULL-TIME BRANCH SECRETARIES:
EDUCATIONAL ACTIVITIES SINCE LEAVING SCHOOL

Type of Education	Proportion Attending	
	Full-Time Officers	Full-Time Branch Secretaries
Technical and Commercial College Courses	37%	30%
Correspondence Courses ..	56%	70%
National Council of Labour College Classes	39%	60%
Workers' Educational Association or University Extra-Mural Classes ..	51%	43%
Schools or Classes run by own Union	58%	63%
Trades Union Congress Courses	38%	30%
Ruskin College or other residential courses over three months	4%	3%
Other	26%	3%
TOTAL	309%	302%

taries, with their burden of clerical and administrative work, find the need for help with office routine and administration. Helping individual members is the most important single duty of the full-time branch secretary, and comes third for full-time officers (just behind correspondence). Negotiating is the first duty of the full-time officer. If the various clerical duties (financial correspondence, etc.) of the full-time branch secretary are taken together they exceed even helping individual members. It seems fairly clear, therefore, that both types of officer think that further training would help them and would prefer training of direct assistance to them in those

TABLE 62

FULL-TIME OFFICERS AND FULL-TIME BRANCH SECRETARIES:
PREFERENCE AMONG SUBJECTS FOR TRAINING

	Preference	
Subject	Among Full-Time Officers	Among Full-Time Branch Secretaries
Industrial Law	41%	37%
Techniques of Collective Bargaining	34%	20%
Economics	32%	17%
Public Expression ..	24%	20%
Management Studies ..	21%	10%
Office Routine and Administration	20%	27%
Wage and Other Agreements	8%	20%

aspects of their work which take up most of their time. It is, therefore, a fairly safe inference that, if training in these subjects could be provided, trade union officers could do their work more easily and could do a better job. The techniques of collective bargaining are not easily taught except in practice, and it would be difficult to find adequate tutors, but there is no great obstacle to providing sound assistance to trade union officers in industrial law and office routine; and trade union executives might ponder whether they do enough for their officers in this respect. It may be suggested that the potential advantages of appointing full-time branch secretaries might not be realized unless the candidates chosen were competent clerical workers.

We also included questions on education in our first questionnaire for lay officers.[1] Thirty-six per cent had not taken part in any educational activity since leaving school, except for the trade union course at which the questionnaire was distributed. The remainder

[1] See p. 233.

averaged about two week-end schools apiece and most had either attended a class or taken a correspondence course. The previous educational experience of lay officers attending trade union residential courses cannot, however, be taken as typical of all lay officers. Another question asked: 'Have you wished there existed a course to help with some particular part of your union work? What did you wish for?' Suggestions for specific subjects were made by 198 respondents and they are worth recording in detail.

TABLE 63

LAY OFFICERS: PREFERENCE AMONG SUBJECTS FOR TRAINING

Subject	Proportion in favour
Branch secretary's work (especially book-keeping); Branch officer's work; 'union procedures'	32
Negotiating, shop steward's duties ..	26
Public speaking, chairmanship and procedure	8
Arithmetic, spelling, grammar, etc. ..	6
Joint consultation	6
Training for full-time officers' work ..	6
Law	3
Others	13
TOTAL	100

The results underline the moral, now recognized by a number of unions, that lay officers need, and are anxious to find, basic training in the conduct of their union duties.

CHAPTER 16

POSTSCRIPT

THIS study has not defined, still less solved, any single 'problem of leadership' in British trade unions. Instead it has drawn attention to some of the many problems of British unions in connection with their officers.

There are problems of selection, problems of promotion, problems of salaries, problems of hours and conditions of work; there are problems of recruitment of branch secretaries; there are problems of maldistribution of work; there are problems of under-staffing and there are signs of over-staffing; and there are many other problems besides these.

Happily not all unions appear to experience the same problems in the same degree. Consequently, it is possible to seek for solutions by comparing the practices, rules and experience of one union with another. We have used this method to try to suggest improvements, and we hope that some of our suggestions will prove helpful and practical. But more important than any single proposal is the conclusion which we think we have established: that by this comparative method the unions can learn to solve their organizational problems in general, and in particular their problems concerning all classes of officer. There is not a union in this country which could not learn from others; and not a union which has not something which it could teach to others. But those who have something to show are often not aware of it; and, even if they are, they do not think of advertising it to others, or do not wish to. And those with something to learn are far too ready to cry that their problems are beyond the wit of man to solve, when all the time some kind of solution (which might at least take them part of the way) is right under their noses in the trade union next door, waiting for them to come and seek it out.

British trade unions have rightly earned the reputation of being wedded to tradition. Their governing committees and conferences frequently prefer to live with their problems rather than to venture into unfamiliar solutions; but they should not be allowed the excuse that no solutions are available.

A. QUESTIONNAIRE FOR FULL-TIME OFFICERS

THE following questionnaire is designed to provide accurate information about union officials which, together with questionnaires from other union officers, will help to create a balanced and informed public opinion. All information about individuals will be kept strictly confidential and the report on this investigation will simply contain statistical summaries of the answers, from which it will be impossible to identify the answers of any individual.

Please answer each question, using the back of the page for any comments you may wish to make.

---

1. Date to-day ....   2. Your age ....
3. Union ....   4. Male or female ....
5. What is your present union post? ....
6. In what town or county do you live? ....
7. What did you do for a living before you became an official? ....
8. How long have you been in your present union? ....
9. At what age did you hold your first voluntary union office? ....
10. What lay offices did you hold *immediately prior* to becoming an official? ....
11. What, if any, other full-time union posts have you had? Please give approximate date of appointment or election to each office. If none, state none.
12. Would you be disappointed if you were not promoted or elected to a higher post in your union before you retire? ....
    If so, would you like to hold the top post in your union? ....
13. Here is a list of trade union aims. Which do you think should be given priority? Please mark *up to three* (mark 1, 2, 3) in order of preference.
    .... Helping members with their individual problems
    .... Higher wages and better conditions
    .... Effective consultation with management at all levels
    .... Creating political consciousness amongst members
    .... 100% organization
    .... Creating unity between all workers
    .... The fullest use by rank and file members of the democratic procedures of the union

14. At what age did you leave school? ....

15. At what sort of school did you finish your full-time education? (Please tick as appropriate from the following list *or write in.*)
.... Elementary or secondary modern
.... Technical
.... Secondary grammar

16. Have you taken part in any of the following educational activities since then? If none, state none. (Please tick *or write in.*)
.... Technical or commercial college courses
.... Correspondence courses
.... W.E.A. or Extra-Mural classes
.... N.C.L.C. classes
.... Schools or courses run by your own union
.... T.U.C. courses
.... Ruskin or other residential courses over three months
.... Any other ....

17. Has this proved helpful to you since as a union official? (Please tick.)
.... Very helpful
.... Moderately helpful
.... Not helpful

18. Could more helpful courses have been devised? ....
If so, what other subjects would you like to see covered? (Please tick *or write in.*)
.... Management Studies
.... Office routine and administration
.... Techniques of collective bargaining
.... Wage and other agreements
.... Economics
.... Industrial law
.... Public expression

19. How many hours do you normally spend on union work in a week?
.... hours

20. How many evenings do you normally spend on union work in a week?
.... evenings

21. How many week-ends do you normally spend on union work in a month? (If less than one a month, please state how often.)
....

22. Please mark from the following list the four *duties* which take up most of your time (mark 1, 2, 3, 4). *Other duties can be written in if necessary.*
.... Attending Branch Meetings
.... Other meetings
.... Financial work

.... Correspondence
.... Other office work
.... Negotiating
.... Recruiting new members
.... Helping members with their individual problems

23. Do you act as Branch Secretary for any Branches? ....
    If so, for how many Branches? ....

24. What is the reaction of your wife or family to the amount of time you spend on union work? (Please tick as appropriate.)
    .... Quite happy
    .... Not at all or only slightly displeased
    .... Moderately displeased
    .... Very displeased

25. Does the union employ a secretary to help you? ....

26. Do you have a car? ....
    If so, did you (a) receive help from the union in buying it? ....
                OR (b) pay for it without assistance from the union?
                ....

27. Please tick or write in other equipment provided for you by the union. If none, state none.
    .... Typewriter
    .... Duplicator
    .... Telephone
    .... Filing cabinet

28. Would you be pleased if your son became a union official? ....
    Please give reasons:

29. Here is a list of occupations ranged according to the generally accepted view of their *social standing*. Please examine this and indicate WHAT YOU THINK WOULD BE THE GENERALLY ACCEPTED VIEW *of the social standing* of the General Secretary of your own union, by writing in 'G.S.' at the appropriate point in the list.
    Would you then indicate WHAT YOU THINK WOULD BE THE GENERALLY ACCEPTED VIEW of the social standing of your own post, by writing in 'own post'.

    1. Medical Officer of Health
    2. Company Director
    3. Country Solicitor
    4. Chartered Accountant
    5. Civil Servant (Executive Grade)
    6. Nonconformist Minister
    7. Business Manager
    8. Works' Manager
    9. Farmer
    10. Elementary School Teacher
    11. Jobbing Master Builder
    12. News Reporter
    13. Commercial Traveller
    14. Chef
    15. Insurance Agent
    16. Newsagent and Tobacconist
    17. Policeman
    18. Routine Clerk

19. Fitter	25. Railway Porter
20. Carpenter	26. Barman
21. Shop Assistant	27. Agricultural Labourer
22. Bricklayer	28. Carter
23. Tractor Driver	29. Dock Labourer
24. Coal Hewer	30. Road Sweeper

MANY THANKS FOR YOUR CO-OPERATION

B. QUESTIONNAIRE FOR FULL-TIME BRANCH SECRETARIES

The following questionnaire is designed to provide accurate information about full-time Branch Secretaries which, together with questionnaires from other union officers, will help to create a balanced and informed public opinion. All information about individuals will be kept strictly confidential and the report on this investigation will simply contain statistical summaries of the answers, from which it will be impossible to identify the answers of any individual.

Please answer each question, using the back of the page for any comments you may wish to make.

1. Date to-day............   2. Your age............
3. Union............   4. Male or female............
5. In what town or county do you live?............
6. What did you do for a living before you became a full-time Branch Secretary?............
7. At what age did you leave school?............
8. At what sort of school did you finish your full-time education? (Please tick from the following list *or write in.*)
   .... Elementary or secondary modern
   .... Technical
   .... Secondary grammar
9. How long have you been a member of your present union?............
10. How long have you been Branch Secretary?............
11. How long have you been *full-time* Branch Secretary?............
12. Do you hold any other union offices? (e.g. District Committee, etc.). If so, what are they?
13. How many members are there in your Branch?............

14. Approximately what proportion of these are women? (Please tick.)
.... Less than 10%
.... Between 10% and 30%
.... Between 30% and 60%
.... Over 60%

15. Is your Branch membership drawn from:
.... a single place of work
.... a single employer with more than one place of work
.... two or more employers

16. Here is a list of trade union aims. Which do you think should be given priority? Please mark *up to three* (mark 1, 2, 3) in order of preference.
.... Helping members with their individual problems
.... Higher wages and better conditions
.... Effective consultation with management at all levels
.... Creating political consciousness amongst members
.... 100% organization
.... Creating unity between all workers
.... The fullest use by rank and file members of the democratic procedures of the union

17. How many hours do you normally spend on union work in a week? .... hours

18. How many evenings do you normally spend on union work in a week? ....

19. How many week-ends do you normally spend on union work in a month? (If less than one a month, please state how often) ....

20. Please mark in order from the following list the *four* duties which take up most of your time (mark 1, 2, 3, 4). *Other duties can be written in if necessary.*
.... Financial work
.... Arrears and meeting notices
.... Membership transfers and the Branch register
.... Benefit claims and payments
.... Other correspondence
.... Branch minutes
.... Helping members with their individual problems
.... Meetings
.... Negotiating
.... Recruiting new members and collecting individual contributions

21. What is the reaction of your wife or family to the amount of time you spend on union work? (Please tick as appropriate.)

.... Quite happy
.... Not at all or only slightly displeased
.... Moderately displeased
.... Very displeased

22. Does the Branch or union employ a secretary to help you? ....

23. Do you have a car? ....
If so, did you (a) receive help from the Branch or union in buying it? ....
OR (b) pay for it without assistance from the Branch or union? ....

24. Please tick *or write in* other equipment provided for you by the Branch or union. If none, state none.

.... Typewriter
.... Duplicator
.... Telephone
.... Filing cabinet

25. Have you taken part in any of the following educational activities since leaving school? (Please tick *or write in*.) If none, state none.

.... Technical or commercial college courses
.... Correspondence courses
.... W.E.A. or Extra-Mural classes
.... N.C.L.C. classes
.... Schools or classes run by your own union
.... T.U.C. courses
.... Ruskin or other residential courses over three months
.... Any other ....

26. Has this proved helpful to you since as Branch Secretary? (Please tick.)

.... Very helpful
.... Moderately helpful
.... Not helpful

27. Could more helpful courses have been devised? ....
If so, what other subjects would you like to see covered? (Please tick *or write in*.)

.... Management studies
.... Office routine and administration
.... Techniques of collective bargaining
.... Wage and other agreements
.... Economics
.... Industrial law
.... Public expression

28. If you were to resign as Branch Secretary do you think there would be anyone willing to take over? ....

29. In your experience, is the ability of your Branch to get a full complement of officers:

   .... Getting harder
   .... Remaining about the same
   .... Getting easier

30. If you do not already do so, would you be willing to serve on higher union committees (e.g. District, Regional and National) if the opportunity arose? ....

31. How often do you meet a District, Regional or National union official on union business? (Please tick as appropriate.)

   .... Once or more times a week
   .... Between once a week and once a month
   .... Between once a month and once a year
   .... Less than once a year

32. Would you be pleased if your son became a full-time union official? Please give reasons.

33. Here is a list of occupations ranged according to the generally accepted view of their *social standing*. Please examine this and indicate WHAT YOU THINK WOULD BE THE GENERALLY ACCEPTED VIEW of the social standing of the General Secretary of your union, by writing in 'G.S.' at the appropriate point in the list.

  Would you then indicate WHAT YOU THINK WOULD BE THE GENERALLY ACCEPTED VIEW of the social standing of your own post, by writing in 'own post'.

1. Medical Officer of Health	16. Newsagent and Tobacconist
2. Company Director	17. Policeman
3. Country Solicitor	18. Routine Clerk
4. Chartered Accountant	19. Fitter
5. Civil Servant (Executive Grade)	20. Carpenter
6. Nonconformist Minister	21. Shop Assistant
7. Business Manager	22. Bricklayer
8. Works' Manager	23. Tractor Driver
9. Farmer	24. Coal Hewer
10. Elementary School Teacher	25. Railway Porter
11. Jobbing Master Builder	26. Barman
12. News Reporter	27. Agricultural Labourer
13. Commercial Traveller	28. Carter
14. Chef	29. Dock Labourer
15. Insurance Agent	30. Road Sweeper

MANY THANKS FOR YOUR CO-OPERATION

C. QUESTIONNAIRE FOR BRANCH SECRETARIES
(OTHER THAN FULL-TIME)

The following questionnaire is designed to provide accurate information about Branch Secretaries which, together with questionnaires from other union officers, will help to create a balanced and informed public opinion. All information about individuals will be kept strictly confidential and the report on this investigation will simply contain statistical summaries of the answers, from which it will be impossible to identify the answers of any individual.

Please answer each question, using the back of the page for any comments you may wish to make.

———————

1. Date to-day...........　　　　　2. Your age............

3. Union............　　　　　　　　4. Male or female............

5. In what town or county do you live?............

6. What do you do for a living?............

7. What *Branch* office(s) do you hold? Please indicate how long you have held each office (e.g. 'Secretary 2½ years').

8. At what age did you leave school?............

9. At what sort of school did you finish your full-time education? (Please tick from the following list *or write in.*)
.... Elementary or secondary modern
.... Technical
.... Secondary grammar

9A. How long have you been in your present union?............

10. Do you hold any other union offices? (e.g. Shop Steward, District Committee, etc.). If so, what are they?

11. How many members are there in your Branch?............

12. Approximately what proportion of these are women? (Please tick.)
.... Less than 10%
.... Between 10% and 30%
.... Between 30% and 60%
.... Over 60%

13. Is your Branch membership drawn from:
.... a single place of work
.... a single employer with more than one place of work
.... two or more employers

14. Here is a list of trade union aims. Which do you think should be given priority? Please mark *up to three* (1, 2, 3) in order of preference.
.... Helping members with their individual problems
.... Higher wages and better conditions
.... Effective consultation with management at all levels
.... Creating political consciousness amongst members
.... 100% organization
.... Creating unity between all workers
.... The fullest use by rank and file members of the democratic procedures of the union

15. How many hours do you normally spend on *Branch* work in a week?
(a) within working hours .... hours
(b) in your own time .... hours

16. Please mark in order from the following list the *four* duties which take up most of your time (mark 1, 2, 3, 4). *Other duties can be written in if necessary.*
.... Financial work
.... Arrears and meeting notices
.... Membership transfers and the Branch register
.... Benefit claims and payments
.... Other correspondence
.... Branch minutes
.... Helping members with their individual problems
.... Meetings
.... Negotiating

17. Do you suffer any loss of pay as a result of union activity? ....
If so, about how much in an average week? ....

18. How much payment do you normally receive as Branch secretary in a quarter? ....

19. What is the reaction of your wife or family to the amount of time you spend on union work? (Please tick.)
.... Quite happy
.... Not at all or only slightly displeased
.... Moderately displeased
.... Very displeased

20. If you were to resign as Branch secretary do you think there would be anyone willing to take over? ....

21. In your experience, is the ability of your Branch to get a full complement of officers:

.... Getting harder

.... Remaining about the same

.... Getting easier

22. If you do not already do so, would you be willing to serve on higher union committees (e.g. District, Regional and National), if the opportunity arose? ....

23. Do you think you would like to become a paid union official?.........
Please give reasons:

24. How often do you meet a full-time union official on union business? (Please tick as appropriate.)

.... Once or more times a week

.... Between once a week and once a month

.... Between once a month and once a year

.... Less than once a year

25. Here is a list of occupations ranged according to the generally accepted view of their *social standing*. Please examine this and indicate WHAT YOU THINK WOULD BE THE GENERALLY ACCEPTED VIEW of the *social standing* of the average local full-time union official, by writing in the word 'official' at the appropriate point in the list.

(NOTE: If you are a member of a union which does not have local officials please indicate the position of the junior officials at head office.)

Would you then indicate WHAT YOU THINK WOULD BE THE GENERALLY ACCEPTED VIEW of the social standing of your own job, by writing in 'own job'.

1. Medical Officer of Health	16. Newsagent and Tobacconist
2. Company Director	17. Policeman
3. Country Solicitor	18. Routine Clerk
4. Chartered Accountant	19. Fitter
5. Civil Servant (Executive Grade)	20. Carpenter
6. Nonconformist Minister	21. Shop Assistant
7. Business Manager	22. Bricklayer
8. Works' Manager	23. Tractor Driver
9. Farmer	24. Coal Hewer
10. Elementary School Teacher	25. Railway Porter
11. Jobbing Master Builder	26. Barman
12. News Reporter	27. Agricultural Labourer
13. Commercial Traveller	28. Carter
14. Chef	29. Dock Labourer
15. Insurance Agent	30. Road Sweeper

26. If you were to become a local full-time union official do you think your *social standing* would:

.... Go up a great deal .... Go down a little
.... Go up considerably .... Go down considerably
.... Go up a little .... Go down a great deal
.... Remain about the same

27. If you were to become a local full-time union official do you think your *earnings,* as compared with your present pay, would:

.... Go up a great deal .... Go down a little
.... Go up considerably .... Go down considerably
.... Go up a little .... Go down a great deal
.... Remain about the same .... Don't know

MANY THANKS FOR YOUR CO-OPERATION

D. QUESTIONNAIRE FOR SHOP STEWARDS AND OTHER WORKERS' REPRESENTATIVES

The following questionnaire is designed to provide accurate information about shop stewards which, together with questionnaires from other union officers, will help to create a balanced and informed public opinion. All information about individuals will be kept strictly confidential and the report on this investigation will simply contain statistical summaries of the answers, from which it will be impossible to identify the answers of any individual.

Please answer each question, using the back of the page for any comments you may wish to make. For the sake of convenience several of the questions refer to shop stewards. If you are a different kind of representative (e.g. convenor, printing chapel officer, etc.) please answer the questions just the same. Your answer to Question 5 will show what office you hold.

----

1. Date to-day ....   2. Your age ....

3. Union ....   4. Male or female ....

5. What office(s) do you hold in your union? ....

6. In what industry do you work? ....

7. What do you do for a living? ....

R

8. About how many people are employed at your place of work? (Please tick from the following list.)

    .... Over 10,000
    .... 2,000 to 10,000
    .... 500 to 2,000
    .... 100 to 500
    .... Under 100

9. In what town or county are you at present working? ....

10. At what age did you leave school? ....

11. At what sort of school did you finish your full-time education? (Please tick from the following list *or write in*.)

    .... Elementary or secondary modern
    .... Technical
    .... Secondary grammar

12. How long have you been in your present union? ....

13. Here is a list of trade union aims. Which do you think should be given priority? Please mark *up to three* (1, 2, 3) in order of preference.

    .... Helping members with their individual problems
    .... Higher wages and better conditions
    .... Effective consultation with management at all levels
    .... Creating political consciousness amongst members
    .... 100% organization
    .... Creating unity between all workers
    .... The fullest use by rank and file members of the democratic procedures of the union.

14. How long have you been a steward? ....

15. Are you subject to regular re-election? ....

16. Have you been opposed (*a*) when first elected ....
                               (*b*) on coming up for re-election ....

17. If you were to resign as shop steward do you think there would be anyone else to take your place? ....

18. How many hours do you *normally* spend on your duties as shop steward in a week?

        (*a*) within working hours   .... hours
        (*b*) in your own time   .... hours

19. Please mark in order from the following list the *three* duties which take up most of your time (mark 1, 2, 3). *Other duties can be written in if necessary.*

.... Discussions with members and shop stewards

.... Rate fixing

.... Taking up grievances with foremen

.... Negotiations with management above foreman level

.... Works' Committee and Joint Consultation Committee, etc.

.... Other meetings

.... Correspondence

20. Do you also collect union contributions? ....

21. For how many members are you personally responsible? ....

22. Do you suffer any loss of pay as a result of your union activities? ....
If so, about how much in an average week? ....

23. Does the management place restrictions in your way which *seriously* hamper you in carrying out your duties as shop steward?

24. In your experience, has there been a case of victimization of shop stewards in your place of work during the last ten years?

25. Are there any other unions with considerable memberships in your place of work? ....
If so, what are they? ....

26. Do *any* workers in your place of work have to be union members in order to keep their jobs? ....
If so, does this apply:

.... In all departments

.... In most departments

.... In only a few departments

Does it apply in your own department? ....

27. Do you serve on any higher union committees? (e.g. District, Regional and National) ....
If not, would you be willing to do so if the opportunity arose? ....

28. Do you think you would like to become a paid union official? ....
Please give reasons:

29. How often do you meet a full-time official on union business? (Tick as appropriate.)

.... Once a week or more often

.... Between once a week and once a month

.... Between once a month and once a year

.... Less than once a year

30. Here is a list of occupations ranged according to the generally accepted view of their social standing. Please examine this and indicate WHAT YOU THINK WOULD BE THE GENERALLY ACCEPTED VIEW of the *social standing* of the average local full-time union official, by writing in the word 'official' at the appropriate point in the list.

(NOTE: If you are a member of a union which does not have local officials please indicate the position of the junior officials at head office.)

Would you then indicate WHAT YOU THINK WOULD BE THE GENERALLY ACCEPTED VIEW of the social standing of your own job, by writing in 'own job'.

1. Medical Officer of Health
2. Company Director
3. Country Solicitor
4. Chartered Accountant
5. Civil Servant (Executive Grade)
6. Nonconformist Minister
7. Business Manager
8. Works' Manager
9. Farmer
10. Elementary School Teacher
11. Jobbing Master Builder
12. News Reporter
13. Commercial Traveller
14. Chef
15. Insurance Agent
16. Newsagent and Tobacconist
17. Policeman
18. Routine Clerk
19. Fitter
20. Carpenter
21. Shop Assistant
22. Bricklayer
23. Tractor Driver
24. Coal Hewer
25. Railway Porter
26. Barman
27. Agricultural Labourer
28. Carter
29. Dock Labourer
30. Road Sweeper

31. If you were to become a local full-time official do you think your *social standing* would:

.... Go up a great deal

.... Go up considerably

.... Go up a little

.... Remain about the same

.... Go down a little

.... Go down considerably

.... Go down a great deal

32. If you were to become a local full-time union official do you think
   your earnings, as compared with your present pay, would:

   .... Go up a great deal
   .... Go up considerably
   .... Go up a little
   .... Remain about the same
   .... Go down a little
   .... Go down considerably
   .... Go down a great deal
   .... Don't know

   MANY THANKS FOR YOUR CO-OPERATION

E. QUESTIONNAIRE FOR PERSONNEL OFFICERS

This questionnaire forms part of an inquiry into trade union officers
(full-time and lay) which several members of this College have been
conducting over the last three years. The bulk of the information has
been collected from the records of the major unions, by local surveys,
and by questionnaires distributed on a national basis to the main classes
of trade union officer. This information, however, cannot supply an
independent assessment of the relative quality and competence of trade
union officers. An assessment of this kind is desirable both for its own
interest, and to allow judgments to be made about different systems of
selecting and training officers, and similar matters. The only class of
people who are in a position to make an informed judgment are personnel
officers who regularly deal with several unions. It would, therefore, be of
great assistance to the inquiry if you would give your answers to the
following questions.

The questionnaire is entirely personal and confidential. No information
relating to individuals or to firms will be published. The report of the
inquiry will contain statistical summaries of the answers from which it
will be impossible to identify the source of any particular answer.

A stamped and addressed envelope is provided for your reply.

---

1. In what area of the country do you work? Please tick as appropriate
   from the following list:

   .... London Area
   .... South of England
   .... Midlands
   .... North of England
   .... Scotland
   .... Wales
   .... Ireland

2. Please list the trade unions with whose full-time officers you have regular contact according to your assessment of the all-round competence of those officers at their jobs (placing the union with the most competent officers first):

      1. ....
      2. ....
      3. ....
      4. ....
      5. ....
      6. ....
      7. ....
      8. ....
      9. ....
    10. ....

3. Please list the trade unions with whose lay officers (shop stewards, branch secretaries, etc.) you have regular contact according to your assessment of the all-round competence of those officers in their trade union posts (placing the union with the most competent lay officers first):

      1. ....
      2. ....
      3. ....
      4. ....
      5. ....
      6. ....
      7. ....
      8. ....
      9. ....
    10. ....

4. Please mark in order of priority (1, 2, 3, 4) the *four* qualities on the following list which you think most important in making your assessments of the competence of trade union officers in answer to Questions 2 and 3. Write in other qualities if necessary.

.... Honesty
.... Ability to control his or her members
.... Skill in negotiations
.... Willingness to accept new ideas
.... Devotion to the principles of trade unionism
.... Intelligence
.... Good contact with his or her members
.... Readiness to talk matters over with management
.... Concern to uphold procedure agreements and undertakings with management
....

5. When either is competent to settle an issue, do you prefer to deal with a full-time official or with a lay official? Please give reasons for your answer.

MEMBERSHIP OF BRITISH TRADE UNIONS

THE only handy source of trade union membership figures is the annual report of the Trades Union Congress, and this covers the membership only of affiliated unions. The Chief Registrar of Friendly Societies collects annual returns from registered unions, but since 1914 has only published totals of membership.

We obtained from his office the membership figures required for this study. Many were the same as those in the Trades Union Congress reports, but a number were different and some of the discrepancies were large. Both for the Engineers and the Mineworkers they exceeded 100,000.

The Registrar's office referred us to the unions for explanations. The major explanation for the Engineers is overseas membership which is returned to the Registrar, but excluded from the Trades Union Congress returns. The Mineworkers exclude members performing national service, retired miners and the widows or orphans of deceased miners, who are retained on the books for certain benefit purposes, and returned to the Registrar.

This second reason applies to several other unions. For instance, the Iron and Steel Trades' Confederation's returns to the Trades Union Congress exclude superannuated and retired members, and also 'an estimated number of lapsed members in respect of whom our records have not been adjusted'.

Since we have used membership figures to construct ratios of different classes of officers to members we are interested in those members who actually make a call on the time of officers. Thus overseas membership covered by its own officers, and retired members or widows and orphans, should be excluded. To do so in every case, however, was not possible. Each union has its own arrangements about who is kept on the books, so that the concept of union membership, in fact, differs from one union to another.

To cut through our problems we have accepted the membership figures as accurate where Trades Union Congress returns and Registrar's returns agree. Where they do not we asked the union concerned to explain the discrepancy, and if the reasons were those of the Engineers, Mineworkers, or Iron and Steel Workers, we accepted the lower Trades Union Congress figure. Two unions remained and in these we accepted the union's view on what constituted a reasonably accurate run of figures.

This seemed the best course in the circumstances, but we could not avoid the conclusion that greater effort could be made to present accurate information to the public.

CATEGORIES OF TRADE UNIONS

SKILLED UNIONS

Blacksmiths' Forge and Smithy Workers, Associated
Boilermakers, Shipbuilders and Structural Workers, United Society of
Coppersmiths, Braziers and Metal Workers, National Society of
Cotton Spinners and Twiners, Amalgamated Association of Operative
Elastic Web Weavers
File Trades, Sheffield Amalgamated Union of
Gold, Silver and Allied Trades, National Union of
Lithographic Printers, Amalgamated Society of
Locomotive Engineers and Firemen, Associated Society of
Metal Mechanics, National Society of
Painters, National Society of
Patternmakers' Association, United
Plumbing Trades Union
Post Office Engineering Union
Power Loom Overlookers, Yorkshire Association of
Printing Machine Managers
Sheet Metal Workers and Braziers, National Union of
Shipconstructors' and Shipwrights' Association
Slaters, Tilers and Roofing Operatives, Amalgamated
Stove, Grate and General Metal Workers, National Union of
Typographical Association
Typographical Association, Scottish
Typographical Society, London
Woodcutting Machinists, Amalgamated Society of
Woodworkers, Amalgamated Society of

EX-CRAFT UNIONS

Building Trade Workers of Great Britain and Ireland, Amalgamated
    Union of
Electrical Trades Union
Engineering Union, Amalgamated
Foundry Workers, Amalgamated Union of
Printing, Bookbinding and Paper Workers, National Union of
Vehicle Builders, National Union of

SINGLE-INDUSTRY UNIONS

Agricultural Workers, National Union of
Bakers, Confectioners and Allied Workers, Amalgamated Union of
    Operative
Blastfurnacemen, Ore Miners, Coke Workers, and Kindred Trades,
    National Union of
Boot and Shoe Operatives, National Union of
Card, Blowing, and Ring Room Operatives, National Association of
Constructional Engineering Union
Fire Brigades Union
Furniture Trade Operatives, National Union of
Health Service Employees, Confederation of
Horse and Motormen's Association, Scottish
Hosiery Workers, National Union of
Iron and Steel Trades Confederation
Mineworkers, National Union of
Post Office Workers, Union of
Pottery Workers, National Society of
Printers and Assistants, National Society of Operative
Public Employees, National Union of
Railwaymen, National Union of
Seamen, National Union of
Tailors and Garment Workers, National Union of
Tobacco Workers' Union
Watermen, Lightermen, Tugmen and Bargemen's Union
Weavers' Association, Amalgamated
Wire Drawers and Kindred Workers, Amalgamated Society of

GENERAL UNIONS

General and Municipal Workers, National Union of
Shop, Distributive and Allied Workers, Union of
Transport and General Workers' Union

WHITE COLLAR UNIONS

Civil Servants, Society of
Civil Service Clerical Association
Clerical and Administrative Workers' Union
Colliery Overmen, Deputies and Shotfirers, National Association of
Draughtsmen, Association of Engineering and Shipbuilding[1]
Musicians' Union
National and Local Government Officers' Association

[1] This union is now (1960) in process of changing its name to the Draughtsmen's and Allied Technicians' Association.

WHITE COLLAR UNIONS (*continued*)

Post Office Controlling Officers, Association of
Radio Officers' Union
Scientific Workers, Association of
Teachers, National Union of
Technical Civil Servants, Society of
Transport Salaried Staffs' Association

UNCLASSIFIED

Building Trade Operatives, National Federation of

APPENDIX 4

TABLE 64

NUMBER OF FULL-TIME OFFICERS BY UNION

	T.G.W.U.	A.E.U.	N.U.G.M.W.	N.U.M.	N.U.R.	U.S.D.A.W.[1]	N.A.L.G.O.	E.T.U.	N.U.A.W.	A.W.A.	N.U.B.S.O.	N.U.P.E.	I.S.T.C.	A.U.B.T.W.	C.S.C.A.	T.S.S.A.	N.U.P.B.P.W.
1921	—	36	—	—	14	115	—	—	—	—	—	—	26	—	—	14	—
1927	—	43	127	—	17	109	—	—	—	—	50	—	28	—	—	14	—
1933	—	32	114	—	16	118	—	18	23	—	58	3	16	—	—	14	—
1939	—	31	130	—	19	122	—	22	26	—	59	19	19	—	7	11	11
1945	504	95	127	76	19	114	—	30	40	—	51	26	19	50	11	13	13
1947	534	109	136	88	20	134	54	32	44	42	58	32	18	52	12	14	13
1951	573	138	151	91	23	136	60	42	46	39	54	37	21	56	12	14	15
1953	566	136	152	93	23	152	63	44	45	42	53	37	20	70	13	14	14
1957	558	138	146	93	23	147	60	45	49	43	51	46	20	71	13	13	14
1959	551	140	148	93	22	147	67	47	50	39	46	46	22	74	13	13	15

[1] Early figures approximate.

254

BRANCH BOOK-KEEPING SYSTEMS

THE answers to our questionnaire for branch secretaries showed us that their financial business was the most time-consuming part of their work.[1] We therefore sought more detailed information from nine unions—all the Big Six except the Mineworkers (whose 'check-off' arrangements reduce their financial business considerably), the National and Local Government Officers, the Printing, Bookbinding and Paperworkers, the Association of Engineering and Shipbuilding Draughtsmen, and the National Union of Vehicle Builders. Information was obtained by interviews with branch secretaries and treasurers, supplemented where necessary by visits to regional or national offices.

Their systems are almost as diverse as the unions themselves. Some are carefully planned and up-to-date. Others are old and less streamlined. One has remained virtually unchanged for forty years. Branch practices vary within unions. One branch secretary was keeping duplicate copies of each collector's book, entailing much work to no purpose, because he had taken them over from his predecessor. All systems, however, require some method of collecting contributions, returns to national or regional offices, and some sort of branch records. We will therefore consider them under these headings.

Collecting

All the branches which we covered had collectors except for a branch of the Engineers which had arranged a 'check-off' with the employer concerned. The Engineers' collecting system is unofficial, however, since the rules prescribe individual payment. The other unions have officially appointed branch collectors, some paid, some unpaid.

Most unions collect contributions weekly or fortnightly. In the Railwaymen contributions are collected as often as branch meetings, and these may be held once a week or once a fortnight, but are normally held monthly. The two White Collar unions (the National and Local Government Officers and the Draughtsmen) pay monthly contributions.

The frequency of collection from the members does not necessarily determine the frequency of payments from collector to secretary. In most unions this is done once a month, but the rules of several unions (including the Transport and General Workers) prescribe fortnightly remittances, whereas the General and Municipal Workers require only

[1] See Tables 32A and B.

quarterly payments. In one branch of the Shop, Distributive and Allied Workers some collectors paid each week or each fortnight, and others once a quarter because they lived at a considerable distance from the secretary.

The more frequent the payments made by members the heavier the work of collectors. At one time monthly payment might have placed a severe strain on the lower-paid worker, and it is significant that intervals are generally longer in the White Collar unions. Now, however, the decline in union dues relative to earnings has reduced this danger. If many branches of the Railwaymen can afford monthly payment, there are few unions which could not do the same.

From the branch secretary's point of view it is the frequency of collectors' remittances which determine the volume of work—the checking of collectors' books, entering their returns and chasing lax collectors. One branch secretary had to see thirty collectors each week to agree their payments. If the General and Municipal Workers find they do not need to insist on payment more often than once a quarter, perhaps other unions could abandon weekly and fortnightly remittances.

RETURNS

The frequency of returns required from the branch in each of the nine unions is shown in Table 65.

TABLE 65

FREQUENCY OF BRANCH RETURNS

Union	Type of Return	Annual Number of Returns
T. & G.W.U.	Weekly or Fortnightly, Quarterly	30 or 56
A.E.U. ..	Fortnightly, Quarterly, Half-Yearly	32
N.U.G.M.W.	Weekly, Quarterly	56
N.U.R. ..	Quarterly, Half-Yearly, Annual	7
U.S.D.A.W. ..	Weekly, Quarterly, Annual	57
N.A.L.G.O. ..	Annual	1
N.U.P.B.P.W.	Quarterly	4
A.E.S.D. ..	Monthly, Annual	13
N.U.V.B. ..	Monthly, Half-Yearly, Annual	15

The figures in the table perhaps exaggerate the range of variation, for the weekly returns of the General and Municipal and Shop, Distributive and Allied Workers are often sent in only once a month. Even so, the differences are striking.

The form of returns also differs. Weekly, fortnightly and monthly returns are basically income-expenditure statements, although they may also give other information such as details of changes in membership. The Shop, Distributive and Allied Workers and the Vehicle Builders require a quarterly return, listing each member and every payment that he has made during the quarter. The Transport and General Workers require the branch register (which records all individual payments) to be sent to the regional office each quarter, apparently for auditing purposes. The Engineers' registers are sent in twice a year and the Vehicle Builders' registers once a year. The single annual return of the National and Local Government Officers consists of a statement of total payments from each individual for the year with various summaries and membership details.

The work of assembling and agreeing a return does not diminish in proportion to the period covered. The preparation of a monthly return does not take four times as long as the preparation of a weekly return in the same form, although the more complex the return, the more time it takes. It seems fairly clear that some unions could adopt less frequent or less full returns (or both) with little or no loss of efficiency.

Branch Records

Branch registers are kept in all nine unions. They give details of each member's payments copied from the collectors' books. In most of them the branch secretaries keep duplicates of the returns which they send in, and branch secretaries in the Engineers and the General and Municipal Workers receive statements from their district or head office. Six of the nine unions also use branch cash books. Branch secretaries in the Railwaymen have three other ledgers to keep.

Conclusion

Other factors influence the amount of work involved in keeping branch books, for instance, the number of friendly benefits and the methods of paying them. And the method of branch book-keeping at the branch has its effect on the volume of work at regional and national level.[1] Nevertheless, we have enough information to make some comments on the differences in the weight of financial work revealed in Table 32B, in which the weighting for financial work is 33 in the General

[1] The volume of financial business at regional or national offices may vary for other reasons also. The Shop, Distributive and Allied Workers keep a record of the payments and movements of each individual at their head office.

and Municipal Workers, 38 in the Railwaymen and the Transport and General Workers, 39 in the Engineers and 52 in the Shop, Distributive and Allied Workers. The average for all unions is 32, but if we exclude the Mineworkers with their 'check-off' and the White Collar unions with their branch treasurers, it is increased to 40.

All three general unions have reduced branch records to a minimum and have clear and simple forms for returns. All three make frequent returns. The advantage of the General and Municipal Workers must therefore lie in the infrequency of payment by collectors to secretaries. It is all the more impressive when we remember that they have the largest average size of branch of the three unions. The Engineers would presumably score well below average but for its additional benefits. It does not, therefore, appear that an unofficial system of collecting contributions entails more work for the branch secretary than an official system. The advantage of the infrequent returns of the Railwaymen seems to be balanced by the difficulty of keeping five different branch books, but it must also be remembered that Railwaymen's branch secretaries spend an unusually large time per member on union business,[1] and the fact that they give the same importance to financial work as other branch secretaries presumably means that they spend more time than others on financial business.

The high score of the Shop, Distributive and Allied Workers is puzzling. Except for the centralization of accounting business at its headquarters in Manchester, the union's system is closely akin to that of the Transport and General Workers, and it is not obvious why centralization should entail so substantial a difference. Its rules provide for a financial secretary as well as a correspondence secretary.[2] It is, therefore, possible that some financial secretaries have filled in the branch secretary's questionnaire and that the preponderance of financial business is the consequence. It seems, however, that the normal practice is for both

[1] See p. 120.

In 1956 the Executive Council of the National Union of Railwaymen set up a special sub-committee to investigate the union's branch book-keeping methods. Although it recommended a number of minor modifications, it described the system as 'as near perfect as possible' and was unable to recommend 'that any book now in use in the branches should be dispensed with'. It also took the view that the Railwaymen had little to learn from other unions in the field of financial administration.

It is our impression that the Railwaymen attach greater importance than most other unions to avoiding branch defalcations. This is a problem which all unions have to face but others require fewer books to be kept without running into disaster. The absence of intermediate financial agencies between the Railwaymen's branches and their head office may also be relevant, but other unions centralize their finances without demanding that five branch books should be kept.

[2] See p. 116.

offices to be held by the same individual, and the answers to our questionnaire given by most of the respondents from the Shop, Distributive and Allied Workers suggest that they did so.

The picture is not so clear as we should have liked to make it, but at least there are grounds for thinking that most unions could find some means of simplifying the financial work of their branch secretaries.

TRADE UNION GROWTH

W E have made reference in the text to trade union growth as a possible test of the quality of trade union officers. Since other factors also affect growth we propose to analyse the change in membership in the last ten years, in order to try to give some estimate of the part played by union leaders and their methods in winning and keeping new members. These are the figures:

	Change 1948–1958
Transport and General Workers' Union	− 4%
Amalgamated Engineering Union	+ 19%
National Union of General and Municipal Workers ..	− 5%
National Union of Mineworkers	+ 11%
National Union of Railwaymen	− 20%
Union of Shop, Distributive and Allied Workers ..	+ 3%
Electrical Trades' Union	+ 27%
National Union of Public Employees	+ 33%
Amalgamated Society of Woodworkers	− 2%
National Union of Printing, Bookbinding and Paper Workers	+ 32%

One influence which might be expected to affect union membership is the size of the industry or industries in which they operate. The expansion of the labour force of the general engineering, motor vehicles and electrical engineering industries is sufficient to account for the growth of the Engineers, and most of the growth of the Electricians. The printing and paper industries have also expanded their labour force by almost a quarter over this period, and this could explain the expansion of the National Union of Printing, Bookbinding and Paper Workers. The decline of the railway labour force has paralleled the fall in the Railwaymen's membership.

Not all unions have responded so easily to the fortunes of their industries. Distribution, for example, has grown far more rapidly, but the numbers of the Shop, Distributive and Allied Workers have increased only slightly. On the other hand, the Mineworkers have expanded while the labour force in the mining industry has suffered a decline. The only possible explanation for the Mineworkers' growth is the effect of the 'check-off' agreements which have followed on nationalization in nearly every coalfield. These agreements have eliminated remaining pockets of non-unionism in the industry. The Shop, Distributive and Allied Workers, on the other hand, have few closed shop agreements outside co-operative undertakings, and the Co-operative Societies have not kept pace with the rest of the distributive trade.

As one might expect, the experience of the two larger General unions reflects the decline in total trade union membership of about 5%. Their wide coverage would prevent changes in any single industry from determining their fortunes. Many large firms have experienced a reduction in production workers over the last few years as new machinery has been introduced, with a consequent increase in their maintenance staffs. There are no figures to measure the strength of this trend, but for what it is worth it has assisted the shift from the General unions to the Engineers and Electricians.

This leaves the Public Employees. The expansion in local authority employment is insufficient to explain their growth. The nationalization of Health Services has brought a more favourable attitude towards trade unionism in many hospitals, which may have helped them. There remains a margin of growth (possibly at the expense of other unions) which may be attributed to the constant pressure for expansion maintained by the leadership of the union. There is also, perhaps, a margin over and above the expansion in the relevant industries for which leaders of the Electricians and the Printing, Bookbinding and Paper Workers can claim credit.

TRADE UNION AIMS

IN each of our four questionnaires we asked an identical question to discover the priority given by the four types of officer to a given list of trade union aims. We were aware that as a means of ascertaining the real priorities of the respondents this was a rather dubious method. It is commonly agreed among social scientists that questionnaires are of very limited use as a way of eliciting reliable information about attitudes, as distinct from factual information. But we did hope that there would be contrasts in the answers of the four types of officer about which it would be valuable to comment.

In fact, the most noteworthy result was the agreement between our respondents on the priorities. Table 66 summarizes the results.

TABLE 66

TRADE UNION AIMS

Aim	Priority given			
	Full–Time Officers	Full–Time Branch Secretaries	'Voluntary' Branch Secretaries	Shop Stewards
Higher wages and better conditions ..	22	26	22	23
100% Organization	25	22	24	21
Effective consultation with management at all levels	13	17	18	19
Creating unity between all workers	12	7	10	14
The fullest use by the rank and file of the democratic procedures of the union	13	13	11	10
Helping members with individual problems	9	10	11	8
Creating political consciousness amongst members	6	5	4	5
TOTAL	100	100	100	100

There are one or two minor differences worthy of attention. Shop stewards rate consultation higher than the others, and this might have been expected, for they spent far more of the time which they give to union business in consultation with supervisors and managers than the other two groups. They might also be expected to attach more importance to unity than other union officers, as they do, because they are by reputation more left-wing than other union officers, because their strength depends on workshop unity and because their unofficial organizations frequently transcend union boundaries. In fact, the enumeration of these reasons makes one surprised that the difference is not more marked. It is not surprising that they are less concerned than other officers with the democratic procedures of the union, for they are less involved in them, and it is understandable, perhaps, that they should be less concerned with individual problems (other than workshop grievances) than are branch secretaries.

We were surprised by the relegation of 100% organization to second place by the shop stewards. When we constructed this question we were confident that stewards would give this aim far greater priority than did branch secretaries, and probably also than officers, for several reasons. They are by reputation the most militant of union officers, and this is a militant aim; the most common method of achieving complete organization is by workshop pressure organized by the stewards; and the power of stewards rests on the strength of workshop organization.

After the event, however, we can suggest reasons for our mistake. It is true that strong workshop organization is the source of shop stewards' power, but it is also true that union officers and branch secretaries may be judged by membership figures; and that the stipends of branch secretaries in many unions are related to membership. The main element in our explanation, however, is that, as we have already noted, the priority given to organization varies *inversely* with the strength of the union. The Mineworkers, for instance, are less concerned with it than are the Building unions. Shop stewards' organization flourishes where organization is already strong. In establishments where organization is weak there are frequently no stewards to be found, because managers have not given recognition to the need for stewards and no one is bold enough to take on the job. Members in such firms may therefore be of no concern to any existing shop steward, but they are still in the care of some branch secretary and some full-time officer who is anxious to expand and stabilize membership in the undertaking. Consequently many shop stewards are less concerned with 100% organization, not because it is not quite as important to them as to other trade union officers, but because most of them are more assured of their hold, and can afford to be a little more relaxed.

The answers of the full-time branch secretaries are slightly eccentric, but it must be remembered that our total sample was only thirty, and it is a sample dominated by two unions.

The answers were broken down by union and union group. Once again the verdicts were almost unanimous, except for the White Collar group. White Collar branch secretaries and shop stewards put far less emphasis on 100% organization and far more on consultation with management than those in other groups.

TABLE 67

TRADE UNION AIMS: WHITE COLLAR AND OTHER UNIONS COMPARED

Aim	Priority given			
	Branch Secretaries		Shop Stewards	
	All Unions	White Collar Group	All Unions	White Collar Group
100% Organization	24%	14%	21%	7%
Effective Consultation with Management	18%	24%	19%	37%

The closed shop is anathema to many White Collar workers; and White Collar unions are strongest in the public service, where their strength has been achieved, for the most part, without making membership a condition of employment. This may explain their low interest in 100% organization. The high priority given to consultation is also understandable. White Collar workers may be expected to think of themselves as closer than wage-earners to management, and therefore to prize close relations with management more than do other groups of workers.

INDEX

268 INDEX

HOURS OF WORK
  Branch secretaries, 120ff, 129, 221.
  „   „   , full-time, 100.
  Officers, full-time, 45, 63ff, 140, 220ff.
  Shop stewards, 154, 158f, 165, 221.

INDEPENDENT LABOUR PARTY, 13.
IRON AND STEEL TRADES CONFEDERATION, 15, 177, 250.
  Branches, 113, 115f.
  Officers, full-time, 39, 254.
    „   „   „   , age, 47.
    „   „   „   , numbers, 40ff, 191f.
    „   „   „   , promotion, 69.
    „   „   „   , turnover, 77ff, 82.
  Staff, 104.

LOCAL DEPARTMENTAL COMMITTEES (Railways), 149f, 153, 164n, 178f.

NATIONAL AND LOCAL GOVERNMENT OFFICERS ASSOCIATION, 7, 18, 20.
  Branches, 113, 255ff.
  Officers, full-time, 62, 215n, 254.
    „   „   „   , age, 47, 191ff.
    „   „   „   , numbers, 40f.
    „   „   „   , promotion, 69.
    „   „   „   , salaries, 57n.
    „   „   „   , turnover, 78f, 81f, 219.
NATIONAL COAL BOARD, 22, 84n, 212f.
NATIONAL COAL BOARD LABOUR STAFF ASSOCIATION, 84n.
NATIONAL COUNCIL OF LABOUR COLLEGES, 228f.
NATIONAL FEDERATION OF BUILDING TRADE OPERATIVES, 28, 33n, 37, 103.
  Officers, full-time, 47f, 77ff, 82.
  Staff, 103f.
NATIONAL SOCIETY OF PAINTERS, 109.
NATIONAL UNION OF AGRICULTURAL WORKERS,
  Branches, 113, 115, 227.
  Collectors, 107f, 222f, 226.
  Officers, full-time, 39, 62, 254.
    „   „   „   , age, 47.
    „   „   „   , duties, 45f, 222f.
    „   „   „   , numbers, 40ff, 194.
    „   „   „   , promotion, 69.
    „   „   „   , salaries, 60, 209.
    „   „   „   , turnover, 77ff, 219.
  Staff, 111.
  Structure, 194.
NATIONAL UNION OF BOOT AND SHOE OPERATIVES, 15, 21.
  Branch secretaries, full-time, 94, 115.
  Branches, 113ff.
  Officers, full-time, 254.
    „   „   „   , age, 47.
    „   „   „   , numbers, 40ff, 191f.
    „   „   „   , promotion, 69.
    „   „   „   , turnover, 77ff, 115.
  Staff, 104f.
NATIONAL UNION OF DYERS, BLEACHERS AND TEXTILE WORKERS, 15.
NATIONAL UNION OF GENERAL AND MUNICIPAL WORKERS, 7, 9ff, 14f, 19f, 260f.
  Branch finance, 255ff.
    „   secretaries, 30, 115.
    „   „   , duties, 118ff, 124f, 255ff.
    „   „   , recruitment, 127f, 130.
    „   „   , remuneration, 98, 134ff.